THE
PASTOR'S
BIBLE STUDY™

VOLUME TWO

A NEW INTERPRETER'S
BIBLE STUDY

THE PASTOR'S BIBLE STUDY™

VOLUME TWO

A NEW INTERPRETER'S®
BIBLE STUDY

Abingdon Press
Nashville

THE PASTOR'S BIBLE STUDY™
Volume Two
A NEW INTERPRETER'S® BIBLE STUDY

Copyright © 2005 by Abingdon Press

This book is printed on acid-free paper.

Cataloging-in-publication information applied for with the
Library of Congress

ISBN 0687055202

05 06 07 08 09 10 11 12 13 14 — 10 9 8 7 6 5 4 3 2 1

MANUFACTURED IN THE UNITED STATES OF AMERICA

Contents

Contributors

David Albert Farmer, the general editor for this series, wrote the foreword for volume two. He is an ordained Baptist minister who taught preaching in seminary. He earned a Ph.D. in New Testament Theology and presently teaches as an adjunct professor of humanities at Wilmington College. Dr. Farmer has served seven congregations and is now the pastor of Silverside Church in Wilmington, Delaware. Farmer was editor of *Pulpit Digest* for eighteen years and *The African American Pulpit* for three years. He is the author of *Pilgrim Prayers for Single Fathers* (Cleveland: Pilgrim Press, 2004), *Teaching Sermons on the Love and Grace of God* (Nashville: Abingdon Press, 1997), and *Basic Bible Sermons on Hope* (Nashville: Baptist Sunday School Board, 1992). He is the coeditor of *And Blessed Is She: Sermons by Women* (San Francisco: Harper & Row, 1990), and contributing author in *The Storyteller's Companion to the Bible: Judges—Kings*, Volume Three (Nashville: Abingdon Press, 1992).

Mitzi Minor, the author of the fifteen Bible sessions on the Gospel of Mark, the gospel of Lectionary Year B for this volume, is originally from Alabama. A graduate of Auburn University, she is currently Professor of New Testament at the Memphis Theological Seminary in Tennessee. Minor earned a Ph.D. in New Testament studies and she is an ordained clergyperson in the Cumberland Presbyterian Church. Her vocational focus has been the intersection of Holy Scripture with our lives of faith. She has written articles on feminist interpretation and women's spirituality, and two books on Mark's gospel that reflect this interest: *The Spirituality of Mark: Responding to God* (Westminster John Knox Press, 1996) and *The Power of Mark's Story* (Chalice Press, 2001). She strives to teach students to take serious Bible study into their own lives as well as into their congregations.

E. Carson Brisson, the author of ten Bible studies on the Second Book of Samuel for this book, earned a Ph.D. in Old Testament studies. He is Academic Dean and Associate Professor of Biblical Languages at Union Theological Seminary and Presbyterian School of Christian Education in Richmond, Virginia. Since 1993, Carson has been Associate Editor of "Between Text and Sermon" in *Interpretation: A Journal of Bible and Theology*. He is also a contributing author in *The God Who Creates: Essays in Honor of W. Sibley Towner*, edited by William P. Brown and Dean McBride, Jr. (Grand Rapids: Eerdmans, 2000). Professor Brisson writes a regular column in "The Gargoyle Speaks" for the Union-PSCE publication, *Focus*. He and his family are currently members of Three Chopt Presbyterian Church, PC(USA), in Richmond.

Thomas McDaniel, author of twelve sessions on the Ten Commandments for this volume, earned a Ph.D. in Semitic Languages from Johns Hopkins University and was for thirty-two years professor of Hebrew and Old Testament Studies at the Eastern Baptist Theological Seminary in Wynnewood, Pennsylvania. Prior to that he was an associate professor at Kanto Gakuin University, Yokohama, and a visiting lecturer in Semitic languages at the Union Theological Seminary in Tokyo and the Graduate Theological Division of the Aoyama University in Tokyo. As an ordained Baptist minister he has served as pastor and interim pastor of churches in Maryland and Pennsylvania. He is the author of *Deborah Never Sang: A Philological Study of Judges 5* (Jerusalem: Makor, 1983). Other publications have appeared in *Biblica and Vetus Testamentum*. Currently, more than fifty articles, as well as a second edition of his monograph on Judges 5 are available online at http://www.ebts.edu/mcdaniel.html.

Mark Wilson, author of eight lessons on cultural diversity and inclusion for this book, earned an M.Div. from Harvard Divinity School and a Ph.D. in sociology from the University of Michigan. He was ordained as a clergyperson in 1987 under the dynamic ministry of the Rev. Dr. Charles G. Adams and the Hartford Memorial Baptist Church in Detroit, Michigan. During his seven-year tenure in that congregation, Rev. Wilson's love and vision of ministry was nourished and greatly inspired. These qualities continued to blossom in his pastorate of McGee Avenue Baptist Church in Berkeley, California. As pastor of this historic African American congregation for almost twelve years, Rev. Wilson's ministry has centered on the spiritual growth of his members and his passion for social justice in the public arena. Dr. Wilson now serves as the Assistant Professor of Congregational Leadership at the Pacific School of Religion, in Berkeley, California.

Thomas C. Davis, author of five sessions on faith and the "spirits" of politics for this book, had planned to work as a college professor, but in 1970 a spiritual awakening in Vietnam changed his course. Davis, who earned a Ph.D. in Christian social ethics (University of Pittsburgh), and later a master's degree in marriage and family therapy (St. Thomas University), has kept one hand in the local church and one in academia for thirty years. He has worked as a campus pastor, church pastor, pastoral psychotherapist, and seminary professor. He currently pastors at the Hanover Street Presbyterian Church, a multicultural congregation in his hometown, Wilmington, Delaware. His passions are peacemaking, writing, and preaching.

Foreword

Welcome or welcome back to *The Pastor's Bible Study*! Some of you are joining this exciting teaching/learning process beginning with this second volume. Many of you have returned to our guide because you found, with thousands of others, that the study and teaching material provided in this New Interpreter's product is excellent in both its scholarship and practical functionality for teachers. Whether a first-time or repeat user of this tool designed primarily for pastors (and other religious professionals, as well as lay leaders) who teach Bible studies on a weekly basis, I'm delighted that we will get to be an ongoing part of your 2005–2006 weekly sessions!

Again in volume two, we offer you more than fifty Bible study preparation lessons. Half of the lessons are "textual," which means that they are based on lectionary-dominant Scripture passages from year B in the Revised Common Lectionary. The other remaining lessons are built around intriguing "topical" themes. Let me introduce you briefly to our superb writers and the materials they have written for you. There are additional biographical details on each gifted writer elsewhere in the volume (or CD ROM if that is your preferred way of using the material).

♦ Dr. Mitzi Minor, Professor of New Testament at Memphis Theological Seminary in Memphis, Tennessee, and a highly regarded Markan scholar and author of books and scholarly articles on Mark, has written fifteen lessons on Mark's Gospel. Establishing Mark squarely as a "Kingdom" Gospel, Dr. Minor shows us how people in Jesus' world reacted to him and the Kingdom. Ultimately, Jesus himself must also respond to his circumstances and challenges. As he does, he advocates inclusivity, ministers to the marginalized, and subverts pure legalism through love. Minor's attention to cultural practices, literary connections, and dynamic themes will make this a captivating study for you!

♦ Dr. E. Carson Brisson, Associate Dean and Associate Professor of Biblical Languages at Union Theological Seminary/Presbyterian School of Christian Education in Richmond, Virginia, has written nine lessons on First and Second Samuel. Having lived several years in Israel and having mastered both ancient and modern Hebrew, Brisson brings nitty-gritty realities to light regarding Israel's rocky transition from a prophet-led collection of tribes to a king-ruled nation. Samuel, Saul, and Solomon are supporting characters, in a sense, to the complex and powerful King David. You will be impressed with his insight into the politics of the time and his relevant applications for today.

♦ You might expect that Dr. Thomas McDaniel, Professor Emeritus of Old Testament at Eastern Baptist Theological Seminary in Philadelphia, Pennsylvania, would have written exactly ten lessons on the Ten Commandments, but he wrote twelve instead; and he could have written more. McDaniel directs us to information about the Ten Commandments that many of us have never known. I guarantee that even seasoned Bible study leaders will have their eyes opened by McDaniel's wealth of information. His close reading of the text and context helps us to rethink other possible interpretations. He provides ample biblical evidence to show the impact that these central teachings had in the life of ancient Israel and the church.

♦ Right in the middle, literally, of writing eight challenging and thought-provoking topical lessons for this volume, Dr. Mark Wilson left a long-time pastorate and stepped full-time (having already taught there on a part-time basis) into the seminary classroom at Pacific School of Religion where he was appointed Assistant Professor of Ministry and Congregational Leadership. A sociologist as well as a pastor and professor, he brings an exciting blend of perspectives to a set of studies about how the gospel challenges multiple oppressors in the world. A diverse set of excluded and ostracized people are liberated by God, in a way that surprises many of us. In Wilson's section, you will find sessions on how to create diverse congregations, making room for the disabled, reviving youth culture, and many more!

♦ Dr. Thomas C. Davis is the beloved pastor of Hanover Street Presbyterian Church in Wilmington, Delaware, where he relishes the challenges of preaching and pastoral care to a congregation that is diverse at several levels. Beyond that work, he is actively involved in inner city justice ministry and interfaith dialogue. His five sessions for this volume focus on what he calls faith and the "spirits" of politics: the politics of compassion, isolation, resentment, and domination. Far from being a commentary on the modern American political scene, he helps us learn how individuals and groups may best position themselves to receive God's love and then to live it out in today's world.

I express my gratitude to the faithful and thoughtful *Pastor's Bible Study* contributors and to the publishing, editorial, and production professionals at Abingdon Press who make *The Pastor's Bible Study*, volume two, a reality. Next year, I look forward to welcoming you all back, along with many new lovers of serious Bible study.

In the meantime, flip the pages—or maneuver around on your CD ROM—to one of these gripping lesson sets. Get pad and pencil (or Palm Pilot or laptop!), pull your *New Interpreter's Study Bible* (also on CD-ROM) closer to where you're sitting, and be prepared to be inspired as you get ready to do one of the major tasks to which you've been called. Teach with understanding and with joy!

David Albert Farmer
Wilmington, Delaware

Introduction

The Pastor's Bible Study is the latest series offered in a line of *The New Interpreter's Bible* products to provide the best in scholarship for the service of the church. Designed to help pastors lead Bible studies for their congregations, this series is intended to enhance the study, teaching, and preaching of the Scriptures.

The results of a recent study conducted among nearly one thousand pastors (male and female) from more than three hundred different churches (urban, suburban, small town, and rural) of various denominations (United Methodist, Presbyterian, Baptist, Lutheran, United Church of Christ, and others) show that seventy-six percent of the pastors regularly teach a Bible study. Most teach an average of five times per month to an adult group. Fifty-one percent regularly offer a Bible study to more than one adult group. More than twenty-four percent of the respondents have a group that meets on Wednesday evenings, and another twenty-four percent have another weekday evening group. Additionally, most pastors are asked to teach a Sunday school class. In their teaching ministry, fifty-eight percent have some type of teaching agenda or philosophy to communicate or implement. On average, it takes pastors approximately four hours to prepare to teach a Bible study.

The Pastor's Bible Study is intended to help pastors meet their teaching responsibilities. Each volume will include fifty sessions written by recognized biblical scholars, professors of preaching and pastoral care, and outstanding pastors and church educators. The fifty sessions studies will include:

♦ Fifteen sessions on one of the four Gospels

♦ Ten sessions from an Old Testament book frequently cited in the lectionary

♦ Ten or twelve sessions on a special topic of interest to the teaching pastor (e.g., pastoral care, faith and practice, social justice, ethics)

♦ Studies of five to eight sessions each on relevant themes for the pastor (e.g., practical issues, inspirational themes)

Whether your study group meets for thirty minutes or an hour, for four weeks or the entire year, the flexible structure of *The Pastor's Bible Study* will meet your preparation needs. Its versatile design is also useful whether you choose to follow the lectionary, the canonical order of the Bible, or a key biblical theme on the Christian life.

As you prepare to lead your Bible study, look for the useful sidebars to the text that will help you provide a meaningful study experience for participants. **Teaching Tips** has ideas that will facilitate class discussion in a variety of creative ways. **Sources** will provide you with resources for further study derived from the lesson studies. **Study Bible** sidebars will indicate points of integration with *The New Interpreter's Study Bible*.* Finally, **Reflection** questions will foster participation, generate group and individual study, and encourage interaction with the biblical text.

Supplementing the six studies and sidebar helps in this volume is a CD-ROM containing valuable data and suggestions for classroom use, such as:

- A video introduction by the general editor
- The full text of *The Pastor's Bible Study: Volume Two,* completely searchable by keywords
- An outline of each lesson
- PowerPoint™ slides
- Supplementary material that can be customized for handouts and screen and video viewing

It is our hope that *The Pastor's Bible Study,* our newest in a line of *The New Interpreter's Bible* products that provides scholarship for the church, will help you lead Bible studies in your congregation, in order to advance and increase the study, teaching, and preaching of the Scriptures.

---

*Note: *The Pastor's Bible Study* frequently cites material from *The New Interpreter's Study Bible*, the recommended textbook for study participants.

THE GOSPEL OF MARK

A STUDY BY
MITZI MINOR

Mitzi Minor, the author of two books on the Gospel of Mark,
is Professor of New Testament at the Memphis Theological Seminary in Tennessee.

THE GOSPEL OF MARK
Outline

Introduction

The Pastor's Bible Study on Mark

S ince Bible study requires us to spend a fair amount of time with a particular biblical text, we'll begin by introducing ourselves to the text. What is this text? Who are we as readers of this text?

I. Locating Mark

I don't remember first hearing the story recounted in Charles Dickens's *A Christmas Carol*, but I remember the impact of learning later that it was written during England's Industrial Revolution. Suddenly Dickens's tale was more than a sweet Christmas story. It was literature protesting the exploitation of vulnerable people like the Cratchits by rich businessmen of the new industrial age like Scrooge. Locating Dickens in his time and place added to my appreciation of his stories. Something similar happens when we locate Mark in its time and place.

Scholars assign a composition date for Mark's Gospel between the years 65-70 C.E.—during the time just before the 66 C.E. Jewish revolt against Rome or while the revolt was underway. Traditionally the community for which Mark wrote this Gospel was located in Rome (Witherington), but recently more scholars believe the community was at home in the Galilee of northern Israel or perhaps just north of Galilee in southern Syria (Blount, Myers). There are implications for locating Mark in such a time and place.

This part of the world was largely rural. The people were mostly peasants living in small villages. They worked long, hard hours in their fields or shops for subsistence wages. Despite their low wages, they were

Sources

From Where Was Mark Written?

See Ched Myers, *Binding the Strong Man: A Political Reading of Mark's Gospel* (Maryknoll: Orbis Books, 1988), pp. 39-87, or Brian Blount, *Go Preach! Mark's Kingdom Message and the Black Church Today* (Maryknoll: Orbis Books, 1998), pp. 55-64 (among others) for arguments in favor of a Galilean or southern Syrian provenance for Mark's Gospel. Some scholars still locate the community in Rome. Those interested in this argument may consult Ben Witherington, *The Gospel of Mark: A Socio-Rhetorical Commentary* (Grand Rapids: Eerdmans, 2001), pp. 31-36.

Sources

Mark and the Jewish Revolt

Those interested in the story of the 66 C.E. Jewish Revolt can consult Myers, *Binding the Strong Man*, pp. 54-69; or Richard A. Horsley, *Jesus and Empire: The Kingdom of God and the New World Disorder* (Minneapolis: Fortress Press, 2003), pp. 15-54. Also see Ben Witherington, *The Gospel of Mark: A Socio-Rhetorical Commentary* (Grand Rapids: Eerdmans, 2001), pp. 31-36.

heavily taxed by Rome, the Herodians who ruled Galilee, and the temple system in Jerusalem. They existed, therefore, on the edge of survival. Should famine or illness or a greater tax burden arise, they were forced to borrow money from upper-class folk who charged exorbitant interest. This caused many peasants to live in virtual debt slavery. They had poor quality food and virtually no access to health care. Is it any wonder that hunger, illness, and indebtedness show up so frequently in stories of Jesus in Galilee?

Peasants might have turned to the chief priests in Jerusalem for help, but the chief priests had cast their lot with the Romans. They cooperated with Rome in order to maintain their power over the temple system in Jerusalem. The temple was not only the center of Jewish worship, it also served as the storehouse for the tithes and taxes required of the people, so that it was the center of the economic system of the day. Furthermore, the chief priests' control of the temple system's religious and economic might gave them political power in the land. Americans are accustomed to our "separation of church and state," but religion, politics, and economics were thoroughly intertwined in first-century Israel.

Thus the chief priests, Roman officials, and Herodians, who comprised less than five percent of the population, were politically powerful and economically well off, and the chief priests could claim God's sanction for their privilege and status. They lived lavishly and could anticipate a life span of sixty to seventy years. Peasants, by contrast, might live thirty to forty difficult years with no voice in the religious-political-economic decisions that affected their lives.

We should not be surprised, therefore, at the discontent and unrest that was ever-present in first-century Israel, erupting periodically in various protests and liberation movements, and finally exploding in full revolt in the year 66 C.E. Jewish zealots wanting to drive the Gentiles from their land, members of messianic movements hoping to restore the Davidic kingdom and apocalyptic groups looking for God to judge Rome's evil joined forces in a violent uprising against Roman oppression in the spring of that year. The days were tense and filled with threats of violence between the Jewish patriots and Romans.

The Markan community was a relatively new community, located on the edge of Israel and socially on the margins of the political, economic, and religious power structures. In the midst of such revolts, tension, and fear during those times, how should the Markan community live out its faith in Jesus as the Jewish Messiah?

2. Locating Ourselves

Nearly 1,950 years after Mark was written, we come to read this text. So, where are *we* located? What questions shape our reading of this Gospel?

There's a good chance that most of us who gather to study Mark already think of ourselves as followers of Jesus. What is it about being a follower that brings us to this Gospel? Are you new to faith so that, sponge-like, you are soaking up as much of Jesus' story as you can? Or have you been a pilgrim on this spiritual journey for a long while? Has your journey recently seemed exhilarating, stagnant, or unsettling? Are you hoping for new insights into your journey or seeking confirmation of old perspectives? What other questions will shape your study of Mark?

There's a good chance that our questions are different from those that shaped the writing of this story, because our social location is different from that of Mark's community. Obviously the twenty-first-Century western world is dissimilar in many ways from the first-century Mediterranean world. In addition, most of us who are reading (as well as writing) a book like this are closer to the mainstream of the political-economic-religious power structures of our culture than we are to the margins of society. Yet the margins were home to Mark's community. How does our different social location, as well as different temporal and geographical locations, affect our reading of Mark?

3. The Text We Will Read

Long ago the church decided that Mark offers meaningful insights to those who want to follow Jesus.

Teaching Tips
Mark's Structure

1. Mark's Gospel is notoriously difficult to outline. Mary Ann Tolbert, in the *NISB* (pp. 1802-1803) divides Mark into two major sections (1:14–10:52; 11:1-16:8) after the prologue (1:1-13). I divide the Gospel into three major sections after the prologue with "geography" being a key (the geography may be as symbolic as it is physical):

Prologue, 1:1–13

  I. Proclaiming God's kingdom in and around Galilee, 1:16–8:26
 II. "On the way" to Jerusalem, 8:27–10:52
III. Proclaiming God's Kingdom in Jerusalem, 11:1–16:8

2. You may want to check Tolbert's outline as you work your way through my organization of Mark's story to see how you would outline the Gospel.

This Gospel presents a particular perspective on what God is doing in the world through Jesus of Nazareth and tells us how people ought to respond to what God is doing if they desire to be faithful.

Mark presents these insights through its narrative. The Gospel writer did not set out to write something akin to a modern historical account of the life of Jesus. Nor did the writer compose a theology book. Instead the writer tells a story. We should take that seriously. Interestingly, people of all cultures, places, and times have told stories. As novelist, Ursula K. Le Guin says, "There have been societies that did not use the wheel, but there have been no societies that did not tell stories" (LeGuin, *Sacred Circles*, 69). Perhaps this reality is due to the narrative quality of human experience: The episodes of our lives take place one after another like a story. We think in stories so that we can weave together the people, dates, and events that fill our lives. Theologian and storyteller John Shea calls human beings "natural narrative beings" who love to tell stories of the experiences that are important to them (Shea, *An Experience Named Spirit,* 107).

Some of the stories we tell entertain us. Others teach us moral lessons. But some stories are retold for generations because they touch a deep, spiritual place in our lives. They are composed of inspired layers of underlying truth that invite but do not force themselves on us. These stories help us understand our own stories. They remind us of who we are, and from whence we have come. They help us remember what it means to be human as God created us to be. We are drawn to these stories because they ring true to our living. As theologian Sallie McFague says, "We recognize our own pilgrimages from here to there in a good story; we feel its movement in our bones and know it is 'right'" (McFague, *Speaking in Parables*, 138). Mark's Gospel is just such a *good* story for us, if we allow it to be.

4. The Reading We Undertake

So, how do we allow Mark to be such a story for us? My experience in churches suggests we rarely ask ourselves how we are reading the Gospels, but I think we must do just that.

Sources
Mark and Story
Ursula Le Guin, quoted in Robin Deen Carnes and Sally Craig, *Sacred Circles: A Guide to Creating Your Own Women's Spirituality Group* (San Francisco: HarperSanFrancisco, 1998), 69. See John Shea, *An Experience Named Spirit,* (Allen, Tex.: Thomas More, 1983), p. 107. On good stories and our own pilgrimages, see Sallie McFague, *Speaking in Parables,* (Philadelphia: Fortress Press, 1975), 138.

Those interested in this perspective on Mark as such a story might read the introduction in my book, Mitzi Minor, *The Power of Mark's Story* (St. Louis: Chalice Press, 2001).

Reflections
On the Margins

1. Would you consider yourself to be more on the margins or in the mainstream of your society and culture? Does it make sense to you that your "place" affects how you read the Bible?

2. Now that you know something about the community for which Mark was written—its "place" on the margins of the society—what was likely happening historically as the Gospel was being written, etc. and how might this knowledge affect your reading of Mark?

3. What brings you to this study of Mark? What are you hoping to discover?

Those of us who have grown up in church often read the Bible badly. Believing we already know what a Bible text says, we don't see what is actually there. In addition, we often read texts through our doctrines. We unconsciously make a text fit what we already believe to be true. Finally, we frequently harmonize the four Gospels and make them fit neatly together, even when they don't.

For this Bible study, let's read Mark on its own terms. Let's set aside what we know about Matthew, Luke, and John and allow Mark to tell its story of Jesus. Let's not assume that Mark confirms our doctrinal views, but open ourselves to new insights, challenges, and possibilities for faithfulness. Let's leave our middle-class comfort zone (for those of us there) and go out to the margins where Mark was written and see what the world and the Gospel look like out there.

Finally, let us read, not for historical or theological information, but for transformation of our living, which is why Mark wrote this Gospel in the first place.

The Kingdom of God Has Drawn Near

The Prologue, 1:1-15

Mark begins his story by jumping right into the events that launched Jesus on his mission. After quoting Isaiah, who had promised that God would send someone to "prepare *the way* of the Lord," Mark announces that John the baptizer appeared in the wilderness preaching a baptism for the forgiveness of sins and announcing the coming of one stronger than he who would baptize in the Holy Spirit (1:2-8). We will find "the way of the Lord," repentance, and the first-century understanding of forgiveness of sins to be important for Mark's story. For now I invite you to some reflection on *repentance.*

Often in Protestant circles repentance is associated with remorse—we've done something wrong, are sorry, and promise not to do it again. I've heard preachers declare that it means turning our lives in a different direction. Neither of those ideas, however, is adequate for understanding repentance in Mark. For Mark *to repent* is closest to the idea of "seeing differently," for if you see differently, you will live differently. Consider the apostle Paul. When he *saw* that God loved Gentiles, he lived his life differently. How could he do otherwise once he *saw* differently? That's what Mark has in mind by repentance, as we shall see.

John the Baptizer

So John is baptizing, calling people to repent, and announcing the Coming One. And then Mark tells us that Jesus of Nazareth was baptized by John. With no preamble or striking introduction, with few words, Mark brings Jesus into the story. But look what hap-

Lectionary Loop

Second Sunday of Advent, Year B, Mark 1:1-8

Baptism of the Lord, Year B, Mark 1:4-11

Third Sunday after Epiphany, Year B, Mark 1:14-20

Fourth Sunday after Epiphany, year B, Mark 1:21-28

Fifth Sunday after Epiphany, Year B, Mark 1:29-39

Sixth Sunday after Epiphany, Year B, Mark 1:40–45

First Sunday in Lent, Year B, Mark 1:9–15

Study Bible
Prologues

Read about the function of "Prologues" in ancient narratives, *NISB*, 1804.

Teaching Tips
Apocalyptic Preaching

The image of John the Baptist as Elijah coming "to prepare the way of the Lord" and Jesus' announcement that "the kingdom of God has drawn near" led many scholars to believe that *(Continued on Page 10)*

pens next: as Jesus came up from the water he saw the heavens ripped apart and the Spirit descending on him like a dove and heard a voice from heaven saying, "You are my beloved son; in you I am well pleased" (1:11).

Jesus of Nazareth

Notice first that *Jesus* saw and heard. In Mark's telling, this event was not a grand announcement to many people but a significant moment for Jesus. So, how might we understand the content of this vision Jesus sees and hears? The heavens were thought to be a great cosmic curtain separating creation from God's presence, but the heavens in Mark's story are torn open, even ripped apart. The Greek verb *schizo* (from which we get schism) is a strong, almost violent, word. Interpreters have long thought this tearing of the heavens means human beings have new access to God. But maybe it also signals that God will no longer be confined to sacred spaces—where we human beings often try to lock God away—but is on the loose in our realm (Juel, *Master of Surprise*, 35-36). So we should not be surprised that when the heavens were torn open, or that the Spirit came down like a dove to Jesus. God is up to something significant, and this Jesus of Nazareth is involved!

The Spirit's first act is perhaps unexpected—the Spirit *drives* Jesus into the wilderness. After saying "yes" to a summons from God, those who embark on a spiritual journey often encounter a difficult moment that tells them the way; though it promises to be God's way, it will not be easy. Driven to the wilderness by the Spirit, Jesus is tempted by Satan for forty days and was with the wild beasts (1:13). Many readers automatically add in their own minds the explicit temptations described by Matthew and Luke. I suspect, however, that Mark hoped we might think along different lines. The associations with Israel's forty-year wandering in the wilderness and Elijah's forty days of travel to Horeb call to mind those who were tempted to quit the journey. Satan's opposition makes clear that Jesus' way will be difficult. We know that with God's help (both the Spirit and angels, vv. 12-13), Jesus did not

(Continued from Page 9)

Mark understood Jesus' mission as an apocalyptic turning point in history. Look up the word "apocalyptic" in several contemporary Bible dictionaries and/or commentaries. Be sure to use new resources, for recent studies have offered exciting new views of the concept. Be prepared to discuss the concept with your group, including Mark's idea that this apocalyptic turning point is currently underway rather than being a future event.

Reflections

A Change of Outlook and in Living

1. Can you recall a time when you *saw* someone or some situation differently and lived differently as a result?
2. What is the impact of considering such a "moment" as an experience of repentance?

Sources

Heavens Ripped Open for God and People

Donald H. Juel, *Master of Surprise: Mark Interpreted* (Minneapolis: Fortress Press, 1994), 35-36.

quit but continued on his journey, because after his forty days in the wilderness, he returns to Galilee to preach (1:14).

Jesus Proclaims the Kingdom of God in Galilee, 1:16-45

In his preaching Jesus announced, "The time is fulfilled and the kingdom of God has drawn near. Repent and believe in the gospel!" In the first-century Mediterranean world, the "kingdom" belonged to Caesar, and the "gospel" was the information about peace and security Caesar brought. Of course his "peace" was wrought by conquest, coercion, terror, and enslavement, but it ended civil wars and brought prosperity to the elites and a few others. Therefore, all people should be grateful to Caesar, follow Caesar's laws, pay their taxes, and be loyal citizens of the empire. This propaganda surrounded and shaped the lives of the people, including the people of Israel. Against this backdrop we can see Jesus' declarations that the kingdom belonged to God, God's kingdom had drawn near, and *this news*, this Gospel, was not just a collection of theologically significant words. They were politically loaded statements!

Christians have tended to focus on the future dimension of Jesus' message of God's kingdom. But the Greek verb translated "has drawn near" is perfect tense, denoting an action that has already taken place but with effects that continue to be felt. Mark has told us that the heavens were torn open, so that God is on the loose in our world (1:10). God's dramatic entry into our space means that transformation is *now* underway. The apocalyptic turning point, God's new age, does not await a future, cataclysmic event—it *has drawn* near! So, "repent," Jesus says. *See* what God is doing in the world! A new way of living is possible! Then Jesus set out to practice his preaching.

We should note that first-century social relations were pyramid-like in arrangement, with Caesar on top ruling over all others who were situated in a complex set of graduated dominations and subordinations. There were a few other "rulers" near the top, but the vast majority of people had little power or worth in this

---

Reflections

Theological affirmations of Jesus as the divine Son of God may make it difficult for us to imagine that he could have been genuinely tempted to turn back from the journey to which God called him. But Mark is notorious for taking Jesus' humanity very seriously.

1. What reactions do you have to Mark's story of Jesus being tempted in the wilderness?
2. What prompts such reactions from you?

Reflections

To Serve or Not to Serve

The Greek word *diakoneo* (meaning to serve, to minister) is used to describe what the angels did for Jesus in 1:13 and what Simon's mother-in-law did in 1:31.

1. Is this verb translated the same in both verses in your Bible?
2. If they aren't, what words are used and what reactions or observations do you have about two different English words being used for the one Greek verb, *diakoneo*?

world and fell to the bottom of the pyramid. The "peace" of Rome was maintained when all citizens knew their place.

So, now let's see Jesus traveling through Galilee calling four fishermen to follow him (1:16-20), touching and healing a woman who got up and ministered to (or with) them (1:29-31), touching and making clean a leper (1:40-45). All of these people were low on the pyramid. Fishermen were course and dirty. Women were, well . . . women. Lepers were the most unclean people in that culture and perhaps should be placed under the pyramid. But Jesus valued them and offered them compassion, respect, and wholeness. In the leper story, Jesus sends the leper to the priests "for a witness to them" (1:44). The witness seems to be, "YOU said I am outcast and unclean, but GOD says I matter!"

Indeed religious institutions (including Christian ones) often seem to create or reinforce the outcast place of certain people, thus becoming arenas where self-righteous superiority fills the air. Consequently, I doubt it's coincidence that, in the midst of these stories of Jesus welcoming outcasts, Mark also tells about Jesus exorcising a demon *in a religious place* (1:21-28). Interestingly, it is the first public event of Jesus' ministry according to Mark.

In our scientific world ancient exorcism stories present a challenge. Some dismiss them as mere ancient superstitions. Others take them literally despite what we now know about viruses, mental illness, etc. Either approach may leave us oddly dissatisfied with their easy dismissal or easy acceptance of demons. In *The Spirituality of Mark* I suggested we learn from scholars who point to the symbolic power of these narratives and see the demons as evoking the presence of evil that threatens life as God intended. Not all of us are comfortable with the idea of "demons," but many of us see ethnic cleansing in Bosnia or Rwanda, the terrible events in Oklahoma City and on September 11, 2001, the effect of addiction or violence on someone we love, the persistence of racism and sexism, and are convinced that evil is present in the world.

From this perspective, Mark 1:21-28 narrates Jesus' encounter with evil within the religious institution in

Teaching Tips
Clean or Unclean?

The ancient understanding of purity/ritual cleanliness/holiness is important in the leper story and will be important again in the Gospel. If you are unfamiliar with newer social science studies of this ancient concept, then do some reading on the topic. You could check the chapter by Jerome Neyrey in *The Social Sciences and New Testament Interpretation*, ed. by Richard Rohrbaugh (Peabody, Mass: Hendrickson, 1996) or the shorter entry in *Biblical Social Values and Their Meaning*, ed. by John J. Pilch and Bruce J. Malina (Peabody, Mass: Hendrickson, 1993), 151-152.

Questions for Discussion
Who Are the Outcasts around You?

A leper was as unclean/unholy as one could get in first-century Israel and was often banished from her or his home. To understand his pain deeply, then, we need to go out to the margins and see where he lived.

1. If you can imagine yourself doing that, what do you think you would see, feel, and experience?
2. Who are the outcasts in your community? Would you say the church in your community (including your own church) has tried to include the outcasts, or has it supported their outcast status?

Capernaum. On the Sabbath he was teaching the people, presumably about the kingdom of God being near, and they were astonished at the power of his words. He was *not* like their usual religious teachers (the scribes, 1:22). At that point evil reared its ugly head. Coincidence?

The demon asks, "What have you to do with us? Have you come to destroy us?" (1:24). If, in the symbolics of the narrative, the demon is asking if Jesus will destroy the world as the human powers have made it, the answer is yes. This is an apocalyptic moment. But he will not do it via violence and conquest like the Romans (and their partners, including some of Israel's religious leadership). He will do it through actions like those in Mark's first chapter—healing, touching, respecting, calling those who've been told they are nothing, enabling them to live in God's kingdom and turn their backs on "their place" in Caesar's pyramid.

So Jesus teaches those gathered to learn and exorcises the demon in the religious institution, and the people call this experience "a new teaching with power" (1:27). No wonder! The kingdom of God has drawn near!

Sources

Understanding Demon Exorcisms

Those interested may read pages 78-79 in *The Spirituality of Mark* (Louisville: Westminster John Knox Press, 1996) for further explanation of this approach to reading exorcism stories.

Conflict Over the Kingdom of God

Conflict and Challenge in a Shame-Honor Culture

Cultural anthropologists tell us the first century Mediterranean world was a "shame-honor" culture as opposed to a guilt culture like our own. We try to change wrongdoers by making them feel guilty. In first-century Israel, people feared being publicly dishonored. Honor was tied to birth status (whether you were born Jew or Gentile, male or female, physically whole, to a priestly or slave family, etc.), which established one's "place" in that world (on Caesar's pyramid). Then the upper class, the elites, demanded that people conduct themselves according to what their "place" was. Men who did so were deemed honorable. Women who did so showed "appropriate shame" and avoided dishonoring their fathers or husbands (Malina, 1981, ch. 2). So, when people said that Jesus, a backwoods Galilean peasant, taught as one having authority and "not as the scribes," and his fame spread broadly (1:22, 28), those already doing the job were bound to check him out, for *they* held places of religious authority. Beginning at 2:1 Mark tells five consecutive stories of conflict between Jesus and the Jewish religious authorities. In each story these authorities hope to dishonor Jesus. In each story they fail. With each failure, the stakes in the conflict intensify.

A Cycle of Conflict Stories on Forgiveness, Fasting, and the Sabbath, 2:1–3:6

The first story (2:1-12) famously recounts four friends who tore a hole through a roof in a house and lowered a paralyzed man to where Jesus was teaching.

Teaching Tips
Honor and Shame

You will want to be familiar with the shame-honor culture of the first-century Mediterranean world. If you aren't already, then you can check Bruce J. Malina, *The New Testament World: Insights from Cultural Anthropology* (Louisville: Westminster John Knox Press, 1981), chapter 1, or *Biblical Social Values and Their Meaning*, ed. by John J. Pilch and Bruce J. Malina (Peabody, Mass: Hendrickson, 1993), 95-104.

Reflections
The Treatment of Women in Antiquity

Women generally were expected to know that they were weak, gullible, not very smart, needy, and thus dependent on the men in their lives—fathers first, then husbands—to tell them what to think and what to do. If a woman tried to think for herself or act on her own, well who knows what kind of horrors she'd get into! So, a woman was to be, appropriately, ashamed of being a woman so she *(Continued on Page 16)*

When Jesus saw *their* faith—do friends sometimes have to believe for us when we cannot believe for ourselves?—he told the paralytic, "Your sins are forgiven." We should know that *sin* in ancient Israel wasn't always a moral failure. It might be, but it might also be such things as an inability to pay one's temple tax or perform purity rituals. The result of sin might be exclusion from the community of God's people so that forgiveness equaled restoration to the community. Further, physical sickness or disability was considered to be punishment for sin.

Consequently, Jesus' words, "your sins *are* forgiven," are significant. The present tense verb in Greek signals Jesus' view that the man's sins are being forgiven *even now* while he is still paralyzed, which would mean his paralysis does not indicate God's judgment on him as a sinner. Jesus' words also mean the man is restored to the community even while he is paralyzed. Once again, Jesus is challenging the "world" as the authorities had defined it! The scribes recognize this, for they question in their hearts, "Who can forgive sins but God alone?" That is, they "get it"; they understand that *Jesus* is claiming the right to announce that God is changing things, but it was *their* place to tell what God was doing. I wonder if, after hearing Jesus speak, they were relieved and ready to leave since this backwoods peasant clearly did not understand "the way things were."

If so, then Jesus interrupts their relief by knowing their questions and challenging them with, "which is easier, to say to the paralyzed, 'your sins are forgiven,' or to say, 'Stand up and take your mat and walk'?" While the power to forgive sins is the more outrageous claim, if Jesus tells the man to walk and he doesn't (which everyone would witness), Jesus would be publicly dishonored. No one would listen to him again. Thus the former (saying sins are forgiven) is easier, so Jesus does the latter (enables the man to walk) and shows that what he says is every bit as powerful as the miracles he does. And he has said that this man is forgiven and restored to the community.

In the second conflict story Jesus calls a tax collec-

(Continued from Page 15) always did what was expected of her, thus not doing anything to bring dishonor on the men to whom she was responsible.

Teaching Tips
A Poem on a Prophet

For those who like poetry, Rumi's poem "What Jesus Runs Away From," which can be found in *The Essential Rumi*, trans. by Coleman Barks and John Moyne (San Francisco: HarperSanFrancisco, 1995), 204, can be helpful for discussion of the religious leaders in Mark's teaching.

tor, Levi, to follow him and then has dinner at Levi's house with "many tax collectors and sinners" (2:13-15). But restrictive eating practices were the norm in this world. Social status and roles determined guest lists. Persons of different social rank usually did not eat together. We've already noted that sinners were outsiders to the community. Tax collectors' contact and collusion with the Gentile (Roman) oppressors led people to assume their non-observance of Torah, making them outcasts too. Thus the scribes ask Jesus' disciples why he eats with such people (2:16). A holy man should know better.

Jesus answers that sick people don't need a doctor; he came to call sinners, not the righteous. His response might trouble religious people who, after all, aspire to righteousness. Does God not care about them (us)? Perhaps the point is that sick people know they're sick, so they seek out healers and trust themselves to such care. Just so, tax collectors and sinners knew they'd been cast outside the circle of God's people. Indeed, Galilean peasants generally, with their poor nutrition, poor health care, and hard lives surrounded by Roman violence, knew about sickness in their midst. Is it mere coincidence that these people were Jesus' first followers? In our time I've heard witnesses to the deep spirituality of many AA meetings—alcoholics also know they're sick. This text suggests God helps those who know that they cannot help themselves, perhaps because they are willing to entrust themselves over to God's power. Religious people are often the ones, then and now, who believe their "religious-ness" makes them better than "those people," i.e., not sick like them, and thus not so in need of God's grace.

Interestingly, "religious-ness" is an issue in the three remaining conflict stories. In the first (2:18-22) Mark tells us that John's disciples and the Pharisees practiced fasting but Jesus' disciples didn't. Some people ask Jesus why not. In the second (2:23-28) Jesus' disciples pluck grain while walking through a grainfield, and the Pharisees ask why they are doing what is "not lawful" on the Sabbath. In the third (3:1-6) the Pharisees, having failed to dishonor Jesus publicly, are

Reflections
An Invitation from Whom?

1. Who are the "tax collectors and sinners" in your world?
2. How would you receive an invitation to come to dinner at their house?

Compare and contrast this situation to Sidney Poitier's performance in the Stanley Kramer film, *Guess Who's Coming to Dinner* (1967), where a young African American doctor engaged to a white Anglo-Saxon woman must undergo the close scrutiny of her mainstream establishment parents (Spencer Tracy and Katharine Hepburn) when invited for dinner.

Reflections
No Problems Here!

In contrast to Mark's community and most of the earliest followers who were from the margins of society, participants in your Bible study today are probably closer to mainstream society. In Mark's story those closer to the mainstream are the ones who don't know they are sick.

1. Is Mark's perspective true of you and/or your community?
2. Are you and those around you aware of wounds among you that need healing, or of growth that needs to happen among you, or is there a lot of satisfaction with the "way things are?" Note also M. Scott Peck's *People of the Lie: Toward a Psychology of Evil* (Simon & Schuster, 1992) where denial and self-deception figure prominently in our modern understanding of evil.

lying in wait for him, watching to see if he will heal on the Sabbath so they can accuse him.

Fasting and Sabbath observance were given as grace to God's people. Fasting is a strenuous practice requiring disciples to set aside physical needs to focus on spiritual ones. It can remind us that we are primarily spiritual (not physical) beings, enable us to discover our deepest needs, and draw nearer to God. Sabbath observance calls disciples to set aside our work for rest and renewal. It reminds us that we are primarily spiritual beings rather than producers and consumers. Thus it, too, can enable discovery of our deepest needs and a closer connection to God.

What Is Up with the Religious Leaders, 3:6?

But religious practices in the hands of those who don't know their need for grace can become another source of oppression. Does the question about Jesus' disciples not fasting suggest that fasting had become a measure of "real" religion? Is it gracious to demand that peasants, such as Jesus' followers, fast to prove their "religious-ness" when enough food was a constant issue? "The bridegroom is with them," Jesus answered (2:19), indicating that a cause for joy has come to these folk. They're not fasting; they're celebrating! This is new wine, he declared further, which needs new wineskins (2:22), suggesting renewal of religious practices.

No wonder, then, that Jesus declared, in the first Sabbath story, that "the Sabbath is made for humankind, not humankind for the Sabbath" (2:27). God gave the Sabbath to free people from viewing life as revolving around their producing and consuming. They were commanded to take a day to rest and reconnect with God and God's people and thus to remember who they are. But those who didn't know themselves in need of such grace had made Sabbath observance into a day for peasants to get in trouble for plucking heads of grain in a grainfield, or Jesus to get in trouble for healing a man's hand.

If peasants generally had trouble with enough food, how much more a man with a withered hand for whom work would be difficult? Such a man came to syna-

Reflections
I'm Sorry, but You're Not Welcome Here

1. Have you ever experienced a religious practice intended to draw you closer to God being used to oppress and alienate you from God?
2. Have you seen this happen to someone else?
3. Discuss the practice of restricting those who receive the Lord's Supper on the basis of how, where, and by whom they were baptized ("closed communion")?
4. Describe what you experienced or witnessed.

Reflections
But We've Always Done It That Way!

How would you evaluate the openness of your church or community to "new wine" or "new wineskins" that God might offer? Whether your answer is "very open" or "not open at all," consider some reasons why you believe that your evaluation is on target.

gogue on a Sabbath when the Pharisees were hoping Jesus would heal so they could accuse him of law-breaking. Jesus called the man into the center of the assembly and asked, "Is it lawful to do good or to do harm on the Sabbath, to save life or to kill?" (3:4). Notice that doing nothing is not an option. When someone is suffering, and others do nothing, they allow the suffering to continue. They do harm. Jesus makes his choice and heals the man's hand, giving him a chance to work again and regain his life. In response the Pharisees leave the synagogue and plot with the Herodians to kill Jesus. This early in Mark's story they perceive a grave threat to their honor and place. What is with them? Why don't they see the paralytic walking and the man's hand restored and rejoice? Why don't they hear Jesus' words about the Sabbath and conclude that God might be on the loose in their world, offering them new wine in God's kingdom? Mark tells us their hearts were hard. So they *are* sick. But they don't know they are. After all, they are very religious!

Teaching Tips
Are You Helpful or Hurtful?

Elie Wiesel tells a story about Job living in Egypt about the same time as Moses did. It illustrates the "problem" with doing nothing when people are hurting. This story, which can be found in *From the Kingdom of Memory* (New York: Schocken Books, 1990), 151, can be helpful for discussion of Mark 3:1-6.

Seeing the Kingdom of God

Calling the People of God (the Twelve), 3:13-19

After a summary statement reminding us of Jesus' work, and that crowds from all over were coming to hear him (3:7-12), Mark tells us that Jesus "went up the mountain" (the place of revelation) and called twelve among his disciples to be with him, proclaim the message, and have authority to cast out demons. Since the names of the Twelve vary among the Gospels, it may be that the number twelve is most significant here. Since *twelve* evokes the memory of the twelve tribes of Israel, its use by Jesus may suggest that he is calling out the true people of God. But a couple of points should be noted. First, the idea of the "true people of God" must not be read as anti-Semitic. All these followers of Jesus were Jews. Second, in Mark's Gospel the word "disciples" is not synonymous with "the Twelve." There was always a group of disciples around Jesus larger than the Twelve. Keep this larger group in mind unless Mark specifically tells us he means "the Twelve."

The First Intercalation: Family Conflict, Conflict with Scribes, True Family, 3:20-35

Then Jesus went home (Capernaum perhaps) and was surrounded again by a crowd. At this point his family came to take him away because "they were saying he is crazy" (3:21). Here is an ambiguous "they" that we also know, as in, "you know what *they* say." Who was calling him crazy? And was his family afraid for him? Embarrassed by him?

Lectionary Loop
Proper 5, Year B, Mark 3:20-35
Proper 6, Year B, Mark 4:26-34

Reflections
Deceiving Liars!

Abolitionists, suffragettes, civil rights activists, contemporary feminists, peace advocates, etc., have all been demonized at times by people within the church.

1. Have you ever been tempted to demonize someone who took a controversial stand?
2. What do you hear this text saying about such a temptation?

The scribes from Jerusalem ("he is demon-possessed"), 3:22-30

We don't know because Mark interrupts the family story to tell about conflict with some scribes who had come from Jerusalem. One of Mark's favorite story-telling devices is to break off one story to tell another and then *return* to the first story. Scholars call this insertion within or around another story/saying an "intercalation." We might think of this framing device as a "Markan sandwich." The effect is to tie the two stories closely together in readers' minds so that they are interpreted together. So what can we glean from these two stories being yoked thusly?

In first-century Mediterranean culture, one's birth status played the most significant role in determining one's place in the world. As we have said, you were born a Jew or Gentile, male or female, into a priestly family or a peasant family, etc. In the first story here, the ones born into Jesus' family are concerned that he is crazy. In the second story, those born into families that produce religious leaders try to dishonor Jesus by accusing him of having "Beelzebul," that is, of being demonic himself. Wow! The two groups in that culture we might most expect to "get" Jesus are the ones who level seriously off-base charges against him!

Jesus responded to the scribes' challenge with parables (3:23). We may be accustomed to thinking of parables as stories Jesus told, but for Mark a parable is any illustration, metaphor, wordplay or other teaching of Jesus that invited hearers to look at their world differently. Here Jesus points out that Satan can't cast out Satan because a house or kingdom divided against itself cannot stand. Rather, one stronger than Satan has come and is plundering Satan's house (3:23-27).

The Family of Jesus ("Whoever Does the Will of God"), 3:31-35

After this confrontation Mark returns to the first story by telling readers that Jesus' mother and brothers were outside calling for him (v. 31). But Jesus asked the crowd around him, "Who are my mother and my brothers?" (v. 33). Then he answers his own question: "Whoever does the will of God is my brother and sis-

---

Study Bible

See notes on Mark 3:23 in the *NISB*, 1811, about parables generally. See also notes about the two "major parables" in Mark on pp. 1812–1814. For further discussion of "parables" and the role they play in Jesus' teaching in Mark, see Mitzi Minor, *The Spirituality of Mark* (Louisville: Westminster John Knox Press, 1996) 13-14.

ter and mother" (v. 35). The word *"whoever"* is key. It evokes for us the radical inclusivity of God's kingdom. Jesus is indeed calling people to look at their world differently. Fishermen, lepers, tax collectors, women, a paralyzed man would all have had lesser status than the holy people of God. But not to Jesus. For Jesus *whoever* does the will of God, regardless of birth status, is his mother, sister, brother, which pretty much makes him crazy, according to the "rules" of that culture.

A final part of this episode needs attention. In the middle story, after Jesus has told the scribes that a stronger one is plundering Satan's house, he warns them that those who blaspheme the Holy Spirit will never have forgiveness. Some, having read this verse out of its context in the Gospel, have feared that somewhere somehow they may have inadvertently committed the "unforgivable sin" and are condemned by God. But Mark tells us plainly that Jesus said these words because the scribes had demonized him (v. 30). That is, the scribes had seen (or heard) Jesus welcome, show compassion, heal, and forgive people who knew pain, want, and exclusion firsthand. But they called his gifts of grace the work of a demon. This sin is not some inadvertent act one may commit by accident but is steadfast opposition to the way God's grace is at work in the world. Those who set themselves in opposition to God's work will not put themselves in the way of God's forgiveness.

The First Teaching Section, 4:1-34

As chapter four gets underway Mark tells us that Jesus is again beside the sea teaching in parables, and a large crowd has gathered. But then Mark does a new thing in his story: Rather than noting that Jesus was teaching and moving quickly to the next story, Mark slows his narrative down and gives us details about the content of Jesus' teaching. It's as if Mark is cueing us that this content is important. We should pay attention.

The Sower Parable, 4:1-9

First Jesus tells the parable of the sower. In a world where peasants lived constantly on the edge of starvation, the failure of a sower's seed would be utter disaster. We can almost feel the peasants in the crowd grimacing as the story unfolds. But then the story twists when the seed that fell in good soil produced thirty, sixty, and a hundredfold. A seven to one return on seed was a good crop. A ten to one return was a bumper crop. So, what is a thirty, sixty or one hundred return? In Jesus' parable, what looked like a disaster is instead an extravagant success! "Let the one who has ears to hear, hear!" he said (4:9).

Disciples, Parables, and Seeing, 4:10-20

Later, away from the crowd, disciples of Jesus (including the Twelve) ask him about the parables (4:10). Notice that "parables" is plural. They aren't asking about the sower parable, but about all of them. Why does he teach in ways designed to turn hearers' worlds upside down?

Jesus answered, "To you has been given the *mystery* of the kingdom of God." In Jewish tradition, a mystery is something that humans can know, but only because God has revealed it. It is a gift. Jesus says that God has given this gift to them. But to outsiders, everything is in parables "so that seeing they may see and not see, and hearing they may hear and not understand lest they turn and be forgiven" (literal translation of 4:11-12). Initially these words seem harsh and troublesome, but closer study yields significant insights. In the Jewish prophetic tradition (see Isa. 6:9) a word from God is often such a challenge that it is rejected by everyone except those radically open to God, thus revealing who is authentically with God and who is not. So, God sends a prophetic word, for example, that birth status does not matter in God's kingdom. Those interested only in a God who affirms their privileged status will reject that word and thus show themselves to be outsiders from God. But those open to what God is doing will receive the mystery of the kingdom, even if it turns their world upside down.

"See what you hear!" 4:21-34

Then Jesus asks them a question: If they don't understand the sower parable, how will they under-

---

Reflections
I Can See Clearly Now!

1. Can you think of a time when you began *to see* the world, or something in your world, or even yourself, differently than you had before? Was the experience difficult? Freeing? What prompted the change (a person you met, an illness, a betrayal, what was it)? Not all such changes are the work of God, but some are.

2. Do you see God at work in the change you experienced? Against that backdrop, how do you relate to Jesus' teaching in Mark 4:1-34?

stand all the parables (4:13)? The point is not that the sower parable is key to all others. Rather, their lack of understanding suggests they are outsiders. Yet, Jesus doesn't give up on them. He explains the sower parable to them (4:14-20) and then challenges them again to "get" the parables in 4:21-25: "Nothing is hidden except to be disclosed," he said. That is, he speaks in parables—in stories, metaphors, and wordplays—precisely so that people have a chance to look at their world differently. So, "see what you hear!" (literal translation of 4:24a). Since we can't actually see what we hear, we know he must mean more than physical sight. He is calling for perception or insight—the kind of sight that enables us to know that neither circumstances nor people are always what they seem to be. External appearances can be deceiving. A tiny mustard seed appears unable to produce a large bush for birds to nest in, but it does (4:30-32). Birth status is no indication of accessibility to the love of God. So, those open to God will see more and more of God at work in the world, and they will live differently because they do. But those unwilling to see will become unable to see God's work at all (4:24-25).

Teaching Tips
See What I Mean?

Almost every time the English translation of Mark reads "take heed," "beware," or "pay attention," the Greek word is *blepo*, "see." Since I am convinced this seeing is a major concern in Mark, I'll translate *blepo* as "see" every time. If you know Greek, you can check for yourself. If you don't, then when you find that I have used the word "see" in the study material, but one of these other translations is used in your Bible, you can know that the Greek is again *blepo*.

The Impact Of the Kingdom of God

Mark follows his presentation of Jesus' teaching with a series of extraordinary miracles. Let's note first that these four miracles aren't recounted to prove either Jesus' power or his divinity. Ancient people didn't understand miracles in such a way. Strange as it seems to us, in the first-century world there were many who claimed, and were believed, to be miracle workers. Miracles alone wouldn't have made Jesus unique. In fact, later in Mark's story, Jesus refuses to do a "sign from heaven" to prove himself (8:11-12). In our scientific world of facts, proofs, and natural causes we may have given too much attention to demonstrating the historical facticity of these stories in order to claim proof of Jesus' unique power as God's son. In so doing, perhaps, we have given too little attention to what Mark's audience may have heard in these stories. For this study let us not *use* these stories to prove anything so that we can hear what the stories are saying.

A Storm on the "Sea," 4:35-41

Jesus has been teaching all around the "sea" (cf. 3:7; 4:1), so when evening came after his parables teaching, he proposed that they cross to "the other side" of the sea (4:35). Interestingly, the "sea of Galilee" wasn't a sea. It was a lake. But Mark calls it a sea, probably intentionally. The vast, unknown, often stormy, filled-with-leviathans entity had become a symbol of evil and chaos. Further, the lake of Galilee was a boundary between Jews and Gentiles—"over there" were "those people." Such an attitude leads inevitably to evil. Is it any wonder, then, that Mark calls this lake a "sea?" We

Lectionary Loop
Proper 7, Year B, Mark 4:35-41
Proper 3, Year B, Mark 5:21-43

Teaching Tips
When Storms Arrive
For those who enjoy poetry, Mary Oliver's poem "Maybe," in *House of Light* (Boston: Beacon Press, 1990), 76, can be a wonderful aid to appreciating and discussing the stilling of the storm story.

should not be surprised that a storm comes up while they're out on this sea (4:37).

Jesus, though, is asleep on a cushion (4:38). The storms of the sea do not threaten him! His followers, however, are not happy with him. They wake him, but not to ask for divine help. (We often read Matthew's version of this story into Mark.) Their words, "Teacher, do you not care that we are perishing?" (4:38), sound angry and frustrated. While they work to keep the boat afloat, he is sleeping. Apparently they think he needs to get up and help bail! Instead, he got up and *rebuked* the wind, which is what he did when he cast out demons (the Greek verb, *epitimao*, is the same verb as in exorcism stories). He told the sea to be still. It did. And *then* he had to ask his disciples, "Why are you afraid? Have you still no faith?" Mark tells us that they "feared a great fear" (the literal Greek) and asked each other, "Who is this that even the wind and sea obey him?" (4:40-41).

Scholars have different views of the disciples' fear. Some consider it a cowardly response, which, along with their question "Who is this?" shows their incomprehension of Jesus and his mission despite all they've seen and heard. Others believe their question is rhetorical, asked not because they don't know, but precisely because they do know, that only God's power controls the sea (see Pss. 89:9, 107:29; Isa. 51:15; Jer. 31:35). Thus, their fear is the natural human response to a near experience of God's presence. I count myself among this latter group. I am struck that there's no mention that they are afraid of the storm. We're told they're afraid *after* Jesus stilled the storm. They know they've encountered God in this man who stills the sea.

A Legion of Demons, 5:1-20

On the other side of the sea, in Gentile territory now, Jesus is immediately met by a demon-possessed man (5:1-2). We learn that the demon's name is Legion (5:9), which is a Roman military term denoting a company of six thousand soldiers (at least). Not surprisingly, the man is uncontrollable (5:3-5). Further, the name "legion" evokes the seemingly unstoppable violence and power of Rome. But Jesus is able to cast the

Study Bible

See "Excursus: Fear of the Lord" in *NISB*, 1455.

Reflections
Fear Of the Lord

Some scholars view the disciples' fear in 4:35-41 as cowardice and incomprehension. Others see their fear as a natural human response to an experience of God's presence.
1. How do you read their fear?
2. What causes you to read it as you do?

Reflections
The Courage to Change

Many people are willing for God to fix what they perceive to be wrong in their world. But many also aren't quite so ready to have God change other parts of their world with which they are comfortable, e.g., to welcome "those people" into "our" church. How do you think you would respond to God calling for change in a part of your world with which you are currently comfortable?

demons out. He gives the demons permission to enter a herd of pigs who then rush headlong into the sea and drown (5:12-13). Perhaps Mark hoped the military terminology would cause us to remember another army (Pharoah's) that drowned in the sea.

The people of the area, having heard of the events, rush out to find the former wild man sitting with Jesus, clothed and in his right mind. Rather than celebrate the end of a menace, however, they are afraid. Like the disciples in the previous story, they are afraid *after* the threat is gone. They beg Jesus to leave them (5:15-17). The healed man, though, begs to stay with Jesus. But Jesus sends him home to bear witness to other Gentiles to what God has done (5:18-20). The word from God is for them too.

An Intercalation: Jairus' Daughter, Woman with Hemorrhages, Jairus' Daughter Healed 5:21-43

When Jesus crossed back over, a crowd gathered around him again by the sea. A synagogue ruler named Jairus emerged to ask Jesus to heal his daughter. Jesus went with him (5:21-24). In another intercalation, Mark recounts the story of a woman with a twelve-year flow of blood who sought healing from Jesus as he was going to Jairus's home. The text emphasizes the hopelessness of her illness (see vv. 25-26). Even so, she believed that a mere touch of his clothes would bring healing, which it did (5:27-29). Apparently, though, she would have sought and found healing without calling any attention to herself (quite in contrast to Jairus). But Jesus stopped, called her out, and blessed her (5:30-32, 34). The woman, *fearing* and trembling, knowing what had happened to her, came forward and told "all the truth" (5:33).

Mark then returns to the first story. While Jesus is blessing the woman, word comes that Jairus' daughter has died. But Jesus tells Jairus, "Do not fear; only have faith" (5:35-36). Jesus goes on to Jairus' home where he tells the mourners that the girl is only sleeping. They laugh at him (5:37-40). In a shame-honor culture, such laughter is ridicule, and his honor is greatly at stake. But Jesus is equal even to this challenge—he raises the little girl to life (5:41-42).

Reflections
Crossing Boundaries

There are some who believe that the boundary lines human beings draw between each other are the source of all the violence and death in the world (see, e.g., James Allison, *Raising Abel: The Recovery of the Eschatological Imagination*, New York: Crossroad, 2000, chapters 1-2). From this perspective Jesus may be seen in these texts as crossing boundaries and erasing such lines and, thus, restoring life to people. What reactions do you have to this theory about human social relations and this view of Jesus' ministry after reading these stories?

Reflections
Gender Bias in Mark?

Three characters (other than Jesus) dominate the story in Mark 14. We are told the names of Judas who betrayed Jesus and Peter who denied him, but not the name of the woman who anointed him, whom Jesus blesses. See also the woman with hemorrhage who was healed by her faith (5:25-34) and the Syrophoenician woman who was a strong advocate for her needy daughter (7:24-30).

1. Feminists suspect gender bias—i.e., women were not important enough to remember—as the reason why we don't know her name. Do you agree?
2. Do you consider the issue of gender bias here to be an important one? Why or why not?

We now find out the girl is twelve-years old, which reminds us of the woman's twelve-year illness, which reminds us these two stories are intercalated. What can we see more clearly when we read them together? The woman's twelve-year illness and the little girl's death both appear hopeless. But neither is. In that culture, neither Jairus's daughter (a family's hopes rested with sons) nor a sick woman should have mattered, but both did. Gender is a key part of these stories. While Jairus openly asked for help, the woman hid her needs and would have hidden her healing, but Jesus goes out of his way to affirm her. He also doesn't hesitate to heal a little girl. In addition, there is fear in both stories.

Reading the Cycle of Miracle Stories Together: When God Draws Near and We're Afraid

But discussion of fear reminds us that there are *four* stories here that are closely connected, for fear is prominent in them all. In the first three, people are afraid *after* Jesus does something momentous. In the fourth Jesus warns Jairus not to fear before raising his daughter from the dead. In the first and fourth stories fear and faith are explicitly contrasted with one another (4:40; 5:36). Perhaps the second and third stories illustrate what is possible in the midst of faith and fear. In the second story the Gerasene people are afraid and beg Jesus to go away (5:15-17). In the third story the woman is afraid and comes forward when Jesus calls her (5:33). The stories suggest that fear is inevitable for us human beings when we realize the presence of God at work in our world (many other biblical stories agree). So, when we are afraid, will we come forward in response to God's call, or will we beg God to go away? Will we have faith in God even when we are afraid of God?

But why would we be afraid when these stories proclaim that no evil—not a raging sea, a legion of demons, a twelve-year illness, not even death—is unconquerable for God? When God draws near evil is exorcised, boundaries between races and genders are crossed, life is restored, there is peace. Can we *see* that this is what life in God's kingdom looks like? This message is what the miracle stories bring to us, not

> ### Reflections
> #### Tell No One
>
> The text does not tell us why Jesus told the healed Gerasene man *to go* tell what God had done for him (5:19) but told Jairus and his wife that *no one should know* what had happened there (5:43). So, we cannot *know* why. But silences in the text invite us to ponder possibilities. What reasons come to your mind for Jesus' different counsel?

proof of Jesus' divinity. In fact, Jesus doesn't want Jairus to tell what happened (5:43), perhaps because he doesn't want to be known as a wonder-worker. No, the miracle stories tell us the good news that happens when God draws near. But this good news also means our world is forever changed. Folks on the other side of the sea are no longer "them" but "us." Gender relations are different. Roman legions can be resisted. Death, in all its forms, can be overcome. Such changes—aren't these the reasons we're afraid?

Some Who See, Some Who Don't

Having told us that Jesus spoke about and then demonstrated God's kingdom drawing near (chapters 4 and 5), Mark will show us in chapter 6 some folks who see, some who don't, and the consequences of their seeing or not.

Back Home in Nazareth, 6:1-6

First, Jesus goes home to Nazareth and teaches in his "home" synagogue. The people are astonished at his wisdom and power (6:1-2). Nonetheless, all they can see is the kid who grew up in their neighborhood, whose family they know well. So they took offense at him (6:3). Are they unable to see past the birth status "rules" of their culture? Do they have a "who do you think you are?" attitude? Are they sure God does not do extraordinary things through ordinary people? However we might name it, the consequence of what they (don't) see is that Jesus can do no great work among them (6:5), which means he cannot bring the life of God's kingdom into their world.

Intercalation: Disciples Sent, Death of John, Disciples Return, 6:7-32

At 6:7 we begin another Markan intercalation. In the first story Jesus sends the Twelve out to do as he has been doing (note 6:12-13). Because the Galilee was dotted with many small villages, they will travel a lot if they hope to speak to many people, so they are to travel light (6:8-9), as we say. They will be relying on the hospitality of those with whom they visit so that they are receiving even as they are giving the gospel to the people. Jesus' counsel that they stay in one home

Teaching Tips
Do You Know the Location?

Look over maps and familiarize yourself with the geography of these stories. Be able to show your people where Herod's territory is, where the feeding account likely took place, where Gennesaret is, etc. Also become familiar with the geography of what's coming next in the story. Geography is important through this part of Mark. The maps 13 and 18 in the back of the *NISB* are helpful.

per village (6:10) is probably about not accepting a "better offer," which would risk dishonor and foster envy and competition among villagers. As Mark will note specifically later, kingdom living is about community, not competition. Jesus also gives guidance for what to do if they are not welcomed and heard (6:11). We might well ask why anyone would not welcome exorcism, healing, and a new way of seeing (repentance). We have noted that the arrival of God's kingdom changes the world as we know it. For some, that kind of change is a huge threat, as we're about to be reminded.

The second story of the intercalation begins with the note that Herod Antipas had heard of Jesus because people saw him as a prophet, maybe even a resurrected John the Baptist (6:14-15). Herod is sure Jesus is John since he had beheaded John himself (6:16), suggesting paranoia on Herod's part. But Herod's comment allows Mark to tell us what had happened to John. Though the text calls him "King Herod," Antipas was really Rome's puppet king in the area. The real political power is always in Caesar's hands. So, in this story, Herod acts like so many who want to be viewed as powerful and important: arrogant, fearful, ruthless, and ultimately pathetic. He threw a lavish birthday party for himself, inviting the military, economic, and royal leaders of the area (6:21). When his daughter danced and pleased him, he made a public, boastful promise to her that led to the request for John's head to be brought on a platter, the last "dish" of the party (6:22-25). The text says that Herod had "feared" John and didn't want to execute him, but since he'd made a public oath before all those important people, his honor was at stake (6:26). Because he is a "king wannabe" and cares what these important people think of him, this supposedly powerful man believes he must do what he does not want to do. The consequence of what Herod cannot see about his desire for power is the gruesome death of John.

Mark returns to the first story by informing Jesus that the apostles had returned and had cast out demons, espoused repentance and cured people (6:30). What do we *see* when we read these two stories together? If John preceded Jesus and was martyred, and Jesus precedes the disciples and will be martyred, what does that bode for disciples? Jesus led the disciples, via the sea, into a deserted place (wilderness) to rest. But the people found them there. Because he had compassion for these "sheep without a shepherd," Jesus taught them many things until late in the day (6:31-34). The scene for the "feeding of the five thousand" is set.

Bread in the Wilderness, 6:33-44

This miracle is the only one recorded in all four Gospels. Perhaps the poverty and hunger of the Galilean peasants caused such a feeding story to leave an indelible mark in the minds of Jesus' followers. Further, the story is told with significant Exodus overtones: God gives bread to the people in the wilderness; an oppressive ruler looms in the background (Pharoah then; Herod now); later there will be a sea story, Jesus will go up on a mountain to pray, and the divine name "I am" will be spoken. The Exodus story evokes God's acts to free and care for an enslaved, suffering people. Royal rulers, including those in Rome, proclaimed that God (or the gods) anointed them to rule, favored them, acted through them, etc., and that their power was proof of their divinely granted privileges. The Exodus story and the story of Jesus say otherwise. The God of the Exodus and of Jesus is the majestic Creator of all that exists, and One who notices, cares for, and acts on behalf of those who are powerless, hungry, and shepherd-less in the wilderness.

We should take note of three other aspects of this story. First is the disciples' disappointing response to Jesus' exhortation that they feed the people (6:37). We'd hope that those who've witnessed Jesus doing the improbable, who've healed and cast out demons themselves, might not so quickly feel hopeless about a situation because of money they don't have. What are they seeing? Second, because the text is silent about *how* Jesus brought this miracle about, some have filled the silence by wondering if the miracle was getting people to share. Without claiming that such is what actually happened, we may still learn by pondering that possibility. How easily would a beaten-down, fearful, hungry people have begun to hoard and hide what little they had and to treat neighbors as enemies who might steal their bread? But what if someone shares five breads and two fish with Jesus, who in turn shares it with those around him and encourages others to do the same? Suddenly, a multitude of hungry people are satisfied, and there are even leftovers! They have a chance to see, then, that their neighbors are *not* enemies, that isolating themselves in fear only furthers Rome's oppression of them, that choosing a we're-all-in-this-together mentality enables them to care for one another, find hope together, and begin to resist the sense that they are beaten. That would be a wonderful miracle! Kingdom living is about such a community. Finally, we should note the repetition of the word "bread." While the English translations go back and forth between "bread" and "loaves," the Greek word is always *artos* (bread). This repetition is not a big deal here, but it sets up well what is coming in Mark's story.

Bread on the Sea, 6:45-56

After the miracle, Jesus sent his disciples back across the sea, that boundary between Jews and Gentiles, while he went up the mountain to pray (6:45-46). What follows is an odd little story in this Gospel. Another storm came up on the sea. Jesus saw his disciples struggling, so he went toward them, walking on the sea (6:48)! But he intended to pass them by—why? The text does not say, and interpreters are baffled. Whatever the reason, the disciples saw him as a ghost and were terrified. But he told them not to be afraid, for "I am," which is the literal translation of the Greek *ego eimi*; this evokes the Exodus story and God's liberating work again. Accordingly, Jesus got into the boat with them and the storm ceased (6:51). Then the disciples were astounded, but not, the text says, because Jesus walked on the sea or stilled the storm, but because they didn't understand about the bread (*artos*). What? Many readers will respond, "Neither do I!" What should they have understood about the bread? What should we? If the disciples' lack of understanding shows their hearts were hardened (6:52), how are

---

Reflections
The Divine Appearance

Some readers think Jesus intended to "pass them by" in the boat (6:48) to avoid frightening them. Others believe Mark intended to evoke God passing Moses by so that Moses could see God's back, which would make this story a *theophany* (a "God-appearing" story). What thoughts do you have about why Jesus would have passed them by?

we then challenged? We must read on in Mark to find answers.

Curiously, the boat trip doesn't get Jesus and the disciples to the other side of the sea. They come ashore at Gennesaret, northwest of Bethsaida, still in Jewish territory (6:53). Mark summarizes Jesus' successful ministry in that region (6:54-56), but perhaps we should note their failure to travel to the other side. What do they (not) see?

The Inclusivity Of the Kingdom

Return to Conflict: Purity Rules and an Honor Challenge, 7:1-5

After a summary report of Jesus' successes and popularity (6:53-56), Mark returns us to the conflict brewing around him. Joining Pharisees to watch him are scribes from Jerusalem (7:1), meaning the temple establishment is now concerned about Jesus.

Mark says that this group noticed some of Jesus' disciples eating bread (Greek, *artos*, omitted in most translations) with unwashed hands. (There is more for us to discover about bread.) Mark then explains Jewish ritual purity practices regarding food and food preparations, which is the "tradition of the elders" (7:2-4). Some have considered this explanation to be necessary for Gentiles in Mark's audience. Perhaps so. But it also highlights the "external" nature of these purity practices: If the food is ritually clean (note: hygiene is not the concern; the issue is holiness), if pots, pans, and hands are ritually clean, then nothing ritually unclean/unholy enters the person eating. The focus of ritual purity is on externals, i.e., boundaries, surfaces, on keeping the "dirt" beyond one's borders. The temple structure illustrates this point. Priests could draw near the Holy of Holies, but those who were unclean could not enter the sanctuary at all so that the "center" would not be defiled. This focus is also what set Jews apart from Gentiles. A Jewish body was more pure than a Gentile body, a male body more pure than a female body, and a physically whole body more pure than one that was less than whole. Again, the importance of birth status is underscored.

> ### Reflections
> #### Jesus Versus the Pharisees
> 1. What would you name as the major issue for the scribes and Pharisees in their conflict with Jesus?
> 2. Was it their Jewishness? The way they practiced their religion? A love of power and privilege? What would you name?

> ### Reflections
> #### Only Pure on the Outside
> Have Christians ever practiced an "external purity?" If your answer is yes, can you give an example?

There is debate today regarding how widespread these purity concerns would have been in first-century Israel. Since most Jews would never be able to go to temple, whether or not they were clean enough to enter the sanctuary might matter little to them. This story suggests, though, that scribes *from Jerusalem* would have been very concerned about purity and that they could use the issue to try to dishonor someone who was considered holy by the people. Further, the practices at issue in this text revolve around eating. New Testament writers frequently mention trouble with meals (e.g., see Luke 14:12-14; Acts 10:9-16; Gal 2:11-14; 1 Cor 11:20-22). Since table fellowship—then and now—brings communities together, and since "kosher" eating practices kept Jews and Gentiles from sharing table fellowship, these practices raised significant questions for followers of Jesus.

So, in a public setting, the scribes and Pharisees call attention to disciples eating bread with unwashed hands and ask Jesus why they "do not live according to the tradition of the elders" (7:5). Such a public challenge is designed to dishonor Jesus.

Jesus' Response to the Challenge: Not Subtle, 7:6-13

Jesus' response is not subtle. First he calls them hypocrites and quotes Isaiah at them (7:6-7). Then he accuses them of abandoning and rejecting God's commandments (7:8-9) and supports his charge with the Corban example (7:10-12). The emphasis in Greek reads: "**Moses** said… but **you** say…". *Corban* refers to an offering dedicated to God so that it cannot be used for other purposes, including care for parents. Jesus' words suggest some were using it to let themselves "off the hook" of parental care and that the religious leadership endorsed the practice (for the money would eventually go to the temple). Thus, he says, they have "made void" the word of God (7:13).

Jesus Subverts Their View of Purity, 7:14-15

Even then he's not finished. He called the crowd (who owns the public setting now?) and said to them that there is nothing outside a person that can defile

Source

Some of the material in this study was originally published in *Lectionary Homiletics* and used with permission. See Mitzi Minor, "Exegesis: Mark 7:31-37, 8:27-37, 9:30-37, 9:38-50," *Lectionary Homiletics* XIV (2003), 41-42, 47-48, 55-56, 61-62.

that person (7:14-15). Thus he has subverted their whole practice of determining (seeing) who is holy and who is not.

Explaining the "Parable" to the Disciples, Making All Foods Clean, 7:17-23

Later the disciples ask him about the "parable" (7:17). Remember that in Mark a parable is any teaching that "stands the world on its head," and this one does. Though Jesus seems displeased with their lack of understanding again (4:10-13), he graciously explains. Purity, he said, is a matter of the heart (7:18-21), which means that a Gentile could be as pure as a Jew, a woman as pure as a man, a leper as pure as a priest. Mark's editorial addition, "thus he declared all foods clean," makes clear his understanding that when the kingdom of God draws near, *everyone* is welcome at the table.

The Syrophoenician Woman and the Children's Bread, 7:24-30

But this kind of radical inclusivity is not easy. Jesus, having rewritten the definition of purity, traveled into Gentile territory (the region of Tyre) where he encountered a Syrophoenician woman with a request (7:24-26). As a Gentile and a female, this woman was automatically unclean to a Jewish man, but there's more. The association of Phoenicia with ancient Jewish struggles over foreign religious practices, especially temple prostitution, means "syrophoenician" could indicate a woman from the "seamier" side of a city. Furthermore, this woman approached Jesus, a Jewish man with a religious vocation to whom she was unknown and unrelated, so that she has stepped out of "her place." She did so on behalf of her daughter, a further liability since sons, not daughters, were the focus of a family's hopes. Finally, her daughter was possessed by an "unclean" spirit, a note that completes the portrait of a thoroughly impure woman—female, foreign, pagan, sexually suspect, inappropriately assertive, and "home" to an unclean spirit.

Thus Jesus' response ("it is not good to take the children's bread [*artos*] and throw it to the dogs,"

Study Bible

See *NISB*, 1822, for comment on the omission of Mark 7:16 from the text. There will be other places in Mark where a verse has been omitted. The *NISB* will have notes on those as well.

7:27) was entirely fitting in that culture. We, however, find his words harsh and troubling. Because we do not want to think of our "sinless Christ" speaking this way, great efforts have been made to "fix" his words (e.g., he was testing her). But the text does not help us. It only gives us Jesus' words without softening them. Perhaps we can be less uncomfortable if we focus on the theological concept of incarnation. How human will we let Jesus be? Interpreters have often thought that Mark gives us Jesus at his most human. This story is a premier example. In it Jesus may be a man still learning and growing in his awareness of God's kingdom. (Is it sinful to be growing still?) Though he himself had declared that purity is a matter of one's heart so that everyone is welcome at the table, when confronted by a thoroughly unclean woman he responded, "But not you." How human is that?

So Jesus has put the woman in "her place," but she will not stay there. She throws Jesus' words back at him: Aren't dogs allowed to eat crumbs (7:28)? Isn't there plenty of *bread*, plenty of God to go around? This time Jesus affirms that she is right and grants her request (7:29), thus signaling his recognition of her purity before God. The woman has "won" her argument with Jesus in more ways than one. It is her riposte to Jesus' challenge.

"Be Opened!" 7:31-37

Mark tells us that Jesus then traveled back toward the Sea of Galilee, though still in Gentile territory, where people bring to him a deaf and mute man (7:31-32). On the surface, we have only another miracle story. But Mark often skillfully arranged his material so that his stories cast a symbolic hue over what surrounds them. Jesus has subverted the purity system of his world and replaced it with purity of heart that welcomes—finally—even a Syrophoenician woman. Now he encounters one who cannot hear or speak clearly. Is this merely historical recording, or is Mark trying to help us see (and hear)? Verse 34 is evocative. First, Jesus sighed. Why? Frustration that people are deaf to God's word? Regret that his ears weren't initially open to the woman? The text does not tell us. We are left

Reflections
Jesus Sighed
Another silence in the text invites us to ponder a bit. So, why do you think Jesus sighed or groaned (Greek, *stenazo*, Mark 7:34)?

with what his sigh evokes within us. Then he commanded the man's ears, "Be opened!" Again, mere historical recording, or do the words leap off the page at readers? This man's ears were opened, and his tongue loosened (7:35). The story ends with Jesus once again ordering people not to tell, but they did, for they were astounded beyond measure (7:36-37).

Bread for the Gentiles, 8:1-10

Since the feeding of the five thousand, we've noted the references to bread (Greek, *artos*) in this part of Mark's story: Jesus fed them *artos* in the wilderness, the disciples in the boat didn't understand about the *artos*, the disciples ate *artos* with unwashed hands, the children's *artos* should not be fed to the dogs. In and around these stories, Jesus has undone the purity rules that divided Jews and Gentiles, making it possible for everyone to come to his table. Now this section of Mark comes to a close with Jesus again feeding bread (*artos*) to a multitude in the wilderness (8:1-10). The story is remarkably similar to the first feeding story: Jesus had been teaching the people for a while, the disciples are clueless, they have but a few loaves and fish to share, yet everyone eats and is satisfied. The key difference is that this feeding happens in Gentile territory. Is this merely historical recording, or is Mark trying to help us see? The boundaries (the sea; the purity rules) have been crossed, the bread has been shared, everyone has been filled. The kingdom of God has drawn near. So, do *we* understand about the bread?

Reflections
Tell No One!

At the end of Mark 7 Jesus tells people *not* to tell what was happening, but they did tell (7:36). We may find Jesus' counsel *not* to tell unsettling.

1. What do you imagine is going on here—are the people telling about the miracles, or are they talking about how everyone is welcomed at the table?
2. Which would bother Jesus, and why?

Teaching Tips
Where Is It Located?

Continue to use maps to highlight the geography of these events, especially to show when Jesus is in Jewish territory and when he is in Gentile territory.

A Second Touch

The Pharisees Do Not Understand about the Miracles, 8:11-13

After the feeding story, another boat trip brings Jesus to another encounter with the Pharisees. They seek a sign "to test him" (8:11). That is, they are demanding proof of the truth of his mission. So, what would prove it to them? What are they willing to see?

Jesus sighs—again—and tells them there will be no signs (8:12). Earlier I mentioned that miracles were not proofs of Jesus' divinity in Mark. Here is good support for that statement. The miracles reveal *to those who can see* what happens when God's kingdom draws near. For those *unwilling to see*, no proofs will ever do. So Jesus gets back in the boat and leaves them (8:13).

The Disciples Do Not Understand about the Bread, 8:14-21

We've been told several times that Jesus crossed the sea, but we come now to the third significant exchange between Jesus and his followers on such a boat trip (see 4:35-41; 6:47-52). Storytellers often tell stories in threes, and the third in a series is often the climactic segment. So we should watch this story closely. Mark tells us that the disciples had brought but one bread (*artos*) with them on the boat (8:14) just before giving us Jesus' words: "Look, see the yeast of the Pharisees and the yeast of Herod!" (8:15). Yeast was a common metaphor in the ancient world for evil. In the context of Mark's story, the "yeast" of the Pharisees and Herod, particularly given the previous story, evokes their unwillingness to see God's kingdom drawing near.

Reflections
Jesus Sighs Again

During a miracle story, Jesus again sighs or groans (Greek, *anastenazo*, Mark 8:12). What do his sighs evoke for you?

Remarkably, the disciples think Jesus is unhappy because they have insufficient bread with them (8:16). As if he hasn't shown that he can provide bread for those who are hungry (8:19-20)! In fact, it appears that Jesus was warning them, not scolding them. But he becomes irate at their response to his warning: "Are your hearts hardened? Having eyes do you not see and having ears do you not hear?" (8:18). All they have been present for, and still he must ask, "Do you not yet understand?" (8:21). Jesus can "do" bread, but he cannot force insightfulness on disciples. They must be willing to see.

A Blind Man Needs a Second Touch, 8:22-26

The boat trip brings them to Bethsaida and an encounter with a blind man (8:22). Is this merely historical recording, or is Mark trying to help us see? After taking the man outside the village, spitting on his eyes and laying hands on him (conventional healing actions in that world), Jesus asks him, "Can you see anything?" (8:23). The question is poignant here. No doubt it should be asked of disciples!

The good news is that the answer is yes; the man can see something. But he can't see clearly. People look like walking trees (8:24). So Jesus laid hands on him again. This time he "saw around" and "saw in" everything clearly (8:25). Some readers are bothered that Jesus seemed to "come up short" on his first healing effort. But Mark hasn't been concerned to prove anything about Jesus' power. Instead, Mark has been interested in telling the story so that readers glean a greater truth than the miracle itself. Is it sometimes true of disciples that we can see something, but we cannot see clearly and need a second touch?

On the Way: Blind Disciples Get a "Second Touch," 8:27-9:1

Jesus then traveled northward for the last time, to the villages of Caesarea Philippi (8:27). To this point he has been teaching in Galilee and north of it. But in this next Markan section he is *on the way*, journeying steadily southward to Jerusalem with his half-seeing followers in tow. These geographical clues signal a shift in the story.

Source

On Mark 8:31 see Ched Myers, *Binding the Strong Man: A Political Reading of Mark's Story of Jesus* (Maryknoll, N.Y.: Orbis, 1988), 244.

So, *on the way* Jesus asked his disciples how others were identifying him. Then he asked, "Who do you say that I am?" (8:27-29). We readers know from verse 1:1 that Peter's answer, "You are the Messiah" (or Christ), is correct. Yet Jesus "*rebuked (epitimao)* them so that they would say nothing about him" (v. 30, a.t.). This verb is the one used when Jesus rebuked demons during exorcisms and the wind during a storm (4:39). It is much sharper than the English translations "warned" or "sternly ordered." Why does Jesus rebuke disciples here? We read on.

"He began to teach them" (v. 31), and he did so openly or plainly (v. 32)—that is, not in parables as before (see 4:34). Here, then, is the "second touch" that he is offering followers. His plain teaching is that the Son of man (not "Messiah") must suffer and die and after three days rise again (v. 31). Surely that is as plain as can be!

The word translated "must" is the Greek verb *dei*, which is literally "it is necessary," or "it is inevitable (Myers, 244). For Mark the word does not indicate that God ordained Jesus' suffering. Since I teach at a racially diverse seminary in Memphis, I often unpack this text for students by asking them if the suffering of civil rights activists was necessary. Was there any other way to expose segregation as a violent, oppressive system instead of submitting to the benign "separate but equal" way of living upon which segregationists insisted? My students invariably answer no. Similarly, Jesus is exposing the evil of the religious leaders' way of living. Their religious, political, economic, and social practices, though centered in temple and torah (the purity code), were *not* just. Their opposition to Jesus' forgiveness, compassion, and liberation of "those who are sick" (2:15-17), their demonizing of Jesus' practices (3:22), and their violent responses to him (3:6; more violence is forthcoming) unveil their intent to preserve their privileged place rather than serve God and neighbor. Jesus' suffering, therefore, is necessary to expose them. If he continues his mission, it is also inevitable.

Peter responded to Jesus' plain teaching by rebuking Jesus (v. 32)! Remember that Peter was rebuked when he named Jesus as the Christ. Does he understand the Christ as a triumphant (Davidic) conqueror of their enemies in God's name, a view apparently alive in first-century Israel (there were several "messiahs" and popular uprisings in this time)? Is he hoping Jesus will replace the current leadership with himself and other disciples? Does he have the title right but the definition wrong? Perhaps, for Jesus rebuked him when he called Jesus the Christ, and does so again here for "thinking human things rather than the things of God" (v. 33).

Then Jesus called everyone together and extended his "second touch." Followers of Jesus must deny self (v. 34). That is, there is no winning, no triumphalism along this way. Those are "human things" serving self rather than God. Pumped-up egos promote the cause of evil as any reading of human history shows. So, followers of Jesus deny self and take up the cross (v. 34). In the first century world "cross" had but one connotation: on it Rome executed those who threatened "the way things were." (Myers, 245) Well, Jesus threatened the way things were by announcing the arrival of God's kingdom as an alternative to the violence and oppression of the religion, politics, and economics of the day. He called followers to join him. They will suffer and appear to be losers, but come on along!

Why should anyone accept Jesus' invitation? *How* can anyone? Verses 35-37 affirm hope in an ultimate sense of *life*, an apocalyptic hope that flows from God and infuses Jesus' followers with life that cannot be taken from them, even by death. Jesus' terse prediction of his own resurrection (v. 31) affirms the same apocalyptic hope. The supreme threat of any earthly power is to kill. But this threat has no power over those with faith that God's life cannot be taken from them. They are free to proclaim God's kingdom and follow Jesus on the way. Their freedom is itself a sign of their life in God.

Thus the issue here is not Jesus' identity. Peter knows who Jesus is. But Peter does not see the mission that goes with the identity: not messianic triumphalism but exposing evil and suffering.

Reflections
Take Up Your Torture Stakes

Rome crucified those whom they considered a threat to the "order" they'd created in the world.

1. At this point in Mark's story, what kind of threat do you understand Jesus to be to the "order" in that world?
2. In that context, how should we hear his call to "take up the cross?"
3. What might "cross-bearing" according to Mark look like in our time, in our world?

Teaching Tips
Rome's Torture Stake

Two thousand years of veneration of the cross have far removed us from Rome's gruesome instrument of terror. Have the class examine and discuss some of the old hymns about the cross of Christ.

1. Do any acknowledge the cross as an instrument of terror? If they do, how?
2. What is the purpose or function of the cross in these hymns?

Some of those standing there, Jesus said, will *see* that God's kingdom *has come* with power (9:1). This verse has bothered readers who understood the kingdom as a future event. From that perspective, Jesus is wrong. But the kingdom is not future (only) in Mark as we have noted. The perfect tense verb "has come" (the continuance of completed action) reiterates that point. And "seeing" isn't about our physical eyes. The bumbling disciples have frustrated Jesus, but this verse affirms that not all followers are blind. Some are going to see that the kingdom has come with power.

The Transfiguration: "Listen to Him!" 9:2-8

Three who haven't yet done so are given another chance. Peter, James, and John went up the mountain with Jesus and saw him transfigured in glory, talking with Elijah and Moses. They heard the voice of God affirm him as God's beloved son (9:2-8). But they also heard God's voice exhorting them, "listen to him!" When he speaks of denying self, taking up the cross, and the arrival of the kingdom to transform their world, listen to him!

Source

Those interested in messiahs and popular uprisings in first-century Israel can read Richard A. Horsley, *Jesus and Empire: The Kingdom of God and the New World Disorder* (Minneapolis: Fortress Press, 2003), chapters 1 and 2.

On the Way: The Second Touch Continues (1)

Elijah Has Come First, 9:9-13

As they came down from the mountain, Jesus ordered the disciples to tell no one about the transfiguration until after he rose from the dead, which prompts questioning about the resurrection (9:9-10). Apparently what they'd just witnessed, plus their Jewish understanding that resurrection happens at the end of the present age and the beginning of the messianic age, caused the disciples to wonder about Elijah as forerunner of the new age (Mal 4:5-6). Perhaps they hoped that if Elijah came first and restored people's hearts to God, then there would be no suffering. But Jesus dismisses that hope: Elijah (John) has come and was treated badly, and "it is written" that the Son of man will suffer also (9:11-13).

Raising a Demon-Possessed Boy, 9:14-29

Returning to the other disciples, they find them disputing with scribes over a demon-possessed boy (9:14-17). Three key aspects of this story call for our attention. The first is the lengthy description of the demon's effect on the boy (9:17-18, 20-22, 26). Clearly this evil is sucking the life from this boy. At one point people even think he is dead (v. 26). But taking him by the hand, Jesus "raised him and he arose" (9:27, a.t.)—the Greek verbs (*egeiro, anistēmi*) are those used for resurrection. The symbolics of the story are telling: evil brings death; God gives life.

The second is the exchange between Jesus and the boy's father. The father's painfully honest response, "I believe; help my unbelief," (9:24), has struck a chord

---

> ### Reflections
> **I'm Only Human!**
> "I believe, help my unbelief"—what response do those words evoke in you?

51

among Christians for generations. Who among us hasn't felt just that way? The good news is: It is enough. Jesus heals the man's son. In addition, Jesus' words, "All things are possible for the one who believes," (9:23) are the first of several similar statements he will make. We should watch this idea unfold.

Finally, there is the disciples' failure to cast out this demon. Earlier they'd been successful at this task (6:13), but not now. When they ask Jesus why, he says this demon only comes out by prayer (9:29), implying they had not prayed. Does this mean they had forgotten from where power over evil derives, that they thought they now "owned" this power? What do they see?

Jesus' Second Passion Prediction, 9:30-37

No wonder, then, that Jesus stays away from crowds and focuses on teaching disciples as they travel through Galilee (9:30-31). He tells them again that he is going to die and, after three days, rise (9:31). This announcement of his fate is the shortest, plainest of his three passion predictions. He says simply that he will be betrayed into human hands, and "they will kill him." Still the disciples do not understand (9:32). Since the words are plain, what do they *not* understand? And why are they afraid to ask? (9:32)

The company journeys on to Capernaum. Now, because Jesus asks them (9:33), we discover that *on the way* the disciples discussed among themselves who was the greatest (9:34). Their lack of understanding is becoming clearer. While Jesus is proclaiming the arrival of God's kingdom, risking his life to expose the evil of "human things" that oppose the kingdom (like status, privilege, power), and trusting in God's life, the disciples hope that their presence with Christ will make them "the greatest." Though Jesus speaks of letting go, they speak of gain. Though he has called them to deny self, they want to boost self even as they are "on the way" with him. Indeed, they do not understand!

Still, Jesus does not give up on them. After all, they have seen something in him and followed him to this point. They even understood enough to be silent—

Reflections
I Was Here First!

1. In Mark 9:34 the disciples appear to want their associations with Jesus to work for their advantage. Jesus seems to disapprove.
2. What is your understanding of why he disapproves?

Reflections
Sorry, You're Not One of Us!

Imagine yourself in the scene in which someone has cast a demon out of another person in Jesus' name. A human being's suffering has been ended in Jesus' name! How do you react? Imagine yourself still there when John and the others arrive and order the exorcist to stop because he's not "following" them. How do you react to this turn of events? What can we learn for our own time from this story? Have volunteers do a class skit of a Christian, unaffiliated with any local church, who provides a shelter for homeless people and receives the greatest opposition from the area churches. About what would some of the opposing churches be most concerned?

embarrassed?—when he asked what they were discussing (9:34). So, Jesus tries again to teach them. To be first, he said, one must choose to be last, that is, a servant of all people (9:35). The irony in the wordplay is wonderful, for if everyone chooses to be a servant, then no one will be "first" (or "the greatest"). Neither will anyone be last. Instead, everyone will be serving everyone else. But note: disciples *choose* to be servants. Even Jesus does not force behavior on followers. He teaches, exhorts, and pleads, but does not force them.

Further, they choose to serve *all* people. To underscore this point Jesus takes a little child in his arms, puts the child in their midst, and embraces the child (9:36). A child in that world was an insignificant part of an adult-oriented culture, without status, honor, or power, meaning that in the public arena children had no "place." But Jesus receives and embraces a child and exhorts disciples to welcome (receive with hospitality; serve) such a child in his name (9:37). Since a child is honorless and powerless, he or she has no "favor" to grant others. Therefore, the only motivation for serving children, Syrophoenician women, lepers, or any others judged as having "no place," is genuine compassion for *all* people. While there is no honor to be gained by serving the least ones, there is a glad outcome to this service. Our "reward" for welcoming them is encounter with God (9:37).

The Disciples and Scandals, 9:38-50

Mark then immediately tells us the disciples stopped someone who was casting out demons in Jesus' name "because he was not following us" (9:38). Notice their complaint that the person "was not following *us*." Us? Don't do such a thing, Jesus said, because "*no one* who does a deed of power in my name will be able soon afterward to speak evil of me" (9:39), and "*whoever* gives you a cup of water in my name . . . will by no means lose their reward" (9:41). See how inclusive he is! See also how he speaks of "deeds of power" as well as "cups of water." *Anyone* who does *any* act of mercy in Christ's name is welcome in Jesus' circle.

Jesus follows with another *"whoever"* statement: "whoever scandalizes one of these little ones who believe in me" would be better off drowned in the sea (42, a.t.)! The Greek verb for *scandalize* denotes causing someone to turn from Jesus' way. Here Jesus is concerned with causing "one of these *little ones*" to turn away. "Little ones" brings to mind the child of 9:36, but would include anyone considered lowly and least.

In verses 43-48 Jesus continues to talk about *scandalizing*, saying that if your hand or foot or eye cause you to do such, then cut it off! He said earlier that nothing compares to the life that is God's gift. (See 8:35-37.) Here he says that scandalizing others risks this life/entering the kingdom, so don't do it, even if you must cut off your hand! Rather, "have salt in yourselves and be at peace" (9:50). In the Old Testament, salt is a symbol of the covenant (Lev. 2:13). In a few verses we've moved from disciples arguing over rank, to conflict with an "outsider" exorcist, to "scandals" in the community. Opposite all of these Jesus offers the peace of inclusive covenant relationships and of service, which is living the life of God and entering God's kingdom now.

A Test: a Question of Marriage, 10:1-12

The company has traveled now to Judea and beyond the Jordan (10:1). "Beyond the Jordan" would be Herod's territory, which may be the reason the Pharisees chose this moment to test Jesus by asking about divorce (10:2). John got in trouble with Herod for criticizing his divorce and remarriage (6:18). Perhaps they hoped Jesus would do the same.

When the Pharisees note that Moses allowed a man to divorce his wife with a certificate, Jesus said that was due to their hard hearts. Since God made us male and female, God intended the two to become "one flesh" (10:4-9). Despite these words, when disciples question him later, Jesus assumes divorces will happen and says that remarriage amounts to adultery (10:10-12). We need to understand ancient marriage if we wish to understand Jesus here.

Marriage in that world was an economic arrange-

Teaching Tip
Seen and Not Heard

Become familiar with and knowledgeable about the "place" of and perspective on children in the first-century Mediterranean world. You can check Bruce J. Malina and Richard Rohrbaugh, *Social Science Commentary on the Synoptic Gospels* (Philadelphia: Fortress, 1992; 2nd ed., 2003).

ment (and a political one among elite classes) between honorable families in the same social class. A woman gained a home. A man gained the means of producing an heir to the family name and inheritance. In Jewish law a man could divorce his wife for several reasons, including not producing a son, but a woman could not initiate divorce. A divorced woman's plight was dire. Jesus' words signaling mutuality and the importance of intimacy, forbidding divorce, and naming a man's remarriage as adultery against his wife thus provided women some protection and made them something more than baby-producing machines in the marriage. Also, prohibitions against re-marriage could prevent the dishonoring of families that produced blood feuds. Indeed, Herod's divorce of the daughter of the king of Nabatea led later to violence in which many Galileans died.

When we bring Jesus' words into our world, we need to remember how differently we understand marriage today. We also need to remember that in Mark, Jesus has already dispensed with food laws and overturned Moses on divorce, both of which were included in the Torah. It is difficult to imagine him saying in any circumstance, "I don't care how much you are suffering, rules are rules."

Study Bible

See "Excursus: Honor and Shame" in *NISB*, 1456-57.

On the Way: The Second Touch Continues (2)

Receive the Kingdom Like a Child, 10:13-16

Following the test about marriage, and still on the outskirts of Judea, people brought children to Jesus so he could touch (bless) them. But the disciples rebuked (*eptimao*) them (10:13), if you can believe that! What do they see?

Jesus is angry with them. We readers should know why. He calls for the children to be brought to him and declares that God's kingdom belongs "to such as these" (10:14). Furthermore, he says, "Whoever does not receive the kingdom of God as a little child, will never enter it" (10:15). When we read these words through contemporary lenses, we likely think of entering God's kingdom by being innocent, trusting, guileless, etc., as children are. But those are *our* views of children. We should remember, as I've suggested, that children in Jesus' world were among the least ones, those without place or honor. They were outside the religious/political/economic "system" the human powers had created. So, when Jesus called that system unrighteous and announced God's undoing of it, children and other "outsiders" were free to join themselves to God's work because they were not invested in the work of human powers. In just this way, we are to receive God's kingdom.

One Who Won't Receive the Kingdom Like a Child, 10:17-22

As they traveled on, a man asked Jesus, "Good teacher, what must I do to inherit eternal life?" (10:17). In a shame-honor culture, his compliment and request for help were a positive honor challenge. Jesus responds by first rejecting the compliment (10:18) and then issuing his own challenge to the man (10:19). Included in Jesus' list of some of the commandments is, "do not defraud," which is technically not a commandment. From the perspective of people in Jesus' world, a person got rich by exploiting and defrauding others, that is, by keeping most people on the bottom of the "pyramid" (through taxes and indebtedness) with only a few at the top to share wealth and power. So Jesus adds "do not defraud" to the commandments. We'll want to watch for why he does so.

The man meets Jesus' challenge. He affirms that he has kept the commandments since his youth (10:20). According to the "rules" of a shame-honor challenge, Jesus ought now to praise the man and declare him blessed with life. Instead, after Mark tells us that Jesus loved him, the only time Mark says such a thing in the Gospel, Jesus tells him he lacks one thing. He must sell all he has, give the money to the poor (those on the pyramid bottom), and follow Jesus (10:21). Now we find out that the man was rich, one of those at the top of the pyramid, one of those who probably defrauded others. Further, he's invested in remaining a part of this system, for he turned away from Jesus' call. He grieved, but he turned away (10:22). He was unwilling to receive the kingdom like a child.

A Hundredfold Blessings with Persecutions for Those Who Do, 10:23-31

So, when Jesus turns to his disciples and declares the difficulty that rich people have entering God's kingdom (10:23-25), we should be able to understand his words. The religious/political/economic system of the day worked for rich people, and they, in turn, worked for it. They had a significant "place" in the world created by the human powers. Thus, it was easier for a camel to go through the eye of a needle (an impossibility) than for a rich person to receive the kingdom like children, like those not invested in the religious/political/ economic system of the day. We should understand now.

But the disciples seem confused. What does their question, "Then who can be saved?" (10:26) suggest?

Reflections
Jesus Loved Him

Mark tells us that Jesus loved the rich man (10:21). Suppose a twenty-first century American read this story and said, "That doesn't look like love to me. If he'd really loved him, he'd have gone after him and not just let him walk away." How would you respond to such a statement?

Teaching Tips
Learn from the Soul-Taker

The wisdom story, "The Soul-Taker," in *One Hundred Wisdom Stories from Around the World*, ed. by Margaret Silf (Cleveland: Pilgrim Press, 2003), 117-118, could be helpful in a discussion of the rich man story.

Since rich people *appear* successful, comfortable, and powerful, do the disciples assume riches to be a sign of God's favor? What do they see? There is still good news here, however. It is possible for rich ones to be saved, for "all things are possible" for God (10:27). God can transform even such a one if he or she is willing. This is the first of two "all things are possible" statements from Jesus (14:36). Remember, we are watching this unfold.

There is even good news about the disciples! Peter points out that they have left everything to follow Jesus, and Jesus seems to affirm Peter's statement. Jesus promises that those who leave homes, families, and fields will receive a "hundredfold" of these in this life and, in the age to come, eternal life. But he adds that these gifts are received *with persecutions* (10:28-30). Living in God's kingdom outside the religious/political/economic system of the day brings blessings, but it also provokes opposition from those invested in that system.

So, *on the way*, going up to Jerusalem, the center of the religious/political/economic system of first century Israel, Jesus' followers are afraid. And Jesus tells them for the third time that he is going to suffer and be killed (10:32-34). As befits the third in a series of three, this prediction gives the most detailed description of his suffering before offering, "and after three days he will rise again."

Jesus' Third Passion Prediction, 10:32-45

Despite these details about Jesus' suffering, James and John ask Jesus to do whatever they request of him. Jesus, being nobody's dummy, asks, "What do you wish that I would do for you?" They ask for the seats at his right and left hands—the seats of honor—when he comes into his glory (10:35-37). *Into his glory!* What do they see?

In response, Jesus asks them if they are able to drink the cup he drinks (see 14:36) and bear his baptism (during which the Spirit empowered him for his mission, 1:9-11). They claim to be able, and Jesus affirms that they will do so (10:38-39). Here is more good news about the disciples. But we should note that the

---

Reflections
Wealth: a Blessing or Curse?

The disciples seem to assume that riches were a sign of God's blessing and favor. Do we make the same assumption today? What response do you have to Jesus' assertion that "it is easier for a camel to go through the eye of a needle than for a rich person to enter the kingdom of God?"

verbs are future tense. They aren't there yet. Even so, only God decides who gets the seats of honor (10:40).

Meanwhile, the other ten have heard and are angry at James and John (10:41). Jesus' response to them, though, suggests they're angry at having been outdone rather than pained that the brothers would ask such a thing. For Jesus reminds them that the rulers of the Gentiles (Romans) "lord over them" and their great ones "have power over them." "But," he says, "it is not so among you!" Rather, as he has said before, to be great or first in God's kingdom is to be a slave and servant of all (10:42-44). This, as we noted before, means no one will be great, first, last, or least because everyone will be serving everyone else. Jesus does not contrast a good versus a bad exercise of power over others. He contrasts power over others versus service to all. In God's kingdom there are neither pyramids and hierarchies, nor structures of domination or subordination. Even Jesus came to serve rather than to be served (10:45)!

Jesus also came to give his life as a ransom for many (10:45). A ransom was paid to buy a slave's freedom, so Jesus will give his life to free people from that which enslaves them. Often while reading Jesus' words, Paul's teachings come to mind (especially for Protestants), so that we assume Jesus means his death is a sacrifice of atonement that frees us from sin. But sin (as we think of it) has not been a major topic in Mark. Instead, we've seen people enslaved by attachment to honor and status, purity rules, demonic powers, fear of persecution, and the religious/political/economic system centered in the temple. Though Jesus doesn't specify how, he declares his death to be an "exodus from slavery," from *whatever* has a person in bondage (rather than a sacrifice of atonement). We will watch this exodus unfold.

Bartimaeus Sees and Follows on the Way, 10:46-52

So they passed through Jericho, drawing ever closer to Jerusalem. Bartimaeus, a blind beggar beside the road, cried out to Jesus for mercy. People in the crowd rebuked (*eptimao*) him. The "rules" of the day said an unclean outcast like Bartimaeus could not even speak

---

Reflections
Was Blind but Now Sees

When Bartimaeus answered Jesus' question with, "Rabbi, let me see," Jesus said to him, "Your faith has saved you." The implication is that a *desire to see* is connected to *faith*. How would you describe that connection?

to someone considered holy. By now, though, we readers should not be surprised that Jesus called for Bartimaeus to be brought to him (10:46-49). Jesus asked him, "What do you wish that I would do for you?" (10:51, a.t.). Interestingly, that question is the same one Jesus asked of James and John in 10:36. They requested seats of honor. Bartimaeus answered, "Rabbi, let me see." Whose request is granted?

Jesus told Bartimaeus, "Go, your faith has saved you." Immediately Bartimaeus saw and then followed Jesus *on the way* (10:52).

The journey to Jerusalem came after the healing of the blind man in Bethsaida who needed a second touch to see clearly. The journey ends with Bartimaeus asking to see, becoming able to see, and following Jesus *on the way*. All along the journey (the way) Jesus offered a second touch to disciples (and readers) as he described life in God's kingdom and the opposition it aroused from those invested in the religious/political/economic system of his world. At the end of this journey, who sees and will follow Jesus *on the way*?

Reflections

1. If Jesus asked you, "What do you wish that I would do for you? (10:51)," what kind of answer would you give?
2. What would you like Jesus to do for you?

Arriving in Jerusalem/At the Temple

Entering the Holy City, 11:1-11

The company has drawn near Jerusalem. The third and climactic phase of Mark's story now begins. Jesus sends two of his disciples into a village with specific instructions to find and acquire a never-before-ridden colt (11:2-3). Some scholars believe these verses show Jesus foreseeing the future, which he will do often while in Jerusalem. Other scholars believe that Jesus had made prior arrangements for the colt involving a password-like phrase, which shows how dangerous it was to assist him openly. Whatever the case, the disciples find the colt as instructed and bring it to Jesus (11:4-6).

As he rides into the city, people spread cloaks and leafy branches on the road. They are connecting his entry to kingly processions and, more specifically, to the triumphant entry of Simon Maccabeus into Jerusalem after driving out the Syrians during the Maccabbean Revolt (1 Macc 13:51; second century B.C.E.). The people also shout hosannas to the one coming in the name of the Lord to restore the kingdom of David (11:8-10). With such a demonstration, they may have been calling for Jesus to be another Simon Maccabeus for them, wanting him to force the Romans from Jerusalem and sit on David's throne as their king.

If so, then we should see Jesus responding with a counter-demonstration. He is not riding the stallion of a great conqueror but a colt, evoking the Zechariah 9:9 prophecy about the triumphant king who is humble. Jesus' way is not violent, his power is not force, and he does not triumph by conquering those who oppose

> ### Study Bible
> Read the comments on Mark 11:1-11 in the *NISB*, 1830-31.

him. As we have seen, the way of the Lord does not involve thinking about "human things" such as these are (Mark 8:34).

After the demonstration, Jesus and the Twelve return to Bethany for the night (11:11). Maybe staying there was simply best for them. Or maybe staying outside the city made an important political and theological statement—Jesus is an outsider to the religious/political/economic system of the city, but his goal was not to become an insider. His goal is a wholly different community.

An Intercalation: Cursing, Cleansing, Effects of the Curse, 11:12-25

Returning to the city the next morning, Jesus saw a healthy fig tree —it was in leaf—but it had no fruit, since "it was not the season for figs" (11:12-14). So, he cursed it (the Greek phrase is clearly a curse; v.21)! Many of us are puzzled by Jesus' apparent temper tantrum, but Mark gives clues for reading this story well. First, the word usually translated as "season" is not the Greek word for ordinary time-keeping (which is *chronos*). Instead, the word used here (*kairos*) denotes an era or an age (as in "the age of Aquarius"). Something more than gardening seasons are afoot in this story. Second, fig trees were often symbols for the spiritual health of Israel in the prophetic tradition (e.g., Jer 8:13, Hos. 9:10). Third, we're about to find that this story is the first in another Markan intercalation. So, we read on.

Arriving in the city, Jesus went into the temple and, in a symbolic act reminiscent of the Jewish prophetic tradition, drove out the sellers, buyers, and money-changers, and stopped anyone from carrying anything through the temple (11:15-16). We're perhaps surprised at such commerce in the temple, so we need to know that these merchants and moneychangers were the "street level" representatives of Israel's redistribution economy. In such an economic system goods and services were gathered into a central storehouse. The PR folks said the goods would be redistributed to those in need. In reality, the leaders made sure redistribution served their own interests. So, in Israel the temple was

Source

For details of the redistribution economy centered in the temple see John H. Elliot, "Temple Versus Household in Luke-Acts: A Contrast in Social Institutions," in *The Social World of Luke-Acts: Models for Interpretation*, ed. by Jerome H. Neyrey (Peabody, Mass.: Hendrickson Publishers, 1991), 233-235; Myers, *Binding the Strong Man*, 300-301.

the storehouse for the excessive burden of taxes, tithes, and other debts controlled by the religious leaders in collaboration with the Herodians and Rome (the intertwining of religion, politics, and economics). Peasants were sometimes forced to sell their lands or family members into debt slavery to pay their temple taxes while the religious and political leaders lived lavishly (*Social World*, 233-35; Myers, 300-301). Quoting from the prophetic tradition (Isa 56:7; Jer 7:11), Jesus declared that the temple was intended to be a sacred space where all people could meet God (a "house of prayer for all nations"; note the inclusivity). But, "you have made it a den of robbers" (11:17).

His prophetic-symbolic act creates concern among the chief priests of the temple. Scribes, Pharisees, and Herodians have opposed Jesus since the synagogue incident in chapter 3. Now he's gotten the attention of the "big boys" of Israel's religious/political/ economic system. Indeed, they want to kill him because they are afraid of him. Why would the most powerful Israelite priests fear a backwoods Galilean peasant? Because the crowd is spellbound by him (11:18). What happens to their place and power if the people begin to *see* what the temple has become, if they *see* what the religious leaders are doing and how they're living, if they *see* the "fig tree" has no fruit?

The next morning as Jesus and the disciples return to the city, they pass the fig tree again, and we're back to the first story of the intercalation. The fig tree has withered to its roots! When we remember the intercalation, we're able to understand Jesus' response to Peter's comment about the fig tree. "Have faith in God," Jesus said. "Truly I tell you, if you say to this mountain ..." (11:22-23). Notice he does not say "a mountain" or "any mountain" but "*this* mountain." Many scholars believe that Jesus refers to the Temple Mount. So, if disciples say to *this* mountain (the temple), "be taken up and thrown into the sea," and do not doubt but have faith, it will come to pass (11:23-24). Jesus cursed the fig tree, and it withered. He has cursed the temple as well. In our time no temple system oppresses us, but there are mountainous evils around

---

Reflections

Is the New Testament Anti-Semitic?

Mark's accounts of Jesus' words and deeds against the temple system (11) and Jesus' conflicts with Jewish religious leaders (1:22; 3:6; 7:5-13; 8:15, 31; 10:2-5, 33) prompt some today to wonder if the Gospel is not anti-Semitic.

1. What are some problems with this line of query?
2. Were not Jesus and (probably) the author of Mark's Gospel also Jewish?
3. Can we assume that the Judaism of Jesus' day was a unified system of beliefs and practices?
4. Many scholars prefer the Judaisms (plural) of the first century.
5. Finally, would it not be more appropriate to think in terms of Jewish sibling rivalry, intramural debates, or Jewish prophetic indictments rather than outside condemnations of Judaism or anti-Semitism?

Study Bible

See "Excursus: Anti-Semitic Interpretations of Isaiah" in the *NISB*, 959.

us. Jesus' words call faithful ones not to despair in the face of such evil. Nor should they adopt an "if you can't beat 'em, join 'em" attitude and cooperate with evil. Instead, have faith in God and pray. The evil (of the temple system) has been cursed and will wither.

Then Jesus, rather suddenly, insists that those who are praying must also be those who forgive (11:25). Remember that "sin" in this world caused persons to be cast out of the community and included such things as not paying temple taxes or keeping purity rules. These things created insiders and outsiders and "places" where people weren't welcome. Forgiveness, therefore, was about restoring outcasts and welcoming them back into the community of the people of God. Jesus has lived and proclaimed that God is all about forgiveness, hospitality, and inclusivity. Only in communities following this *way of the Lord* can God be at work bringing in the kingdom and casting evil, like that of the temple system, into the sea.

An Honor Challenge, 11:26-33

So, they arrive in the temple again, and the chief priests, scribes, and elders confront Jesus. His prophetic-symbolic act in the temple had challenged their honor as those who decided how the temple should function. Now they respond, asking him, "By what authority are you doing these things?" (11:27-28). While the question is directed to Jesus, these officials no doubt want the crowd to remember that they have been appointed to the chief positions, they wear the vestments of power, they make the decisions, they *look like* people of authority, and that Jesus looks like the Galilean peasant that he is.

Jesus responds with his own question: "Was the baptism of John from heaven, or was it of human origin?" Jesus has put the religious leaders in a bind. If they say, "from heaven," Jesus will ask them why they didn't listen to John. But if they say, "human origin," they fear the crowd because the people believed John to be God's prophet. So they say they don't know. The Galilean peasant has asked the religious leaders a religious question they can't answer! In a shame-honor setting, their non-answer brings dishonor. Since they've dishonored themselves, Jesus need not answer their original challenge (11:29-33).

Two aspects of this confrontation deserve further consideration from us. First, notice that the religious leaders never ask themselves, "From where did John's baptism come? Might God have sent him?" They show no interest in discovering the truth about John. They are only concerned to save face and preserve their place in that world.

Second, this episode raises the question of authority acutely. From whence does it come indeed? The religious leaders had positions, titles, finances, Roman support, and the ability to put people to death, yet they feared the crowd, avoided questions of truth, and were unable to do as they wanted. Jesus was a peasant, unauthorized and unofficial, with a motley crew following him, who would be executed by the powers. But he freely sought and spoke the truth of God as he knew it, and the religious leaders could not stop him, even with death threats. So, what is true authority? This story says it doesn't reside in positions, titles, and force. In what, then, does it reside? Do we recognize it when we see it? Will we *see* it?

Reflections
Authority that Dictates or Inspires

The religious leaders' question to Jesus, "By what authority do you do these things?" brings the question of true authority to our attention.

1. How would you say our culture understands authority?
2. How would you describe or define true authority?
3. Think of someone who has exercised true authority in your life.
4. What made that person authoritative for you?
5. When have you seen religious authorities (including Christians) acting like the chief priests, scribes, and elders from this story?

Conflict in the Temple

Jesus Tells the Parable of the Vineyard, 12:1-12

Immediately after the chief priests' challenge to Jesus failed to dishonor him, Jesus goes on the offensive; he "began to speak to them in parables" (12:1). The parable Mark records in 12:1-9 revolves around a vineyard, which was an oft-used image for Israel (e.g., the "vineyard of the Lord," Isa 5:1-7). It also involves an absentee landowner and the tenant farmers who rebel violently against him. Interestingly, by using their wealth and political connections to exploit desperate peasants, many chief priests had become absentee landowners themselves, holders of large estates in the countryside that were worked by tenant farmers. One of their great concerns would have been rebellion by their tenants. With the vineyard in this parable evoking Israel, the landowner would be God, which means the religious leaders must identify themselves with the tenants. So, Jesus tells a parable that casts them (Mark 12:12) as doing to God what they feared having done to themselves!

Noteworthy also, the tenants in the parable plot against the landowner's son precisely because they know the identity of the son. Sometimes people participate with evil out of ignorance or because they are deceived. But sometimes they know exactly what they are doing. The religious leaders aren't like the disciples who are blind. They understand what Jesus is proclaiming, but they deliberately reject it. So, what will God do in response, Jesus asks? The answer: God will bring judgment on the tenants, give the vineyard to others, and elevate the "rejected stone" (i.e., the

---

Reflections
Fear of Losing What Has Been "Acquired"

After the parable of the vineyard, the religious leaders are again afraid of the crowd. What thoughts, insights, or questions does their "fear" evoke for you?

abused son) to the position of chief cornerstone (12:9-11). The "chief cornerstone" quote from Psalm 118:22-23 was one of the favorites of the early church.

The religious leaders would have acted out the parable right then and arrested Jesus, but they feared the crowd (Mark 12:12). Twice we've been told they feared the crowd, and once that they feared Jesus because of his impact on the crowd. Why are they so afraid of the people? How much authority do they really have?

The Challenge of the Pharisees and Herodians, 12:13-17

With Jesus having now attacked the temple and the chief religious leaders directly, with the crowd on his side and Passover drawing nigh, the leaders apparently feel they have to respond quickly to Jesus lest he cause a revolt to break out. They will now challenge Jesus in an effort to dishonor him. First they send Pharisees and Herodians to ask him about paying Roman taxes (12:13-15). American Christians may have heard Jesus' answer, "Give to Caesar the things that are Caesar's and to God the things that are God's," (12:17) interpreted to mean that government has an important role in the world (so people must pay their taxes), but we must never forget what we owe God. That interpretation, however, is based on the American experience of separation of church and state, which didn't exist in first-century Israel. As we've noted, religion, politics, and economics were inextricably intertwined in Jesus' world. We've also noted that Roman rule was forced and Roman taxes were oppressive and exploitive, filling the peasants' world with violence, debt, and starvation. It's hard to imagine Jesus claiming the Roman government had an important role in the world so that people should pay their taxes.

We can better understand his response by attending first to his demand that one of his questioners bring him a denarius. Since a denarius had Caesar's likeness on it (12:16), faithful Jews wouldn't carry one so as not to break the second commandment (no graven images). But one of those testing Jesus had one. Where would he have gotten this unclean coin? Against that

---

Reflections
Christ is Our Cornerstone

The "chief cornerstone" text from Psalm 118 appears here (and parallels in Matt 21:42; Luke 20:17), Acts 4:11, Ephesians 2:20, and 1 Peter 2:7. What thoughts do you have about why this Scripture became a favorite of the early church?

Teaching Tips
Learning about Fear

Having seen fear as part of a number of stories in Mark, and with the third instance of the religious leaders' fear being part of this study, now is a good time to do some further reading on fear in Mark in preparation for leading this study. For some helpful insights, see Mitzi Minor, *The Power of Mark's Story* (St. Louis: Chalice Press, 2001) chapter 4.

backdrop, we can read "Give to Caesar … Give to God" as telling us to, "Pay the one you owe" (Myers, 1988). Did Israel's leaders owe God or Rome for their privileged positions? Given whom they owed, what would *they say* to the people about paying Roman taxes?

The Challenge of the Sadducees, 12:18-27

Then the Sadducees, the party from which the chief priests derived, challenged him with a question about resurrection. They didn't believe in resurrection (12:18) because they recognized only the written torah as authoritative. Thus they rejected oral traditions, prophetic texts (no promises of a coming messiah), and apocalyptic texts (no apocalyptic hope for judgment on evil, the renewal of creation, or resurrection). Their question about a woman married to seven brothers uses the Torah's provisions for levirate marriage (Deut. 25:5-6) along with a physical view of resurrection (i.e., life after death will be the same as life now) to ridicule Jesus' affinity for both prophetic and apocalyptic traditions in Judaism (Mark 12:19-23).

But Jesus will not be easily ridiculed. In response he denounces their blundering assumption that life in God's realm will match life in their world. "For *when* they rise from the dead, they neither marry nor are given in marriage," (12:25) is directed at the scenario they proposed. The apocalyptic hope of many Jews, including Jesus, was about the subjugation of evil and the triumph of God's love and justice for *all* of creation. Therefore, patriarchal marriage, in which a woman could be passed from brother to brother as if she herself did not matter, will not exist in the time of the resurrection. Then he declares that the Torah itself bears witness to the resurrection (12:26). So they are "hugely wrong" (12:27) because they know neither the Scriptures nor the power of God to give life.

The Challenge of a Scribe, 12:28-34

At this point a scribe, who's watched the dispute and *sees* that Jesus has answered well, asks a question: Which is the first commandment (12:28)? By now we expect nothing positive from a scribe, yet this one *sees* something. Is his question another test, or is it genuine? We read on.

Jesus' well-known answer gives two "first" commandments so that loving one's neighbor as oneself is intertwined with loving God with all of one's being. Nothing in the law is greater than loving in this manner (12:29-31). The scribe agrees! After repeating the two "first" commandments, the scribe adds that loving God and neighbor is "much greater" than all whole burnt offerings and sacrifices (12:32-33). His statement is significant. Burnt offerings and sacrifices were part of worship in the Temple wherein only certain Jewish males could participate. Those who led this worship and those who participated in it were surely more holy and more honored than everyone else! But a scribe, one of those who benefited from this Temple system, agrees with Jesus that loving God and neighbor is "much greater" than such a system. And loving is inclusive. Anyone—Jew or Gentile, male or female, leper, fisherman, Syrophoenician woman, blind beggar—can choose to love God and neighbor. So, is this scribe ready to give up his temple-based privilege and join Jesus' inclusive servant community? "You are not far from the kingdom of God," Jesus told him (12:34).

Pushing this Scribe, 12:35-40

Then Jesus is on the offensive again with two comments about scribes. We might wonder if he is "pushing" this scribe who is "not far from the kingdom" to *see* more. First he asks the crowd how the scribes can say that the Messiah is David's son when, in a psalm attributed to David, David himself calls the Messiah "Lord" (12:35-37). Fathers do not call their sons "lord!" Jesus' rhetoric not only disputes the scribes' interpretation of the psalm, it also challenges the notion that the Messiah will sit on David's throne as a political ruler. Jesus' mission had political implications, as we have seen, but not aspirations for political power.

Then Jesus called the crowd to "*see* the scribes" who like to appear religious and occupy places of honor in the marketplace and at banquets. But all the while they say long prayers for the sake of appearance, and they "devour widows' houses," (12:38-40), either by embezzling from widows' estates over which they've been made trustees or by the general injustice of the temple system of which they are a part. *See* them, Jesus says. No matter what they look like, they do not conduct themselves like righteous people.

The Widow with Two Coins: Praising Her Faith or Cursing the Temple? 12:41-44

As if to underscore the last point, Mark tells us that Jesus went and sat down opposite the temple treasury to watch the people bring their money. Amidst the wealthy people, he saw a poor widow throw in two copper coins (12:41-42). The traditional reading of this story is that Jesus praises her great faith for giving her last two coins, "her whole living," to God (12:43-44). But attention to the literary context raises another possibility. Jesus cursed the temple system as a "den of robbers," described its leaders as rebelling against God, and denounced the scribes for devouring widows' houses. So, when he calls attention to this widow and her last two copper coins, he may be pointing again to the consequences of the corrupt and unjust temple system that took "her whole life" rather than praising her faith.

So, at the end of chapter 12, what do we think about all Jesus has said and done in the temple? If we were that scribe, would we be ready to give up our temple-based privileges and enter the kingdom of God?

Reflections
Jesus' Anguish over the Robbing of the Poor

The traditional reading of the story of the widow with the two coins is that Jesus praises her great faith because she gave "her whole living" to God. In this study I suggest that attention to the context in Mark calls us to see Jesus as pointing out the effects of the temple system which has robbed this poor victim of "her whole living." Discuss the implications of this second reading. Which of the two readings do you prefer and why?

Reflections
Can You *See* the Poor?

If you'd been sitting with Jesus across from the temple treasury watching rich people put impressive amounts of money in, do you think you'd have seen the widow putting in two copper coins? If you had, would it have been because of the contrast with the rich folks, or because you were interested in her story? How often is someone like her *invisible* to us? What do we learn about Jesus that she wasn't invisible to him? Do you *see* the poor and hurting today?

Judgment on the Temple, Apocalyptic Hope

The Temple is Doomed, 13:1-4

After seeing the widow throw in her last two coins, Jesus and company leave the temple for the last time. Is it a coincidence? At this point one of the disciples remarks at how impressive the temple appears (13:1)! What do the disciples see?

Not surprisingly, Jesus is less than impressed with the great stones. Not one of them, he says, "will be left here upon another; all will be thrown down" (13:2). His statement prompts four disciples, later when they are at the Mount of Olives opposite the temple, to ask Jesus what we might call an "end of time question": "What will be the sign that all these things are about to be accomplished?" (13:3-4)

There is Also a Future Hope

We've been saying throughout this study that in Mark the kingdom of God *has drawn near*, that an apocalyptic turning point *has come* so that the way of the Lord is being lived out among Jesus' followers now, that God is giving them *life* now. But there is also hope for a future when the present evil order will be finally overcome, judged, and put away so that God's love and justice reigns in the age to come. It may even be that a taste in this life of what Jesus offers (an inclusive servant community without structures of domination in which people are healed and freed from whatever has bound them) intensifies the longing for the fulfillment of God's reign. Apparently, the destruction of the temple was thought by some in first-century Israel to be tied to the end of the present age and the beginning of this new age. Thus, when Jesus announced the tem-

Lectionary Loop

Proper 28, Year B, Mark 13:1-8
First Sunday of Advent, Year B, Mark 13:24-37

Teaching Tips
Secret Revealings of the End of Time

Do some reading on first-century Jewish apocalyptic thinking in preparation for leading the study of Mark 13. A good source is N. T. Wright, *The New Testament and the People of God* (Minneapolis: Fortress Press, 1992), 299-334. I summarize Wright's views on pp. 99-100 of *The Power of Mark's Story* (St. Louis: Chalice Press, 2001).

ple's doom, the disciples ask about the sign that the end is almost here.

"See that No One Deceives You!" 13:5-8, 21-23

Jesus' response is blunt: "*See* that no one deceives you!" (13:5). His words are an imperative, short and to the point: Be perceptive, insightful so that you aren't scammed! Some will make messianic claims, some will point to wars, earthquakes, and famines, but "this must happen." The Greek word for "must" here is the same word we saw before (*dei*) that means necessary or inevitable. So, events like these are inevitable, "but the end is *not yet*" (13:6-8).

Similarly, in 13:21-23 he warns his followers about false prophets, those who claim "here is the Christ," and even some who will do signs and wonders in order to deceive others. "But YOU see," he says, "I have told you all things beforehand" (the "you" is emphatic in the Greek).

For "No One Knows," 13:32-36

So, in his long response to disciples' questions about "when the time will come?" Jesus is quite insistent that we see and not be deceived by those who claim to know that specific events are *the* sign that the end is coming. The key reason he offers for such insistence is that no one knows—not angels, not even Jesus. The unfolding of God's purposes for creation is God's business alone (13:32). Note how Jesus hammers this point in 13:32-36: "no one knows" (32); "you do not know" (twice 33, 35). Could Jesus be more clear or forceful in his words?

The text does not tell us *why* we do not know, but it may be worth speculating a bit. We might quickly realize that if we focus on what may happen in the future and when, we are not attending to the present ways we are called to live and serve in God's kingdom. Relatedly, focusing on the future can be a means to avoid suffering on behalf of God's kingdom in the present. We already saw the disciples, coming down the mountain after the transfiguration, wondering about Elijah coming first (9:9-12). Some have thought they might have hoped that Elijah would come first and restore people's

> ## Reflections
> ### The End is Now!
> ### Turn or Burn!
>
> Three times in 13:32-35 Jesus says "You don't know" when the end is coming. Furthermore, he insists that God alone knows. Yet people keep writing books and creating websites that speculate about when the end will come, and other people buy those books and visit those websites in droves. Why do you think that is happening?

> ## Reflections
>
> Jesus warns us in Mark 13 about those who would deceive "even the elect" that this or that event is *the* sign that the end is here (or near). What reasons or motives might such people have for wanting to so deceive us? Money? Power?

hearts so that the Messiah—and they—wouldn't have to suffer as Jesus said. A similar kind of idea has certainly been used to tell people that they ought not be worried about present injustice or engage in struggle to change the way things are because God will "fix" everything in the future. In other words, focus on the future promotes denial and avoidance. God's kingdom is better served by our not knowing God's timetable.

But the Promise of Apocalyptic Fulfillment Remains, 13:24-31

And yet there remains the promise of ultimate fulfillment. The sun and moon won't shine, stars will fall, heavenly powers will be shaken, and the Son of man will come in great power and glory! By this poetic language, characteristic of apocalyptic speech and literature, Jesus promises that the world as we have known it will be undone, for God's power and glory will prevail when God's purposes are fulfilled. Then Jesus will send out angels "and gather the elect from the four winds, from the ends of earth to the ends of heaven" (13:24-27). Notice the sweeping poetry of the last part of Jesus' promise: There is nowhere that any follower can be lost or missed! Nowhere!

We may not know when the fulfillment will come, but 13:28-31 insists it is near, even "at the gates." Scholars who study the first-century Mediterranean world by methods developed in the social sciences tell us that a sense of "not long" is what we should expect from a peasant society. With their lives so difficult, their concern was for today, tomorrow, and the next day. They might think of the time between seed and harvest, or how long till a pregnant woman gave birth, but never about a faraway future. Thus, by insisting that these events will happen in a time frame his people understand, Jesus asserts the sureness of the promise. Ironically, we who think very differently about the future, read, "This generation will not pass away until all these things have taken place" (13:30) and fear the promise may have failed. Chronologically speaking, the words are inaccurate, but if we attend to the context, we hear the sincerity and assurance that Jesus hoped to convey.

Reflections
No Time to Bleed

Jesus promises the coming of the Son of man in glory will lead to the gathering of the elect. But he also states that living faithfully in this world will result in trials and suffering. The call he offers us is a difficult one. Some have described our culture as a "haven't got time for the pain" culture.
1. How is Jesus' difficult call being announced by the church today?
2. And how will it be heard in this culture?

Such promises offer us two things. One is an awareness that there is more to life than this moment. What we may call an apocalyptic perspective on life reminds us that God's life transcends this moment, this breath. God is at work even now drawing the kingdom near and renewing creation. We are invited to participate in that work and thus to be part of something greater than ourselves. Further, the promise of being "gathered with the elect" frees us from fear of death or personal loss and, therefore, empowers us to pursue righteousness and the transformation of the world. Rather than "pie in the sky," authentic apocalyptic hope gives us the courage to take up our crosses in the present for the sake of the gospel.

Bearing Witness in the Present, 13:9-20

Which is exactly what followers of Jesus must do. "You will be handed over to councils; and you will be beaten in synagogues, and you will stand before governors and kings because of me," Jesus said (13:9). But these struggles will serve as witnesses (testimonies) to them and result in the gospel being proclaimed in all nations (13:9-10). Is it a difficult calling? Yes, and Jesus does nothing to sugarcoat it: brother will betray brother, a father his child, and those who bear Jesus' name will be hated (13:12-13). He even adds the characteristic apocalyptic warning that as the end draws nearer, things will get worse, so that those in Judea (Jerusalem) must flee immediately (13:14-20). There's a good chance that the threat of Jewish revolt against Rome (which was likely happening as Mark wrote these words) adds a sobering tone to Jesus' words. Both Jesus and his hearers knew what Rome did in response to revolt. Thus Rome's violence is an illustration of how evil responds to those who struggle for God's justice and freedom. But Jesus also promises that the Spirit will enable followers to bear their witness in such moments (13:11), that God will shorten "those days" (13:20), and that those who persevere—who continue to resist evil and insist on living in God's kingdom rather than Caesar's—will be saved (13:13).

> ## Reflections
> ### Freedom to Serve
> Many will have heard apocalyptic hope described as "don't worry about anything because God will take care of it by and by." In this study, however, drawing on recent scholarly work, I understand Jesus' apocalyptic teaching as liberating us from fear of death so that we can live lives of righteousness now. How do you respond to this view of apocalyptic hope and this interpretation of Mark 13?

> ## Reflections
> ### Hang in There
> In times of pain and uncertainty, perhaps especially communal uncertainty, the question, "Where are we headed?" seems to rise naturally from human hearts. In the weeks and months following September 11, 2001 many Americans wondered if the end of the world was near. After reading and studying Mark 13, what do you think Jesus would have said to Americans during those post-September 11 days?

"Keep Awake!" 13:37

Jesus began his response to his disciples' question about "when" with the blunt imperative, "See that no one deceives you." Apocalyptic hope has serious consequences. We catch a glimpse of life in God's kingdom, strive to live such a life even now, and taste enough of it so that we long for its fulfillment in "the age to come." But the Caesars of the world are intent on forcing us to live in their kingdoms. Consequently, living in God's kingdom brings hope and joy, plus struggle and suffering (see 10:29-30). Speculating about when the end comes is pointless and distracts us from living in God's kingdom. It isn't our business anyway. Our business is to bear witness in the power of the Spirit! Jesus ends his response with the challenge to "Keep awake!" which he says twice (13:35-37). Don't be distracted by those who speculate about "when." Don't be dismayed by the struggle. Keep awake and see. Those who persevere to the end will be saved!

Preparing for Trial and Betrayal

An Intercalation: a Plot to Kill, the Anointing, the Accomplice 14:1-11

With Jesus' words just spoken, "Keep awake" (13:37), still reverberating through readers' minds, Mark 14 opens with a grave-sounding intercalation. First, having failed to dishonor Jesus and turn the crowd against him, the religious leaders decide to kill him (14:1). But not during Passover (14:2). With a heavy Roman presence in Jerusalem alongside Jewish pilgrims remembering their deliverance from Egypt, the execution of a popular prophet could spark a riot.

Meanwhile Jesus is back in Bethany at the home of Simon the leper, a simple note reminding us of Jesus' understanding of God's kingdom. Simon's leprosy may have been healed (or in remission), yet the designation stays with him, marking him as outcast. But Jesus sits at a table at his house (14:3). As if that isn't statement enough about God's kingdom, in walks a woman with a flask of expensive ointment that she breaks open and pours on Jesus' head. In Jewish tradition (male) priests anointed the heads of kings. But here is a woman anointing the head of a Galilean peasant. What is the meaning of this? We read on.

Some disciples protest that the ointment should have been sold and the money given to the poor. Jesus defends her: We can do good to the poor whenever we will (Deut 15:11), but she "has done a beautiful thing" to Jesus (Mark 14:4-7). He will not pit acts of social justice against individual acts of devotion. He affirms both. But he has more to say: "She has anointed my body beforehand for its burial" (14:8). He interprets

Study Bible

On Jesus and foreknowledge of events in this final week, see *NISB*, 1831 (11:1-11) and 1838 (14:2-16).

her act as a prophetic sign action illustrating what lies ahead for him. Thus this woman, not the twelve (male) disciples, "gets it," and somehow Jesus knows that she does. In Christian theology Jesus has often been called "king," but in Mark this woman anoints him, not for political power, but for death at the hands of the political powers. For doing so Jesus blesses her: "wherever the good news is proclaimed in the whole world, what she has done will be told in memory of her" (14:9). Except it rarely is told.

Now we return to the first story of the intercalation, the plan to kill Jesus. Judas, one of the Twelve, agrees to betray Jesus to the religious leaders. They promise him money, and he looks for an opportunity (14:10-11). So what do we *see*? The religious leaders and one of the Twelve sell out Jesus, while a woman, one of the "least ones" in that culture, "wastes" money to show her devotion to Jesus and her understanding of his mission. People are not always as they appear to be.

The Supper, 14:12-31

The day of the Passover meal arrives. Scholars are divided again over Jesus' instructions to his disciples about whom to follow and what to say to the owner of the house where they will share the meal (14:12-16). Are they the result of his foretelling what will happen, or has he made prior arrangements involving stealth and "passwords" because of the danger he faces? Whichever it was, the meal is prepared, and the Twelve come with Jesus to share the supper.

As they are eating, Jesus drops a "bombshell": One of those eating with him will betray him (14:18). They are grieved and begin to ask, one by one, "Not I?" (14:19). Then Jesus clarifies—the betrayer is one of the Twelve, one who is dipping bread into the dish with Jesus, which, as a side note, might suggest that there were more than the Twelve at the table. What is clear is that betrayal will come from someone close to him (Ps 41:9). How much more painful when that is the case!

During the meal, some comments on the Passover itself would have been expected. Instead, when it is time to speak, Jesus talks of his death. First he took

> ## Reflections
> ### How Many Were Really There?
> 1. What is the impact of imagining that there were more disciples than the Twelve at the Last Supper?
> 2. More eyewitnesses?
> 3. Other disciples (including women) beyond the Twelve?

bread (*artos*), blessed, broke, and gave it to them, saying, "This is my body." Remember our encounters with bread in Mark 6–8 wherein boundaries were crossed, bread was shared, and there was enough for everyone? For doing such work, Jesus' body will be broken. Then he took the cup, gave thanks, and shared it with them, calling it "my blood of the covenant" (14:22-24), a phrase referring to the ceremony which binds God and God's people together (see Exod. 24:8). By sharing the bread and cup the disciples bind themselves to Jesus and his mission to draw God's kingdom near. They also bind themselves to Jesus' suffering, to the *broken* body and *spilled* blood, for God's kingdom. Significantly, then, the last word here is a reminder of their apocalyptic hope (Mark 14:25).

They sing a hymn and go out again to the Mount of Olives, where Jesus drops another bombshell: They will *all* desert him. Still he offers hope, promising that, after he is raised, he will go ahead of them to Galilee (14:26-28). When Peter protests that he will not desert Jesus, Jesus prophesies Peter denying him three times. But Peter insists, "Even if I must die with you I will not deny you." The others agree (14:29-31). Perhaps we are accustomed to thinking of Peter as being "all talk," as spouting bravado that actually means nothing. It's possible, though, that Peter meant exactly what he said.

They go to Gethsemane for Jesus to pray. Mark has recorded Jesus praying three times, at the beginning (1:36), near the middle (6:46), and now at the end of his journey (14:32), all at night. Before going off by himself, he tells Peter, James, and John how troubled he is and calls on them to "keep awake" (14:34; remember 13:35-37). Going further, then, he prays, "Abba father, for you all things are possible; remove this cup from me" (14:36). This is now the third time we've seen the assertion (or a close variation) that all things are possible for God. It's time to discuss these. Our understanding of the assertion must take into account that it was apparently *not* possible for God to accomplish God's will *and* have the cup pass from Jesus. It was also apparently *not* possible for Jesus to

> ## Reflections
> ### Is Night Time the Right Time?
> Mark records Jesus praying three times, all at night (1:35, 6:46, 14:36). What do you think: Is it symbolically significant that Mark tells us he prayed "at night"?

get the rich man to sell everything and follow him at the time the second assertion was made (see 10:24-27). I suspect we have taken "all things" in these statements to mean "anything we might think of." If such is true, then why not just pray for the disciples to *see*? Or pray away all the suffering Jesus keeps promising will come to faithful followers? But Jesus has said that suffering is inevitable, even necessary. The context of Mark, then, indicates that "all things" means "all things necessary to accomplish God's purposes for creation." So Jesus asks three times for the cup to pass, but he also asks for God's will to be done (14:36-41). It is *not* possible for both to happen, so he will do God's will.

Meanwhile, the disciples are sleeping rather than keeping awake. The betrayer arrives, surrounded by a mob with swords and clubs as if they were itching for a fight. As it turns out, some disciples want to give them one! When Jesus is seized, one of the disciples draws a sword and slashes off the ear of the high priest's slave (14:43-47). Surely we must ask: What was a disciple of Jesus doing with a sword? Jesus, however, stops the brewing fight with his words: He is not a bandit (i.e., one who used violence against Rome), and they could have arrested him openly in the temple any time. Thus he names and shames the lynch-mob at this night scene that they've created. But, he says, let the Scriptures be fulfilled (i.e., he accepts his suffering at their hands, 14:48-49).

At this point, the disciples forsook him and fled (14:50). The strange note about the young man (the Greek word is *neaniskos*) following, covered only by a linen cloth that gets snatched from him so that he ran away naked (14:51), may be a word picture portraying the disciples' shame (nakedness was shameful in Jewish tradition). I am struck that the disciples, despite their struggle to see, stayed with Jesus until the moment they realized he wasn't going to fight. They even had a sword (more than one?) with them in Gethsemane. Earlier Peter had said he would die with Jesus. I wonder if they were quite ready to fight and die with Jesus. If they won the fight, great! But even if they lost, they'd be martyrs. Either way they'd be honored

> ## Reflections
>
> In Mark we've had two assertions that "all things are possible for God" (10:27; 14:36; see also 10:38-39). In this study I take Mark's context into consideration and interpret those sayings to mean that "all things necessary to accomplish God's purposes for creation" are possible. Read again 14:36 focusing on what *God* wants. Does that interpretation make sense to you? Why or why not?

> ## Reflections
> ### Jesus the Terrorist?
>
> In our time we've watched the development of the phenomenon of the terrorist "suicide bomber"—one who is willing to kill and also die to be celebrated as a martyr by his or her people. Maybe that phenomenon gives us a new paradigm for understanding Peter's insistence that he would die with Jesus and the disciple having a sword in Gethsemane (14:29-31, 46-50). Might they have been willing to be "suicide martyrs" for their cause and their people? If that's possible, why would you say Jesus rejected such a plan?

by their people. Jesus, however, wasn't going to fight, so they fled. They would die in a blaze of glory, but they would *not* do what Jesus was doing. They were committed to winning their cause but not to the renewal of all of creation. They had not kept awake, so when the crucial moment arrived, they were thinking the things of humanity. And they fled, shamefully.

Bearing Witness at Trial, at Death

**The Last Intercalation: Peter, Jesus on Trial,
Peter's Denial, 14:53-72**

Those who seized Jesus in Gethsemane took him to the high priest, where the religious leaders had gathered and were waiting. But Mark also tells us that Peter followed "right into the courtyard of the high priest" (14:53-54). If we don't know how the story plays out, for a moment our hearts lift—perhaps Jesus isn't completely forsaken! We will also learn that this note about Peter serves as the first part of the last Markan intercalation.

The middle part of the intercalation is Jesus' trial before the council or Sanhedrin. Much has been written about the historical inaccuracy of Mark's account, since the Sanhedrin did not meet at night. But we've seen Mark to be more concerned with the symbolic significance of what he writes than with the mere reporting of facts. Certainly this trial is a "dark" moment, for it is not a trial for justice but a "kangaroo" court. Council members weren't determining guilt or innocence but looking for testimony to justify what they'd already decided to do: condemn Jesus to death (14:55). Their witnesses even gave false testimonies that did not agree (14:56-59; Deut 19:15-19). Mark, though, allows one report of the false witnesses to convey a profound irony in this Gospel. Mark's Jesus never says that he will destroy the temple "made with hands" and in three days build another "not made with hands," so the witness is false—on the surface. On a deeper level, Jesus' teaching about the kingdom of God anticipates the destruction of the temple system that the religious leaders had established. For just this reason this "dark" trial is taking place.

The high priest finally gave up on his fruitless false witnesses and addressed Jesus himself. First he tried to get Jesus to respond to the lies, but Jesus was too smart for that tactic. Then he asked Jesus directly, "Are you the Messiah?" We now hear Jesus' ringing confession: "I AM!" Furthermore, Jesus' apocalyptic faith is that they will "see" him seated at God's right hand, coming with the clouds of heaven (14:60-62)! But his confession leads to another of the ironies of this scene—there were apparently no consequences for those whose false witness broke covenant with God and God's people (Exod 20:16; Deut 19:18-19), but for telling the truth (as Jesus and his followers understand it) Jesus is condemned to die by the religious leaders (14:63-64).

In response to Jesus' truthful witness, the religious leaders begin the process of dehumanizing Jesus (14:65). It's difficult to hurt a person badly if we recognize the common humanity we share, so treating a person as less than human provides some rationale for those who torture their victims. Nazis did it to Jews; white supremacists do it to non-whites. In this instance the dehumanizing includes labeling him a criminal, spitting, beating, and mocking Jesus, as well as taunting him to "prophesy."

We return to the story of Peter in the courtyard. Three times someone there insists that Peter was with Jesus or was "one of them." Three times Peter denies the charge, the third time even cursing and swearing an oath that he does not know the man (14:66-71). At the moment of the third denial the cock crowed again, and the last irony of this scene surfaces. While the religious leaders taunted Jesus to prophesy, his prophecy regarding Peter was coming true. While Jesus bore witness and gave up his life for the gospel, Peter denied Jesus to save his own life. But as he broke down and wept (14:72), we may wonder what his life was worth to him in that moment (8:24-38).

Pilate, 15:1-20

Chapter 15 begins as morning dawns and the religious leaders hand Jesus over to the Roman procurator,

Reflections
Saving Your Own Skin
Peter broke down and wept when the cock crowed after he had denied Jesus (14:72). What thoughts and feelings are evoked in you by this moment in Peter's story? Read also and reflect on Mark 8:34-38.

Pontius Pilate (15:1). Since Jewish leaders could put someone to death, why would they hand a Jew over to Pilate for execution? Pilate's question, "Are you the king of the Jews?" suggests the religious leaders had charged Jesus with insurrection, not blasphemy. Again, why? The text doesn't say, but we may wonder if Mark understood the religious leaders specifically to want Jesus crucified. The Romans crucified those from the lower classes who they suspected might rally the masses against Roman rule. The purpose was to terrorize others who might have similar ideas. Perhaps the religious leaders intended to halt any messianic movement brewing in Israel, not only to preserve their privileged positions but also to prevent a popular revolt that would surely bring violent Roman reprisals.

Traditionally, Pilate has been read as reluctant to condemn an innocent man (15:10, 14) but too weak to stand up to the scheming of the Jewish religious leaders (15:11-15). That portrait doesn't match what we know from other historical sources in which Pilate is brutal and cruel in putting down threats to Roman rule. Indeed, that portrait may not fit Mark (if we don't read Matthew and Luke into Mark). We should probably understand Pilate here as manipulating the crowd by turning them into a vengeful mob and collaborating with the religious leaders, whom he no doubt despised. In the end he got what he wanted—the execution of a Jewish troublemaker without a riot in the city.

Some might be surprised that Pilate was willing to release Barabbas, a known insurrectionist who'd already killed, but crucify Jesus who refused violence in Gethsemane (15:15). On the surface, Barabbas might appear more dangerous. But Rome knew violence, and they could do it bigger and better than Barabbas did. If Jesus, however, got people to *see* a radical new way to live… No, that kind of revolution could not be tolerated. Jesus must die.

After further dehumanization of Jesus, "they led him out to crucify him" (15:16-20). The soldiers compelled Simon of Cyrene (whose sons, Rufus and Alexander, were apparently known to Mark's community but unknown to us) to carry the cross and take

> ## Reflections
> ### How Crafty Was Pilate?
> Traditionally Pilate has been viewed as too weak to follow his own convictions, so that he went along with the Jewish religious leaders although he knew they were wrong. Recently some scholars have suggested that's not an accurate reading of Pilate in Mark. Pilate was prefect over Judea for at least ten years. If he were a foolish Roman official, Pilate would not have had such a lengthy tenure in this turbulent part of the empire. Therefore, they see him as collaborating with the religious leaders to get rid of a problem, manipulating the crowd and orchestrating events to get what he wanted. Which view of Pilate seems true to Mark's story to you? Why?

Jesus to Golgotha, "And they crucified him" (15:21-24). Mark gives no details about the crucifixion itself, for which we are probably glad. It was a horrific way to die. Rome did not invent cruelty, but we might believe they worked to perfect it.

Mark's portrayal of the scene surrounding the crucifixion is equally stark and bare. No followers are present. Jesus doesn't say, "Father, forgive them," or any other of the gentler words from the cross that other Gospels recount. We're told the inscription of the charge against him read "The King of the Jews," which was probably intended to mock him, but we (the readers) know that he's been anointed. We're told he was crucified between two bandits (not thieves or robbers), two who plotted violence against Rome, but we know that Jesus rejected violence. We're told these bandits, some passersby, and the chief priests and scribes mocked him, taunting him to "save himself" (15:25-32), but we know that he has lost his life for the gospel. We're even told the chief priests called out, "Let the Messiah…come down from the cross now, so that we may see and believe" (15:32), and we know the irony in their words. Miracles do not lead to sight. Our insightfulness enables us to see the miracle that God is doing. But the religious leaders had already chosen not to see.

Is it any wonder, then, that Mark tells us that darkness covered the land (15:33)? Whether this is historical fact or not, we know this was indeed a "dark" time. In the midst of the darkness Jesus screams, "My God, my God, why have you forsaken me?" (15:34). The same words begin Psalm 22, a lament psalm. Wrapped in darkness, no friends or followers beside him, Jesus feels abandoned even by God and laments his fate in the words of his tradition. In this dark moment it appears for all the world that the religious leaders were right. They have won. Jesus looks like a deluded fool, a crazy man. "Then Jesus gave a loud cry and breathed his last" (15:37).

Then we're told the temple curtain was ripped (the Greek verb is *schizo*) in two (15:38), an event that has been variously interpreted. Does it signal further judg-

Reflections
How do You See It?

The chief priests claim that if Jesus came down from the cross they would "see and believe." If we read the centurion positively (as I do), then he saw how Jesus died and said that Jesus was truly God's Son.

1. Do you know more people like the chief priests or like the centurion?
2. What about you—who have you been more like?

Reflections
He Was Subjected to the Most Cruel and Vicious Tortures

In the months that I worked on these studies Mel Gibson's movie *The Passion of the Christ* was making news. Gibson devoted a significant portion of his movie to detailing the gruesomeness of the crucifixion. Mark gives us four words (three in Greek): "And they crucified him (15:24)." See also Mark's concise mention of Jesus' mockings and beatings (14:65; 15:19). What thoughts do you have about Mark's sparse account versus Gibson's dramatic details of torture and agonizing death?

ment on the temple for Jesus' death? A further ripping apart of the divide that existed between God and human beings? An expression of God's grief? The text doesn't clarify. But it does tell us a most curious thing next: The Roman centurion who was facing him, having seen how Jesus died, said, "Truly this man was God's Son" (15:39). Until this moment no one in the story has said of Jesus what readers are told in the Gospel's opening line, "Jesus Christ, the Son of God" (1:1). Now the most unexpected person, a Roman centurion, says it at the most unexpected time, *when he saw* how Jesus died. It is so unexpected that some scholars believe the centurion's words are only further mockery of Jesus. But other scholars, myself included, believe that so much of Mark has been about *seeing* what is unexpected that having a Roman centurion *see* what others have not seen fits the story well. But we are left to ask ourselves, what is it about seeing Jesus die that enables him to see God's Son? Is it possible for us to *see* what he saw?

Teaching Tips
What Did He See?

Divide the group into three or four to brainstorm and discuss the following: What did the centurion see (15:39)?

Allow each group to respond in its own way, e.g., poem, a drawing, song, list of possibilities. Give the group *at least* ten minutes to brainstorm and five minutes to report its findings to the class.

There You Will See Him

Women Witnesses at Jesus' Death and Burial, 15:40-47

Jesus is dead. After the fact, we find out that some followers—some of the women including Mary Magadalene, the "other" Mary, and Salome—watched from a distance (15:40-41). For Mark this is a brief note probably to tell us who reported the events of Jesus' death, but it gives us some interesting information. These women were always there (from Galilee to Jerusalem), following and ministering with Jesus (or for him or to him). The Greek verbs for following (*akolutheo*) and ministering (*diakoneo*) are *the* discipleship words of the early church. So, this note reminds us again of the radical inclusivity of God's kingdom, that it was the "outsiders" who seemed to understand Jesus best, and who didn't completely forsake him.

At evening, Joseph of Arimethea, a member of the council who was waiting for the kingdom of God, asked for Jesus' body and saw to it that Jesus was entombed, albeit hastily (15:42-47). Joseph is an interesting—and ambiguous—character who appears in all four Gospels at Jesus' burial. In other places he's called a disciple, though a closeted one. It's not clear in Mark that he's a disciple. He may be merely a compassionate man, or a Jew who doesn't want the body to defile the Sabbath. What is clear is that this stranger, rather than Jesus' closest followers, provides for Jesus' burial. Two of the women disciples witness the event so that they know the tomb's location.

> ## Study Bible
> Read about the shorter and longer endings in Mark in *NISB*, 1844-45.

The Women Go to Anoint, Flee the Tomb in Fear and Silence: The Issue of Mark's Ending

After the Sabbath these women go to anoint Jesus' body *when the sun had risen*. There has been so much darkness in the story lately that we may sense a first flicker of hope now that the sun has come up again. The women wonder what to do about the stone at the tomb but arrive to find it already rolled back. Entering the tomb they find a young man (Greek: *neaniskos*) dressed in a white robe, which is the clothing of vindicated martyrs (see Rev. 6:9-11). He has astonishing news: Jesus "has been raised, he is not here." Thus he confirms Jesus' amazing predictions of his death and resurrection (8:31; 9:31; 10:33-34). Then he announces that one final prediction of Jesus will be satisfied: He tells the women that Jesus is "going ahead of you to Galilee; there you will see him, just as he told you" (see 14:28). Everything about the story prior to this moment, especially regarding Jesus' predictions and their fulfillment, have prepared readers to expect satisfaction again. We await, perhaps with eager anticipation, the tale of the meeting in Galilee. Instead we learn that the women fled from the tomb and said nothing to anyone because they were afraid (16:1-8).

Then we are told nothing more. The best manuscripts of Mark end at 16:8. Modern English Bible translations usually include a "shorter" and a "longer" ending, but these were added in the fourth and late second centuries, respectively. What we have from Mark's pen ends at 16:8.

Some scholars believe Mark wrote more, but the Gospel's ending has been lost. They base their belief on the following evidence. First, the grammar at the end is odd (the last word in Greek is *gar*, which means "for"). Second, as noted, the story causes us to *expect* a meeting with the resurrected Christ in Galilee. Third, the ending at 16:8 is unsatisfying. And fourth, they believe Mark is most like ancient biographies in terms of genre, and an ancient biography would never end in this manner.

I count myself, though, among those scholars who believe Mark intended to end at 16:8. The grammar is odd, but it's not impossible for Mark to have written it this way. The other three reasons really come down to the issue of whether or not the ending is satisfactory. Mark may be *most like* ancient biographies, but that doesn't mean Mark was writing primarily as a biographer. It's more likely that Mark wrote this Gospel as a pastor or teacher or spiritual guide to challenge and encourage Christians as they followed Jesus on the way of the Lord. Spiritual teachings or guidance are often open-ended, leaving disciples a conundrum to resolve or a question to answer. See, for example, the Desert Fathers and Mothers, or even the book of Jonah. From this perspective, I don't find Mark's ending unsatisfying at all.

Making Sense of the Ending of Mark

But it is unsettling. Can we make sense of it? Let's return to the words of the young man in the tomb and work our way to the end. He knew the women were looking for "Jesus of Nazareth, who was crucified," and he tells them, "He has been raised; he is not here" (16:6). My experiences with church people suggest that many of us have weak resurrection theologies. We often imagine that on Easter morning Jesus woke up, stretched, yawned, and walked out of the tomb much the same as before (as in Mel Gibson's film, *The Passion of the Christ*). That view, however, is closer to resuscitation than to the proclamation that Jesus was resurrected. We need to *see* the difference between resurrection and resuscitation. What did Mark mean by, "he has been raised?"

Careful considerations of Mark tell us these things: (1) Mark is an apocalyptic Gospel from an apocalyptic community; (2) resurrection and apocalyptic thinking are linked in the Gospel (see 8:34-38, 9:9-13, 12:18-27); and (3) Mark was like apocalyptic Jews whose reflections on resurrection occurred in the midst of their apocalyptic hope for the renewal of creation in the age to come. Weaving these points together brings the following suggestion: If for Mark resurrection is an apocalyptic event that happens at the end of the present age and the start of the age to come, *and* Jesus is resurrected, *then* the present age is already passing

---

Reflections

What Did You See?

What is the most significant insight, new perspective, challenge, or transforming moment that will stay with you as a result of your study of Mark?

Reflections

In both this study and my book (*The Power of Mark's Story*, 98-101), I interpret Jesus' resurrection in Mark in this way: (1) If for Mark resurrection is an apocalyptic event that happens at the end of the present age and the start of the age to come, and (2) Jesus is resurrected, then (3) the present age is already passing away and the new age has begun. Thus Jesus' proclamation that the kingdom of God has drawn near is dramatically confirmed!

1. What responses do you have to this interpretation?
2. How does it confirm what Jesus said and did in Mark's Gospel?
3. What implications does this have for us today?

away and the new age has begun (Minor, 98-101). Jesus' proclamation that the kingdom of God has drawn near is, therefore, dramatically confirmed!

So, if they go to Galilee, they will see the resurrected one (16:7)! Galilee brings to mind Jesus' journey through that region and from there to Gentile areas, crossing boundaries and sharing bread, announcing that God's kingdom has drawn near. It is not only a place but also a symbol of Jesus' mission. If the disciples go "there," they will *see* him. What kind of seeing? What if this is not just seeing an appearance of the resurrected Jesus with their physical eyes but the kind of *seeing* Mark has been calling for all along? What if they "go to Galilee" in the sense of joining themselves to Jesus' mission and *see* that Jesus is resurrected, that is, the age to come has arrived, the renewal of creation is possible and is happening, and they are part of it? These may be the implications of the young man's words to the women.

So the women, in response, run from the tomb and say "nothing to anyone," because they are afraid (16:8)! Most of us have likely thought of Jesus' resurrection as unambiguously good news. We love the idea that the "good guy wins," that life is stronger than death, that Jesus is alive. We love Jesus' resurrection for Jesus' sake. But the women's fear, flight, and silence suggest there is a flip side to consider. Guatemalan poet Julia Esquivel has written about being "threatened" with resurrection. Are the women threatened? Think of the advantages for them if Jesus stayed dead. Any hatred they felt toward the religious leaders or Roman officials would be justified, since those people killed someone they loved. The same would be true of any vengeance they might plot. Or they could understandably think, "nothing ever changes, so why bother?" and just go home to the lives they'd led before Jesus. They could even be forgiven for yielding to despair. Jesus' death was no doubt difficult enough. How much easier it would be (after all they've been through) if he just stayed dead rather than being resurrected, returning to Galilee, and calling them to follow! For if he is resurrected, then God is indeed at work drawing the kingdom near. Nothing

> ## Reflections
>
> The women's fear, flight, and silence at the end of Mark suggest there is a "flip side" to the good news of Jesus' resurrection. What responses do you have to the idea that Jesus' resurrection is also threatening?

> ## Reflections
> ### If I'd Been There . . .
>
> If you'd "been there," if you'd gone to the tomb with the women that morning, what do you think you'd have done in response to the young man's words?

will ever be the same, including their lives! It may be that this kind of insight has scared the women speechless.

Are We Headed to Galilee?

So, what happens next? Mark doesn't tell. We are stranded with the women's fear, flight, and silence. Literary critics tell us that when a narrative ends well, readers are content that the story does not go on. Mark's ending does not give us that closure. Instead, it leaves us unsettled, wondering, with unanswered questions. How could they? Did they never tell? What should they have done? Sooner or later we may get around to, "Well, if I'd been there . . . What would I have done?" Maybe that's the point.

Are we ready to *see* that Jesus is resurrected, the kingdom of God has drawn near, and the renewal of all creation is underway? Are we ready to cross boundaries, share our bread, practice the radical inclusivity of God's kingdom, serve one another, cast out evil, heal, and forgive? Are we ready to bear suffering at the hands of those invested in the world as the human powers have ordered it?

Through Mark's story "we are there" for these words: He has been raised. Go to Galilee. There you will see him. So, as this study ends and you walk out the door, are you headed in the direction of Galilee?

What About Mark?

Suppose someone said to you, "We're about to study Mark at my church. I heard you've just done that. Do you think I ought to sign up?" What answer would you give the person?

Reflections
Are You Going?

At the end of this study, are you ready to "go to Galilee"?

THE BOOK
OF SECOND SAMUEL

A STUDY BY
E. CARSON BRISSON

E. Carson Brisson is Associate Dean for Academic Programs, Associate Professor of Biblical Languages at Union Theological Seminary and Presbyterian School of Christian Education in Richmond, Virginia.

Introduction

The Pastor's Bible Study on Second Samuel

Overview and Introduction: a Cycle of Stories

For communities of faith, the biblical books we now know as 1 and 2 Samuel preserve one of the richest and most colorful story cycles in the Old Testament. These narratives are at once personal and theological; they are about relationships among people, and they are about the relationship between a people and its God. They were told, written, collected, and edited not simply to preserve history or to tell an entertaining, and at times shocking tale, but also to make claims about life and the obligations of a life lived before Yahweh. They were written to teach both individuals and a community the ways of Yahweh and the way that both individuals and the community formed by Yahweh could and should live with: each other, those considered outside the community, and the community's God.

Hannah

It is clear from the beginning that these stories are deeply human. We meet a woman named Hannah, the beautiful feminine Hebrew word for "grace" or "favor." But Hannah knows anything but "favor." She is barren in a society that viewed barrenness as a sign of God's displeasure. Hannah reaches for what little power she may have in her setting. She desperately prays for a "male child." She promises to dedicate such a child to Yahweh for the rest of his life if Yahweh will only favor her petition.

Ironically, Hannah's need and her silent form of prayer result in her running afoul of the established religious authorities of her time (1 Sam 1:9-18). The

Study Bible

Read the Introductions to First and Second Samuel in *NISB*, 391-2, 439-40.

Teaching Tips

How About Hannah?

1. Divide the class into groups of three or four to read and discuss Hannah's situation before and after the birth of Samuel (1 Sam 1:1–2:21).
2. Sample queries: Who is Hannah? What has caused her great distress? What has she done in response to it? How were some of her actions misunderstood by Eli? How did God act on Hannah's behalf? What was her response to God's gift? (Allow about fifteen minutes in small groups.)
3. Then, have each group relate to the class Hannah's situation, through words, music, song, or art (five to seven minute presentations).

priest, Eli, mistakes her unspeakable grief for wicked behavior. Behavior tends to matter in 1 and 2 Samuel. Eli thus accuses her of drunkenness. But this clash turns out to be a foreshadowing of great change to come—a reversal of destinies. The time of former authorities, the Elide priesthood, is fading. A new day is dawning. Hannah's need and her petition are about to become the surprising means by which the God of Israel, Yahweh, will accomplish the divine purposes by providing new leadership for the people (1 Sam 3:19–4:1). Typically, Hebrew religion will not simply make a propositional statement based on logical or philosophical reasoning. Instead, it will tell a story such as Hannah's—full of detail, humanity and particularity. The story invites those who hear it to discern and ponder the ways that Yahweh is active in history.

Upon this foundational account of divine provision for Hannah, a great cycle of stories will be built. This cycle will stretch all the way through 2 Kings. It will trace, not in neat statements but in wonderfully complex plots, driven by gifted and flawed characters, how new leadership emerges for the nation of Israel during a period that stretched from around 1000 B.C.E. to the middle of the sixth century B.C.E.

Samuel and Saul

Hannah does give birth to a son, Samuel. The account of Samuel's birth and destiny is immediately followed by stories of Saul, Israel's first king. Saul is cast in both light and shadow. He is portrayed with an ambivalence that seems to reflect the conflicting perspectives with which the emerging institution of monarchy was met in Israel. Some greeted it; some resented it; even Saul himself may not have understood it (1 Sam 10:24-27).

Saul is tall but shy. He is brave but impatient. He is anointed by God's prophet, but he comes into conflict with that prophet. He can be magnanimous, but he can be furiously jealous. He can be filled with an overwhelming zeal for God's purposes, but he can be tragically at odds with those same purposes. For a people who still remembered and still recounted in their sacred history a time when they had no king to rule over them—no king except Yahweh—Saul's reign runs a tragic course. Even their God's heart, they claim, and the heart of God's prophet Samuel, are made heavy by the person and ruler that Israel's first monarch turns out to be:

> Then the word of the Lord came to Samuel: "I regret that I made Saul king, for he has turned back from following me and has not carried out my commands." Samuel was angry, and he cried out to the Lord all that night (1 Sam 15:10-11).

Saul and David

As Saul's star falls and fades, David's rises. David's story will dominate

1 and 2 Samuel and reach into the first two chapters of 2 Kings. Due to certain theological themes that attach themselves to David's name, his saga will in fact stretch beyond his time and continue to be part of Israel's living story right into the time of the emergence of early Christian thought. The New Testament will mention David's name no fewer than fifty-nine times, and the title "Son of David" appears in the Gospels frequently as a term associated with Israel's complex messianic hope.

David actually enjoys three introductions in the story line of the books of Samuel and Kings. In the early verses of 1 Samuel 16, David, Jesse's youngest son, enters the story. David, having not been deemed important enough by Jesse to call in from shepherding sheep when Samuel visited his family in Bethlehem, is subsequently and privately anointed by the prophet at Yahweh's command. Later in the same chapter, David is brought to the royal court where his musical ability comforts a tormented Saul. In chapter 17, following an introduction that does not acknowledge the earlier statements about David (v. 12), David emerges as an errand boy who becomes a giant-slayer and draws the admiration and fateful curiosity of the king: "Saul said to him, 'Whose son are you, young man?' And David answered, 'I am the son of your servant Jesse the Beth-lehemite'" (v. 58; cf. 1 Sam 16:17-22). The fact that Saul does not know who David's father is, according

> ## Study Bible
> See discussion on Son of David and Israel's ideal king in *NISB*, 225-26, 974-75, 2278.

to 1 Samuel 17:58, cannot be harmonized with the earlier account in 1 Samuel 16:17-22 in which Saul explicitly calls for Jesse's son David to be sent to him. What we now have may represent different strands of the tradition being brought together to form one larger narrative with a greater theme that did not trouble those who preserved the texts in their present form (*NISB* 2269).

David, Israel's secretly anointed king-in-waiting, is presented as a young, charismatic musician and warrior who obeys his father, soothes Israel's deteriorating current king, slays giants, wins hearts, beguiles enemies, becomes an outcast from the royal court, walks a thin line between heroism and treason, demonstrates zeal for God's law as understood and practiced by the guardians of his nation's religion, and finally takes the throne himself (with help from his friends and Yahweh).

On the threshold of David's ascension to the crown the account we know as 2 Samuel begins. Second Samuel will examine why David, who was not of the line of Saul, will become the king when Saul dies. This fascinating story will be told along a major fault line. On the one side, there will be tales of David's glory. On the other, there will be accounts of his dark decline. In his glory, David will consolidate religious and political power in Jerusalem, unite the Hebrew tribes—to a degree not seen since they entered the promised land—expand Israel's power over her neighbors, and receive a unique and unprecedented promise from Yahweh. But in his steep decline, David will be unable to control himself, his house or his court, and will sow a bitter harvest for his family and friends. In the process of David's rise and decline, a parade of characters will march across the text, all different yet all playing a role in God's relationship with Israel and all people. (cf. Gen 12:1-3). We meet beautiful Bathsheba, loyal Uriah, courageous Nathan, conniving Absalom, ambitious Joab, wicked Amnon, dignified and abused Tamar, wise Abigail, and a host of minor players trying to survive the intrigue swirling around who will and who would be Yahweh's king for Yahweh's people, how this could be known, and what it would mean for the nation.

Reflections
Priests, Prophets, and Culture

1. How and when should religious structures function to support cultural norms?
2. When and how might religious structures challenge and change cultural norms?

Reflections
The Rule of God and the Rule of People

What are the differences between a theocracy and a democracy? What are the assumptions about God, religion, power and the rights and responsibilities of individuals that lie behind these two different forms of government?

Session 1

Text and Context

Canon

As a literary unit, the books of Samuel and Kings constitute one continuous narrative. Scholarly consensus is that they did not begin that way. Layers of tradition and earlier versions of stories seem to have been artfully brought together in the composition of these texts. Not everyone agrees where one layer begins and another ends. The approach taken in this study is not to try to decipher the particular layers of each of these texts, but to look at the story they tell as they now stand. This may be called a "canonical" approach to the material. That is, it takes the text "as is" and tries to discern what meanings it may render that offer guidance to contemporary readers and communities of faith (*NISB*, 2263) who, though they may not always agree among themselves, already consider these texts to be important to, and in some way formative for, the life of faith.

Translation

As they first appeared in written form, the four books of Samuel and Kings formed two scrolls, one for the material in 1 and 2 Samuel and the other for the material in 1 and 2 Kings. The division of these stories into four separate books arose out of translation. When these stories were translated into Greek so that they could be read by Greek-speaking Jews and other Greek speakers, in a version known as the Septuagint, it took nearly twice the space to write the Greek as it had to write the Hebrew. Hence, two Hebrew scrolls resulted in four Greek books. In this first Greek translation, the books were given the titles I, II, III and IV Kingdoms.

> ## Study Bible
> See "Translations of the Hebrew Text" in *NISB*, 2244-45.

An early version of the Old Testament, printed in the sixteen-century in Venice adopted this four-fold division. Subsequently, translations of these texts into English have divided the material into four books, though the titles I, II, III and IV Kingdoms used by the Septuagint have given way to the titles 1 and 2 Samuel and 1 and 2 Kings.

Why "Samuel?"

There is no consensus as to why the first two books as we now have them, 1 and 2 Samuel, bear the name of the prophet. Some schools of thought reason that because the books are associated with other prophetic books called the "Former Prophets" in the tradition of the Old Testament, the title Samuel was used to reinforce that connection. Others argue that the books bear Samuel's name because the story of his birth, dedication and destiny, with which 1 Samuel begins, make him the foundational character in all that follows. A more compelling reason may be that as the individual who serves in the tradition as a "bridge" personality between the turbulent waters of the failed leadership of the period of the judges (cf. Judges 21:25) and the emergence of the idea of a divinely-sanctioned monarchy (1 Sam 8:21-22), Samuel's role is unique. The incredibly poignant passage, known as Samuel's "farewell speech," gives us a glimpse of that stature and uniqueness.

One of the groups responsible for editing Samuel and other books from Deuteronomy to 2 Kings used the technique of farewell addresses to sum up what was most crucial about an individual's contribution to Yahweh's people. Samuel's speech, which is charged with theological/ethical implications, is one such passage. This speech reveals a vision for leadership at once simple and sublime:

". . . I am old and gray, but my sons are with you. I have led you from my youth until this day. Here I am: testify against me before the Lord and before his anointed. Whose ox have I taken? Or whose donkey have I taken? Or whom have I defrauded? Whom have I oppressed? Or from whose hand have I taken a bride to blind my eyes with it? Testify against me and I will restore you." They said, "You have not defrauded or oppressed us or taken anything from the hand of anyone . . ." He said to them, "The Lord is witness against you, and his anointed is witness this day, that you have not found anything in my hand." And they said, "He is witness" (1 Sam 12:2b-5).

God and King

It is remarkable that in Samuel's farewell address God and king are presented as equivalent entities that may bear covalent witness for or against him. The people validate this close association of God and king in their reply, "He is witness." Samuel's day of leadership is indeed passing. A new day in Israel has surely come. The idea that royal and divine authority may be closely identified has emerged by the time this passage appears. It is an idea that will drive the texts through the books of Samuel into the books of Kings, and despite vigorous echoes of opposition in the other places by those who long for the days of leaders like Samuel, it will play a significant role in Israel's history for centuries to come. The identification of God and king will resonate with empires thousands of miles and years away.

Context

First and Second Samuel may be divided into five major movements. Taken as a whole, these five sections accomplish two major goals. First, the books present a literary record that explain how Israel moved away from former kinds of authority toward, for a window of time, a monarchical model of government. Second, 1 and 2 Samuel proclaim that the crown came to rest on the head of David and his "house" because the God of Israel, the one true God who had rescued the people from slavery, guided them through the wilderness, and gave them a land to call their own, was also directing their history in similar benevolent ways.

The idea of monarchy did not emerge among the Hebrew people without considerable opposition.

> **Study Bible**
>
> See "Excursus: Biblical Ambivalence to Government" in *NISB*, 407-8.

> **Study Bible**
>
> Read and discuss Romans 13:1-7; 1 Timothy 2:1-2;1 Peter 2:13-17; Titus 3:1. See also "Excursus; Christians and Government," *NISB*, 2029. What historical and cultural factors may have been important when these texts were written?

Hence, the stories that we have in 1 and 2 Samuel are drenched with tensions between prior models of authority and the coming new future. As is still the case, any centralization of power involves the loss of power in more localized settings. For this period of Israelite history in particular, the move toward a king threatened the authority of tribal systems. Those systems were based on family and extended family structures first, and then tribal councils of elders whenever a family system failed or was perceived to fail, or whenever a need (village agriculture), too large to be faced by family units alone, emerged.

During the period of the judges, authority could come to rest on a particularly charismatic individual who would unite various tribal units to face a temporary threat too great for individual tribes—for example, Deborah's leadership against the military forces of Sisera and northern Canaan. But such leadership during the period of the judges was not imbued with royal authority. Indeed, mighty leaders such as Deborah and Gideon were celebrated not as monarchs, but as temporary and expedient agents of Yahweh. Yahweh's preferred response to kings, non-Israelite, during the period reflected in the book of Judges, was to crush them (cf. Judges 5). Even the first Israelite who would be king found his ambition ran afoul of Yahweh and brought him and his community to quick ruin (Abimelech in Judges 9).

Teaching Tips
Render to Caesar
Read and compare Mk 12:13-17, Matt 22:15-22, Lk 20:20-26. See *NISB*, 1833 on Mark 12:17 and Mitzi Minor's study of the Gospel of Mark, Session 10 under Mark 12:13-17.

Literary Structure

The situation changed from the time of Israel's Judges. Other nations had kings. As the social structure of Yahweh's tribes in Canaan developed, and as they began to interact more and more through trade and expansion with the surrounding peoples, the need for and question of more centralized authority increasingly presented itself. First and Second Samuel take up these issues.

1. Samuel the Prophet, 1 Samuel 1:1–7:17

This unit traces how Samuel, through the prophetic office, is chosen by Yahweh to be God's divine remedy for the collapse of the old. This section also addresses the need for more consolidated governance during this period. Israel's former institutions can no longer sustain it as the covenanted people of Yahweh. So Yahweh, ever faithful, will reshape these structures for a new future.

2. Samuel and Saul, 1 Samuel 8–15

This section is marked by two strong characters: the aging but divinely-guided prophet/mentor Samuel, and the young, divinely-chosen monarch, Saul. This section explores how these two individuals and the offices they represent will coexist. Saul's authority rests on three pillars: his anointing by God's prophet, the gift of God's spirit, and martial prowess. Samuel's authority rests on his mother's answered prayer and pledge to Yahweh, his divine calling, and, later, his righteous resume.

Saul turns out to be a fine military leader, but, probably reflecting the views of anti-monarchical editors, he is a poor religious leader. This failing will lead to personal disaster for Saul, which, in a social structure that always looked upon the strengths and weaknesses of the monarch as reflecting those of the nation, will also result in a national crisis involving the transfer of power when Saul's days are ended. Will the next king be of Saul's line? If not, how will Yahweh transfer the ruling authority? Why will it not be done in the same manner as the other "grown-up" nations and their gods? This is a weighty question for a people whose governing assumption is that Yahweh determines all leadership and governance for them.

3. From Saul to David, 1 Samuel 9–2 Samuel 5:10

The purpose of this unit is to erase any possibility that the throne of Israel could possibly pass to a descendant of Saul and to firmly refute any idea that the crown comes to David without the sanction of Israel's God. As might be anticipated, the transfer of power is anything but bloodless. David, however, in the editor's point of view, shows practical instincts and proper regard toward a divinely appointed king, and manages to avoid being directly involved in any acts of sedition or outright treason against King Saul, "the Lord's anointed" (2 Sam 1:14).

Indeed, in a gesture that is both politically astute and well within the boundaries of norms of punishment for his time, David passes a terminal sentence on the Amalekite who seeks to ingratiate himself to David by dispatching the gravely wounded Saul (2 Samuel 1:9-16). Note that David also refuses to accept any guilt for the Amalekite's death.

4. David's Rise to Kingship, 2 Samuel 5:11–10:19

This unit chronicles David's gradual but successful rise to king of the southern and northern Hebrew tribes, and his masterful consolidation of political, military, administrative and religious authority. Within these chapters, all obvious contenders to the throne are slain. A central capital, Jerusalem, is established at a location that offers great military and political advantage. Despite claims in the book of Joshua (Josh 21:44) age-old enemies still seem to be very much around

(Judg 1:1), are reduced in strength and don't pose the threat that they have in the past. The ark of Yahweh, the most sacred object of Israelite religion, is dusted off and brought into Jerusalem amidst great fanfare and feasting. David declares his intent to build Yahweh a house because of what God has done for him, but this only inspires Yahweh to promise to make out of David's descendants a royal "house" (dynasty) that will never end. In an editorial summation that casts Israel's second king in a most favorable light, David is said to administer "justice and equity" to "all his people" (2 Sam 8:15).

5. David the Flawed King, 2 Samuel 11–21

The final major narrative section of the Samuel scrolls paints a different picture. David the darling of providence has become David the deeply flawed human being. These chapters trace the king's tragic personal decline and the cruel war unleashed as a result. The question of succession quickly arises again. Who will be king when David is dead? These chapters explore the story of the transfer of power to unlikely Solomon, who will bring Israel's first experience of a united throne to an end.

Sources and Editing

Scholars identify various groups of stories and traditions that have been compiled and shaped to produce the relatively coherent account in 1 and 2 Samuel. These materials in oral and written form served as sources for building the larger narrative. Among the most important of these early sources identifiable in the books of Samuel are accounts that had particular interest in the ark, stories that focused on Saul as person and king, and accounts that concentrated on David, his rise to power, and the deadly struggle to succeed him that took place within his own household. The editors who handled these stories deliberately sought to construct a literary expression of their belief that their God was actively shaping their history. They wanted to pass on this faith in Yahweh to subsequent generations through their written tradition.

Above all, the editors sought to bear witness to the

character and purposes of the God made known to them in the promise of covenant to their ancestors (Gen 15:17), their divine rescue from the bondage of Egypt (Exod 3), their miraculous deliverance from the sea and Pharaoh's army (14), the gift of the sacred law on Mt. Sinai (20), guidance through and provision in the howling wilderness (Exod 15-16; Num 10:11–36: 13), and the promise of a land to be their very own (Deut 11). All of these traditions, deliberately folded into their account of the rise of monarchy in Israel, provided a deeper context within which to understand more contemporary matters for the community. The same God who had been faithful in ever-changing situations before, Yahweh, was now being faithful to the nation in the midst of its struggle in newly emerging sociological circumstances. Put theologically, the slaves and pilgrims in the wilderness struggle to keep hope alive. Hope is often the challenge for groups with little power. Now, having come into land ownership and international relations as a state, slaves and pilgrims had to struggle to do what the texts, particularly Deuteronomy, call "remembering."

In this context, the call to remember does not imply simple intellectual recall. It meant the people were to conduct themselves in ways pleasing to Yahweh in order to continue to prosper in their new, landed situation. This was important for the people in general and was especially incumbent upon the king as the representative of the nation. The cost of not "remembering" would be catastrophic.

Some scholars detect in the Samuel texts a strong bias warning that in order to "remember" Yahweh's ways the prophetic office would always be needed as a corrective to the power of monarchy. This strand of the tradition is probably original, dating from before the Babylonian exile. Other scholars detect a strand that looks back on this era from exile (or after exile) and view the monarchical idea of leadership in Israel as a disaster that played a major role in "forgetting."

Both 1 and 2 Samuel as we know have them stand within the larger literary work known as the Deuteronomistic History. The influence of this work stretches

Teaching Tips
Israel's Credo and the Church's Kerygma

Divide the class into two groups: one to read and discuss Joshua 24 and the other to do the same with Acts 13:15-42. Give each group fifteen minutes to read and discuss the following questions:

1. Identify and list the major events that God has done on behalf of God's people, e.g., God brought/led them out of Egypt.
2. Why are these events so important for Israel/the people of God?
3. To what extent was God active in these events on behalf of God's people?
4. What were the benefits of these events for the people of God?
5. What kind of response to God was expected of the people as a result of these divine events on their behalf?

Allow each group about five to seven minutes to report its findings to the class.

from Deuteronomy through 2 Kings. Within this narrative the promised land is gained and lost; the southern and northern tribes unite under one throne and then divide again; the people of Yahweh win and lose wars, prosper and suffer deportation, take and lose Jerusalem, build the Solomonic temple and see it looted and burned. They see Yahweh as she "weeps bitterly in the night, with tears on her cheeks" (Lam 1:2a). The question of Yahweh's role in all of the above is raised with searing intensity. The mark of the Deuteronomistic historian/theologian editors can be seen throughout much of this saga. These editors sought to offer guidance to God's people particularly with reference to the possibility and reality of loss, and were convinced that divine standards had to be followed to forestall divine judgment. They evaluated how well or how poorly each of Israel's united and divided monarchs adhered to Yahweh's commands. The measure of such a "good" king is provided in a well-known passage from the law book of Deuteronomy (17:18), from which the term "Deuteronomist" is derived:

> When you have come into the land that the Lord your God is giving you, and have taken possession of it, and settled it, and you say, "I will set a king over me like all the nations that are around me," you may indeed set over you a king whom the Lord your God will choose. . . . When he has taken the throne of his kingdom, he shall have a copy of this law written before him in the presence of the levitical priests. It shall remain with him and he shall read in it all the days of his life, so that he may learn to fear the Lord his God, diligently observing all the words of this law and these statutes, neither exalting himself above other members of the community nor turning aside from the commandment, either to the right or to the left, so that he and his descendants may reign over his kingdom in Israel (Deut 17:14, 18-20).

This passage is foundational to understanding at least one important standard by which the monarchs

---

Reflections

The Use and Abuse of Power

1. What constitutes proper authority and what does not?
2. How will authority be exercised among the people of God?
3. Under Yahweh, what are the legitimate and illegitimate uses of power, then and now?

are judged who march, pray, stumble, flee, and serve across the pages of Samuel and Kings are judged. In short, the position of the Deuteronomists was that even Yahweh's king, or especially Yahweh's king, is subject to Yahweh's will and character as these are revealed in the divine law. The king must be versed in the law in order to administer the law justly. Royal practices that might interfere with this sacred duty, that might "turn away" the king's heart from Yahweh's mandates, are prohibited:

> You may indeed set a king over you whom the Lord your God will choose. One of your own community you may set as king over you; you are not permitted to put a foreigner over you, who is not of your own community. Even so, he must not acquire many horses for himself, or return the people to Egypt in order to acquire more horses, since the Lord has said to you, "You must never return that way again." And he must not acquire many wives for himself, or else his heart will turn away; also silver and gold he must not acquire in great quantity for himself (Deut 17:15-17).

Read in the light of these passages, the accounts of Samuel and Kings bring many issues to bear. Saul's sacrifice before battle (1 Sam 13) is not simply a strategic expedient and a hasty breach of protocol. It is a royal and dangerous usurpation of duties reserved to a counterbalancing priestly/prophetic sphere of authority. David's infidelity is not only a personal wrong and a crime. It is an abuse of theocratic power on several levels. The king should have been with his army, not playing the voyeur on his rooftop after a nap. He should have been serving in the field with his commanders, not preoccupied in bed. (He is not accused of rape, but the story of the rape of Tamar, 2 Sam 13, placed one chapter after David takes Bathsheba to his bed, may strongly suggest his status as king made his initiative with Bathesheba tantamount to rape.) David should have been prepared to care for the orphans and widows of those who fell in battle, not involved in causing the former and caressing the latter. Solomon's

---

Study Bible

Read "The Time of the Monarch and the First Temple," in *NISB*, 2274-76.

Reflections
Power Corrupts

1. What still tempts people in places of power today?
2. Read again Deuteronomy 17:14-20.
3. What general principles can be gleaned here for people in authority today?

many marriages, not to mention his numerous horses and dazzling wealth, raise the question of how his "heart" might be caused to "turn away" from the very statutes and laws he is charged to ponder constantly and uphold diligently. Ahab's theft of Naboth's vineyard at the cost of Naboth's life, vile in and of itself, is also carefully portrayed as a cynical misuse of divine law up the "chain of command" against an individual who "righteously" refuses to part with his vineyard in keeping with sacred law. Deuteronomy 17:6, ironically a section of text placed very near stipulations setting boundaries on royal authority, calls for at least two witnesses in cases that may result in the death penalty. There are indeed two witnesses against Naboth. But both of them conspired with the throne and village elders. They lied and said that Naboth "cursed God and the king" (1 Kgs 21:8-14). Naboth was then stoned to death. Conversely, the reform of King Josiah, bloody and frightening by our standards, is seen as the renewal, albeit too little too late, of Yahweh's rule over the promised land. It is the people's last best hope that that land will not be lost and Yahweh will not be forgotten.

Let There Be No Dew or Rain: the King Is Dead

Second Samuel Begins with Stunning News: Yahweh's King Is Dead.

Lectionary Loop
Proper 8 or Third Sunday after Pentecost, Year B, 2 Samuel 1:1, 17-27

And there is even more bad news. To press the point of Israel's vulnerability given its defeat on the slopes of Mt. Gilboa, the Philistines, the Darth Vaders of Hebrew history, have hauled Saul's royal armor off to display in the temple of their goddess and have hung his decapitated body (The message is that Israel itself is "headless.") out as a trophy! Had it not been for the valor and stealth of a few good men from a village east of the Jordan River, and their meticulous attention to religious rules regarding fasting, the situation would be entirely hopeless. With the end of Yahweh's king does Yahweh's rule also end? It is clear that Yahweh's presence, whatever it means, does not mean that Yahweh's people are shielded from the vicissitudes of history. In fact, if anything the claim of Yahweh's presence intensifies the sense of loss felt when the house of Saul and not Saul's army, but what they believed to be "the army of the Lord," are destroyed (2 Sam 1:12). The question of where to go from here could not be more urgently raised on a practical or theological level. As this question hangs in the air, the exquisite poem, known as the "Song of the Bow" but perhaps better named the "Song of the Shattered Bow," appears in the narrative (2 Sam 1:17-27).

When Up Is Down

David's lament begins with a cry resulting from the profound disorientation. Israel's world has been turned upside down. Israel's mountainous region is considered to be its most secure strategic feature. Heights are a place of advantage where a smaller, less-equipped force may hold off superior numbers and technological advantage for quite some time, a lesson not lost in some regions of the world to this day. But in the poem, it is precisely upon Israel's "heights" that the very worst of events has occurred. The point is that the place of the nation's strength has now become the very place of its most manifest weakness. No enemy could fail to see this fragility.

Gazelle

David amplifies the sense of vulnerability and tragedy with which the poem opens by referring to Saul and Jonathan as the nation's "glory" (v. 19, Heb., Ṣĕbî'), perhaps best translated "beauty." The Hebrew term is literally the noun for gazelle (2:18), a creature held in wonder and esteem in the Israelite imagination because of its power, speed and graceful agility, especially in harsh terrain. It would be astounding—morally, theologically and aesthetically—to see a gazelle slain in the heart of its own habitat. So too is it stunning to imagine Israel's royal house crushed and humiliated on the heights of Gilboa.

The Mighty

At this juncture in the poem, the first occurrence of the refrain that will be used to suture the entire piece together is heard: "O how the mighty have fallen!" (2 Sam 1:19). This refrain will occur again in vv. 25 and 27. The effect of this repetition is to elevate the poem to a profound wail expressing the overwhelming presence of sorrow. Restraint, at least emotional restraint, in the face of grief and tragedy is not the value present here.

The clause also contains two other significant signals. First, it uses the verb "fallen." This is a technical term often employed to depict those who die pursuing a cause and whose deaths may be considered untimely in the sense that they cancel not simply the plans of the deceased but the promise of what the deceased's life could have meant to the community. The definite noun rendered here "the mighty" (Heb., gibôrîm) might best be translated "the champions (v. 19)." It is widely used in the Hebrew Bible not only to communicate valor and martial prowess, but also to denote those who are favored with Yahweh's counsel, wisdom and prudence. Yahweh can personally be referred to with this word as the "mighty one" of Israel (Ps 106:8; Job 12:13; Pro 8:14).

The use of the term here raises the stakes around the death of Saul and his sons. Specifically, if the nation's "champions"—the best the people could put forward and also the ones chosen directly by Yahweh to lead and endowed with characteristics of Yahweh—have been slain on Mt. Gilboa, what then becomes of Yahweh's intentions for the chosen people? Have they also perished?

Hush

The anxiety of this question is expressed in the double prohibition contained in the first couplet in verse 20:

> "Tell it not in Gath, proclaim it not in the streets of Ashkelon . . ."

In other words, don't let this word get out among the five-city Philistine confederation on our western border! The mention of Gath, in particular, conjures up the ghost of the Philistine champion Goliath, for Gath was his home town (1 Sam 17:4, 23). The news in the hands of Israel's perennial nemeses, the Philistines, will provoke mockery, be a humiliation, and will raise the prospect of further military action against a weakened people of Yahweh.

Rain and Oil

A more proper response to catastrophe among the chosen people of the God who creates and redeems is to appeal to the natural order itself to render a verdict. Creation is often called as a witness to matters between Israel and its God in both the wisdom (e.g., Job 38–41) and the prophetic strains of the tradition (Hosea 4:2-3; Amos 9:14-15; Micah 6:1-2; 7:1-2).

David's cry for nature itself to depart from its ordained patterns (2 Sam 1:21) is not simply poetic expression. It has a theological basis and implications.

> **Study Bible**
>
> See "Excursus: Life After Death in the Old Testament," in *NISB*, 434-35.

The people of Yahweh are connected to the land literally and religiously in a life-sustaining relationship. It is the very terra firma "flowing with milk and honey" (Exod 3:8) that is for them a primary expression of Yahweh's provision and protection. Significant rainfall means crops. It means life. It represents God's favor just as drought can signify the removal of that favor. Rainfall is also tantamount to a sacramental signal in the religion of the people. It is quite tangibly one of the differences between being in the land of promise rather than in the land of bondage:

> For the land that you are about to enter to occupy is not like the land of Egypt . . . where you sow your seed and irrigate by foot like a vegetable garden. But the land that you are crossing over to occupy is a land of hills and valleys, watered by rain from the sky, a land the Lord your God looks after (Deut 11:10-12a).

Therefore, David's dramatic request for the rain to stop is actually a multivalent moment in the poem. It is a profound expression of grief. But it is also a question: Has there been a fundamental shift in Yahweh's relationship with the people now that Yahweh's first king is slain? Is the covenant goodness of Yahweh, tasted with thanksgiving in the gift of rain, still effective?

The second half of this same verse puts the matter more plainly and in a somewhat poetically veiled manner. Saul, who had once been anointed with oil by God's prophet and about whom it had been proclaimed on that very occasion "You will save them [Israel] from the hand of their enemies all around," (1 Sam 10:1-2) is now compared to a shield that is no longer properly maintained (2 Sam 1:21b). Shields were regularly rubbed with oil to keep them supple, ready to resist attack. Saul's shield will no longer require oil and thereby symbolizes the defenseless circumstance of the people.

Saul and Jonathan

At this point the poem becomes very personal (vv. 22-23). Symbolic references are dropped. The names of two of the deceased are spoken plainly. It is striking that Jonathan, who is never designated as heir to the throne, but who represents throughout the stories of 1 Samuel the question of hereditary succession, has achieved a level in the poem covalent with the officially chosen and anointed Saul. Justification for this, without ever being explicitly stated, is derived from the accounts of the steadfast love and friendship that formerly existed between Jonathan and David, at first approved of by Saul himself (1 Sam 18:1-5; 19:1-7; 20). Jonathan's friendship with and faithfulness to David, though Jonathan does not know it, protects Israel's next king. For this, Jonathan is greatly esteemed.

The presence of Jonathan's name in David's lament also serves to soften the isolation and potential problems Saul's name alone would provoke given Saul's dramatic fall from Yahweh's grace (1 Sam 15:10-34). At 2 Samuel 1:24, the floodgates of sorrow are opened. In contrast to the "daughters" of the Philistines who would have danced for joy over the news, the women of Israel are called upon to "weep," perhaps a reference to professional bands of mourners who participated in funerary rites, oftentimes for wages. In this case, the mourners are to remember how they have benefited at the hands of the fallen, receiving from Saul and Jonathan dazzling portions of the spoils of their victories (v. 24.)

Verses 25 and 26, building to conclusion, conspicuously exclude any mention of Saul, and repeat the thematic refrain of the poem, "O how the mighty have fallen!" The verses boldly concentrate solely on the death of Jonathan, twice citing him. This technique masterfully accomplishes two goals. First, it underscores David's affection for Jonathan (1 Sam 18:1; 20:17) to such a degree that it completely submerges what is obvious: someone is going to benefit from the fact that Jonathan is no longer a possible successor to his father, and David will be that someone. Second, it establishes David's loyalty to the house of Saul through his grief over Jonathan, thus removing from David any taint of being at cross purposes with Yahweh, who chose Saul as Israel's first king.

> ## Reflections
> ### A Strong Friendship
> 1. What are the dynamics of David and Jonathan's personal relationship?
> 2. What were the high points and the low points of the friendship?

> ## Reflections
> ### Good Grief
> Why is it important to eulogize loved ones? Consider the importance of honor for the deceased as well as the acceptance of death as a part of grief expression.

Shattered Bow

The lament draws to a close by eloquently suggesting that Saul and Jonathan, Israel's "weapons of war," were valiant but, in the end, inadequate for the task of leading Yahweh's people. Jonathan himself had prefigured such when he gave his robe, armor, sword, and bow to David as tokens of covenant loyalty between them (1 Sam 18:1-5), an act sealed with approval in the editorial comment that "all Israel and Judah loved David; for it was he who marched out and came in leading them" (1 Sam 18:16). Out of the fall of the Saulide house a vacuum arises. Is this the end of Israel's independence? Are the Philistines coming once and for all? Will the land of promise become the land of loss? Is sorrow the last word? Or, will Yahweh's purposes and Yahweh's people survive this catastrophe? If so, what shape will that survival take?

> ### Reflections
> #### A Nation at Grief
> Consider times in modern history when the death of a key leader brought a grieving nation to its knees—for example, the death of President John F. Kennedy in 1963. In what specific ways did the sad event seem to unite the nation?

Stronger and Stronger; Weaker and Weaker

There was a long war between the house of Saul and the house of David; David grew stronger and stronger, while the house of Saul became weaker and weaker (2 Sam 3:1).

Next

The beautiful lament of 2 Samuel 1:17-27 notwithstanding, the texts in their final form disclose the bitter strife that attended the question of who would succeed Saul. This phase of the narrative, 2 Samuel chapters 2–4, reports the all-too-human scramble and intrigue that attended Israel's first attempt to transfer power during the monarchy. There is an interesting tension in the story. David's lieutenants get blood on their hands, but David himself never does. At every turn David seems to gain from the losses that Saul's house experiences, but he is never portrayed as being directly responsible for those losses. The pro-Davidic stance that 1 Chronicles takes on David's rise to power is well-known. The Chronicler reports none of the struggle mentioned in the eighty-three verses of 2 Samuel 2-4. Rather, in a mere two verses he solves the question of how Yahweh's crown could fall from Saul's head and land on David's:

So Saul died in his unfaithfulness; he was unfaithful to the Lord in that he did not keep the command of the Lord; moreover, he had consulted a medium, seeking guidance, and did not seek the guidance from the Lord. Therefore, the Lord put him to death and turned the kingdom over to David son of Jesse (1 Chron 10:13-14).

From the Chronicler's point of view, Saul's unfaithfulness is basically a failure to demonstrate loyalty

> **Teaching Tips**
> **Theological bias?**
>
> Have someone read 1 Chronicles 10:13-14 to the class. Next, discuss how this Chronicler's summary of the transfer of Saul's royal power to David is so different from the interpretation that we find in 2 Samuel 2-4. Then ask: Does the Chronicler seem to have a *more* pro-David bias than what we find in 2 Samuel? Does the account of struggle in 2 Samuel seem to be more historical explanation or description? If so, why? Finally, read *NISB*, 443 on 2 Samuel 2:12—3:5 and 588 on 1 Chronicles 10:1-14.

125

("remember") or show reverence to Yahweh, illustrated most dramatically by the erstwhile king's consultation with soothsayers and mediums after the king himself had banished these very persons from Israel (Cf. 1 Sam 28:3, 7).

To Be King: Four-step Program

The path David takes as he grows "stronger and stronger" can be observed in four significant steps.

Step One

Perhaps taking advantage of credits accrued during an earlier period in which he might be called the "Robin Hood" of Judah (Cf. 1 Sam 22:5; 23:1-6), David's first step is to take his wives and his troop of experienced warriors and shift his base of operations, with Yahweh's blessing (1 Sam 2:1), to the town of Hebron, about nineteen miles south of Jerusalem. This area is controlled by the Calebites, kinsmen of Abigail's late (and foolish) husband, Nabal. David's marriage to Abigail may have made it easier for him to make this move. In Hebron, David finds himself proclaimed king by the southern alliance of Hebrew tribes, the people of Judah. David's first official act is to send a message of encouragement to Saul's former allies, the brave people of Jabesh-gilead who recovered Saul's body from the Philistines. David's praise constitutes an appeal to them to transfer their allegiance from Saul's house to David's.

David's overture to Jabesh-gilead, though the point is lost in many translations, employs a double reference to one of the most important terms in the Hebrew Bible, the word *hesed*. Concerning what the residents of Jabesh-gilead have done, David says, "May you be blessed by the Lord because you showed this loyalty (*hesed*) to Saul your lord, and buried him!" (v. 5b). David continues, "Now may the Lord show steadfast love (*hesed*) and faithfulness to you!" (v. 6a)

Neither the translation "loyalty" nor the translation "steadfast love" adequately capture the heart of the term *hesed*. A clearer translation might be, "Since you, Jabesh-gilead, have done the right thing for Saul . . . may Yahweh in return do the right thing for you." The

---

Reflections

The Ways of God in Both the Old and New Testaments

Read Exodus 34:6-7; Jeremiah 9:23; Joel 2:13; Jonah 4:2. What parallels might be drawn between the Hebrew concept of Yahweh's *hesed* and New Testament understandings of the character and ways of God? Read, e.g., Romans 5:1-2, 17 and Ephesians 2:4-5, 8-10.

term *ḥesed,* most often translated as "steadfast love," should not be confused with contemporary understandings of love as an emotion. The word is much more directed toward doing than feeling. There are plenty of references to the feeling we call "love" in the Hebrew Bible. Read the story of Jacob and Rachel or the Song of Songs, for example. But *ḥesed* has more to do with what one does than with how one feels. It signifies repeated, habitual acts of kindness and help— the practice of discerning and doing "the right thing" in the face of needs. These acts are born out of orientation to the needs themselves rather than one's particular feelings for or against those in need.

The word is used in the Hebrew Bible approximately eighty times, referring to the God who practices *ḥesed* and to the people of God who receive God's *ḥesed* for themselves and are shaped by it to the end that they extend it to others (Cf. Exod 20:5-6; 34: 6-7; Num 14:18; Deut 5:9-10; Jer 9:23; 32:17-18; Hos 6:6; Joel 2:13). In terms of its application to the God of Israel, it is the crown jewel of the orthodox confession of Hebrew faith:

> . . . for I knew that you are a gracious God and merciful, slow to anger, abounding in steadfast love (*ḥesed)* and ready to relent from punishing
> (Jonah 4:2c).

> O mortal, what is good; and what does the Lord require of you, but to do justice, and to love kindness (*ḥesed)* and to walk humbly with your God?
> (Micah 6:8)

In terms of its use with reference to the community desired by the God of steadfast love, it is placed both in the Mosaic tradition and in the prophetic tradition at the heart of the ethic that takes root among Yahweh's people:

Ḥesed signals acts that are consistently and repeatedly kind, concrete, merciful, and fair, rather than randomly right. These acts of *ḥesed* are so consistently right that they define the relationship in which they are practiced. The relationship reveals the characters of those relating to each other. In Hebrew thought, it is

---

Reflections
Ḥesed Today

Read Micah 6:8 and Zechariah 7:8-10.
1. What might *ḥesed* entail in a situation where one party has done irreparable harm to another?
2. How might an individual or a community discern what constitutes *ḥesed* in various situations?
3. What is the relationship between *ḥesed* and motive, between *ḥesed* and feelings?
4. Is selfishly motivated *ḥesed* still *ḥesed*?

Yahweh who is characterized by and the source of unfailing *ḥesed.*

Step Two

David's appeal, freighted though it is with reference to the Davidic succession that he hopes will lay claim to the people, is not entirely successful. This failure sets in motion the second stage of David's rise to power. Abner, Saul's military commander, makes a bid for authority through manipulating Saul's only surviving son, Ishbaal. This chaotic situation is to be expected. There is no orderly process for the transfer of authority in the society. First Samuel brought us bloodletting between armies. There will be some of that in 2 Samuel. But in 2 Samuel one is more likely to meet friends and former allies and servants and family members at each other's throats. Victims tend to know their assailants (*NISB*, 439).

Violence on a small scale erupts when young men loyal to Abner, representing the house of Saul, and young men loyal to Joab, representing the house of David, engage in a duel at Gibeon. (2 Sam 2:17-23) There is a brief moment (vv. 24-32) when it seems that both sides reach a settlement. It may be possible for there to be some compromise, some sharing of power, between the two vying factions. But negotiations collapse, and full-scale war over the throne breaks out. A major theme of 2 Samuel is now revealed: conflict between those who would see David come to reign and those who want the house of Saul to be continued. Though a temporary resolution to this struggle will be effected shortly, the long-standing divisions between northern and southern tribes that it reflects will never go away, and will in time tear the nation apart (cf. 1 Kgs 12:16-19). David himself will live to see the deadly political machinations that attended his rise to power repeated among those who would be king after him, and to give experienced advice (1 Kgs 1:5-53; 2:1-46) on the dealings with leftover enemies.

Step Three

Abner's growing strength in what is left of Saul's house (2 Sam 3:6) provides, ironically, the impetus for

---

Reflections
A Blood-Shedding Campaign to Office?

Back then:

1. Reading 2 Samuel 2-4 as a tract for establishing good government, how do you think the final author/editor would want us to understand: Errors to avoid? Examples to follow? Duties to perform? Promises to claim?

2. How is the authority of God invoked in this section?

Here now:

1. How do you see David portrayed in this section?

2. How are the heirs and followers of Saul portrayed?

3. Who wins and how?

4. What would politics look like today if some of these measures were carried out to insure the "proper" transfer of power?

5. Do you see God working in the midst of or *in spite of* these hostile events? Explain.

David's third and perhaps decisive step toward gaining leadership over a united Israel. Now Saul had a concubine whose name was Rizpah daughter of Aiah. And Ishbaal said to Abner, "Why have you gone in to my father's concubine?" The words of Ishbaal made Abner very angry; he said, "Am I a dog's head for Judah? Today I keep showing loyalty to the house of your father Saul, to his brothers, and to his friends, and have not given you into the hand of David; and yet you charge me now with a crime concerning this woman …" (2 Samuel 7-8)

Abner bypasses a consultation with Ishbaal about Saul's concubine that causes a rift, and promises to deliver to David "all Israel." An alliance between Abner and David, with David paramount and Abner a powerful subordinate, seems to be growing. David manages as part of his dealings with the Abner/Ishbaal faction to have Abner return one of his wives, Michal, daughter of Saul. This is an incredibly shrewd maneuver. It removes the threat that Michal might claim rule over the tribes still loyal to Saul and acts as a clear token of the covenant or treaty that the two competing camps have struck. It also raises the possibility of there arising, from the union of Michal and David, an heir to the throne who is of both the house of David and the house of Saul (although we are told later that it will never happen).

Abner does not enjoy his alliance with David for long. Joab slays him for personal reasons (2 Sam 3:27-28). The Deuteronomistic editor ensures that David is not implicated in Joab's vengeful act (v. 26) and that David's heirs are assessed no guilt (v. 28). The editor at the same time lays a foundation for ruining Joab and for removing his heirs as a threat to the throne (v. 29). With Abner gone and David's hands still clean, with half the crown already on his head and Michal back by his side, only Ishbaal stands between David and complete victory over Saul's house.

Step Four

Thus the stage is set for the fourth and final step in David's rise to power. That step is anticlimactic. David has carefully distanced himself from any wrongdoing as Saul's possible heirs and successors fall one by one. Ishbaal has already demonstrated he is unfit to rule by failing to control Abner. Now we are told that when Ishbaal heard of Abner's death, his courage fled him and with it, "all Israel" was cast into renewed anxiety. It is only a matter of a very short time before unfit Ishbaal is assassinated by Benjaminites seeking to impress David favorably. They have, of course, made a fatal mistake. David cannot possibly hope to be considered Yahweh's chosen king if he ascends the throne using as rungs the dead bodies of those who were of the lineage of the first king Yahweh appointed. Perhaps to remind everyone of his innocence with respect to Saul's death, another person who has aided David's cause is put to death. No one is left to challenge David for the throne. "Then all the tribes of Israel came to David at Hebron . . . and they anointed David king over Israel (2 Sam 5:3)." The former king (along with his heirs and generals) is dead. Long live the king.

Study Bible

Read "Excursus: Biblical Ambivalence in Government," *NISB*, 407-8.

1. Do you think the difficult transition from tribal confederacy to monarchy is a necessary one? Why or why not?

2. What are some positive and negative evaluations of the monarchy? Do the positive outweigh the negative?

For God, for King, for Country

David then perceived that the Lord had established him king over Israel, and that he had exalted his kingdom for the sake of his people Israel (2 Sam 5:12).

As the editorial view summed up in the above verse states, despite the mayhem and death that preceded his coronation, David takes the throne under the aegis of divine blessing and with the hopes of the nation placed upon him. One failed monarchy is risky enough, especially with Philistines for neighbors. David symbolizes a fresh start and has been chosen to rule "for the sake of" Yahweh's people, Israel. It is clear that, at least for now, there is no golden cord of inheritance descending from heaven, passing through the throne of one monarch and extending to that of the next monarch. If anything, the cord connecting one throne to the other is crimson, stained with blood. This makes the claim that the king is Yahweh's elect all the more stunning. It is no small feat of master storytelling to pull off an account so soaked with violence, yet so drenched with the belief and claim that somehow, through it all, Yahweh is providing leadership for the future. Yahweh is looking for a king who is "after his own heart." This is how David was described earlier in 1 Samuel 13:14. Fidelity to God, then, trumps being heir to the throne by birth, at least in the sight, or hindsight, of the Deuteronomistic editors.

The idea that David is an individual "after God's own heart" and that from him will follow forever the rulers through whom Yahweh will bless and govern the chosen people will take deep root in the Hebrew community. A thousand years hence the question for those

Lectionary Loop

Proper 9, Fourteenth Sunday, Fourth Sunday of Pentecost, Year B, 2 Samuel 5:1-5, 9-10

Teaching Tips
David and Jesus

Divide the class into two groups. Compare Jesus' entry to Jerusalem (Mark 11 or Matthew 21) with David's assuming his kingship (2 Sam 5). Other biblical texts may be consulted.

1. Have one group find some general similarities between David and Jesus. Discuss also how these similarities may have influenced Jesus' reception by the crowd?
2. Have the second group find the key differences. Discuss how and why they are significant.
3. Allow fifteen minutes for small group study and discussion.
4. Have each group share its findings with the class (at least ten minutes for each side).

131

whose hopes are quickened by a carpenter's son from the back hills of Galilee will be, "In what way is he related to David (cf. Matt 21:9-11, 14-16; Mark 11:9-10)?" The question will also plague all the kings who take the throne after David, and bedevil empires, from Babylon to Rome, who seek to place their own puppets on the Hebrew throne.

Jerusalem

David perceived "that the LORD had established him king over Israel ..." (2 Sam 5:12). David will now secure and consolidate his grip on the throne through a series of military, political and religious successes. David is about to get some things done. David first needs a gesture that will help him unite the northern and southern factions of the Hebrew tribes. The Jebusite city of Jerusalem, situated on the political fault line between the northern and southern Israelite factions—will provide a neutral geographical location for his plan to be king of all of Israel—Dan in the north to Beer Sheba in the south. As a mountain city, Jerusalem has two appealing assets in addition to its politically strategic location. First, it is relatively easy to defend, guarded on all sides except the north by valleys and ravines. Second, from the beginning, Hebrew cosmology has associated mountains with the abode and place of revelation of its God (cf. Exod 3:1, 12; 19:1, 12, 23). Jerusalem will afford just the kind of town in which Yahweh, so to speak, will feel right at home. So, David sees, comes, conquers, and settles in the city.

Conquests

David's next step, as 2 Samuel explains, is to turn to broad military conquest. Saul may have been the primary cause of his own undoing, but as the end of 1 Samuel makes clear, the Philistines were the proximate cause. David will make it a priority to do what Saul was never able to do: contain the Philistines in such a manner that they never again constitute a serious military threat to Israel. To that end, doing "just as the Lord had commanded him to do," David "struck down the Philistines from Geba all the way to Gezer" (2 Sam 5:25).

It is also significant that David's military exploits mentioned later in the narrative are presented as having extended across the Jordan River. David is said to have defeated the kingdoms of the Transjordan who had vexed the Hebrew people since the period of their wilderness wanderings. Whereas Saul's military conquests had been tenuous, David's are glorious—so much so that the summary editorial statement made about David's command of the military situation knows no bounds: "And the Lord gave victory to David wherever he went" (2 Sam 8:6, 14).

Righteous Rule

But David is not just Yahweh's warrior. He is also characterized as adept at domestic affairs. In times of war it is the primary duty of the monarch to provide protection. In times of peace the ideal Yahwistic king is to safeguard the twin pillars of idealized theocratic society, Ṣēdēkǎ, fair dealings in the civil and economic realms, and mišpat, the honest application of legal judgments in the courts regardless of the status or lack of status of the persons to be judged (2 Sam 8:15; *NISB*, 2274-75).

Though one of his own sons, Absalom, will claim otherwise and make it the chief point of his seditious remarks against his father (David), the narrator's view on the matter is that David is as impeccable with the scepter as he is with the sword: "So David reigned over all Israel; and David administered justice and equity to all his people" (2 Sam 8:15).

Three points should be noted about this brief but important description of David's jurisprudence.

First, the little modifier "all" is cited twice. This stresses that Davis was not unfair to the northern tribes (Israel) who pledged allegiance to him after the civil war between the northern Saulides and David's followers from the southern tribes. The claim here is that David did not privilege one group over the another. It is this very issue that will fester during Solomon's reign and explode within verses about Solomon's death (cf. 1 Kings 11:41–12:17). It is also on this very point that Absalom, as noted above, speaks sedition and foments revolt by the northern tribes against his

> **Reflections**
> **A Bloody Good King!**
> Is David's violent rise to power reconcilable with the Hebrew idea that the king will be the arbiter of social justice and equity? Explain.

> **Reflections**
> **Who Is Fit to Lead the Nation?**
> What are the characteristics of a good and just "ruler" in a modern democracy?

father, long before the ultimate collapse of the north-south tribal confederation:

> Absolom used to rise early and stand beside the road into the gate: and when anyone brought a suit before the king for judgment, Absalom would call out and say, "From what city are you?" When the person said . . . "of such and such a tribe in Israel," Absalom would say, "See, your claims are good and right; but there is no one deputed by the king to hear you." Absalom said moreover, "If only I were judge in the land! Then all who had a suit or cause might come to me, and I would give them justice." . . . so Absalom stole the hearts of the people of Israel (2 Samuel 15:1-6).

Second, the noun phrase "justice and equity" used in 2 Samuel 8:15 should be viewed inclusively. It seeks to gather in the wide sweep of daily life whose welfare would fall under the purview of the king, including but not limited to the legal sphere.

Third, the statement describing the values that characterized David in his royal role as judge place him in an ideal light with respect to the regulations for a good king laid down in the Deuteronomistic legislation. They stand in stark relief against the portrait of a preoccupied Saul laying aside every principle of jurisprudence to vengefully pursue an innocent David, only to end up declaring of David, "You are more righteous (sādîk) than I . . ." Saul also predicts that David is the kind of person that Yahweh will select as (the next) king (cf. 1 Sam 24:16-20). For a good summary statement from the anti-monarchial party claiming that the "ways" of any king will by definition fail to be just and equitable, and rejecting the idea of monarchy altogether based on the claim that Yahweh alone is the chosen people's real and only Sovereign, refer to 1 Samuel 8:4-18. In this text, the elders of Israel told Samuel to appoint a king as his successor to rule over them, like other nations.

> ### Reflections
> #### In God We Trust
> How have issues of separation of church and state been challenged in recent years? Why?

David Danced . . . with All His Might

D avid danced before the Lord with all his might;
David was girded with a linen ephod. So
David and all the house of Israel brought up
the ark of the Lord with shouting, and with the sound
of the trumpet (2 Sam 6:14-15).

The Ark

David's genius for consolidating his reign and for
uniting the Hebrew tribes around a theocratic ideal is
related in 2 Samuel 6. The cornerstone of his effort to
solidify his grip on power consists of his relocation of
Yahweh's ark, the most important religious artifact of
his people. It was transported from the village of
Kiriath-jearim (1 Sam 7:1-2), here called Baale-judah
(2 Sam 6:2), to Jerusalem. Before examining how
David used the event, we should locate the meanings
and importance of the ark of Yahweh, sometimes
called the "ark of the covenant" in Hebrew traditions.

It its broadest sense, the power of the ark lay in its
identification with the time of the wilderness wanderings and the emergence of the Mosaic law. It represented and hearkened back to what is sociologically known
as a "type-time," a period of their history when unique
experiences shaped the community's identity and destiny. What emerged as normative about the wilderness
period was not the sense of vulnerability or rebellion
against Yahweh that the biblical texts make no attempt
to hide. Rather, what emerged as, and was celebrated
as, life-sustaining was the memory of Yahweh's provi-
dential guidance through the wilderness. The consensus
among the people, and particularly the Deuteronomistic
editors, was that God's providence reached its religious

Teaching Tips
Draw a Picture of the Ark

Divide the class into groups of three
or four. First, ask someone in each
group read the descriptions of the ark
of the covenant in Exodus 25:10-22;
40:20-21. Next, have each group
select someone to draw an image of
the ark according to the descriptions
read. Finally, have each group share
the drawing with the class.

Question to consider: Why was the
ark of the covenant regarded as the
central symbol of God's presence
with Israel? See "Special Note,"
NISB, 123. Allow about fifteen minutes of small group time and five minutes for the presentation. Provide
paper and crayons and/or colored
pens and pencils for each group.

peak in the giving of the divine law to Moses on Mt. Sinai. The ark, in a practice reflected in synagogue protocols to this day, was built to be the receptacle of the divine law, the place where Yahweh's statutes could be stored, honored and preserved, and the means whereby the tablets of the law could be transported by a pilgrim people (Exod 25:16).

The ark not only had tremendous religious value, it also had great military significance, a point that David the warrior could not have missed. The relationship between the ark and warfare plays a significant role in 1 Samuel. When Eli learns that his sons have perished in battle, we are not told of his reaction. But when the aging priest is told that the ark of Yahweh, taken down to the battle to inspire the Israelites and terrify the enemy, has failed to stem the Philistine tide and has been captured, he is stunned and dies. His death signals the end of Elide authority and serves as a catalyst for the full emergence of Samuel.

Finally, the significance of the ark is best understood as we read about the Hebrews and their religion at the time of their leaving Mt. Sinai and settling in Canaan. During their journey to Mt. Sinai, the people were guided by a pillar of cloud by day and a pillar of fire by night (Exod 13:21) that appeared before them and represented Yahweh's presence. They are, as they flee Egypt and approach Mt. Sinai, little more than a horde of former slaves at the mercy of each other and the wilderness. But, when they depart from Mt. Sinai, they are much more. They have received on that height (a usual place to meet gods during this period) Yahweh's divine law that will mold them into Yahweh's people. They are now an army of God on the march, rather than former slaves on the run, ready not simply to escape their chains but to claim by force (with the blessing of their God) the "promised" land.

They have constructed a tabernacle in which to house their sacred law nestled in the "ark of the covenant" (Exod 40:1-21). While they are still guided by cloud and fire, these sacramental phenomena are now coordinated with the movements of the tabernacle and the ark containing Yahweh's laws. Though the

> ## Reflections
> ### Moral Law
> ### and Faithful Community
> What is the relationship between ethical norms and the formation of faithful community?

details are not clear, the ark gains prominence in the several strains of traditions about it that have been woven together. In fact, the ark has become so important that it can even be said that it is now the ark itself, not just the people, that is on pilgrimage. The ark, signifying Yahweh's actual, legal and martial presence, now providentially guides towards Yahweh's promised land those who, having once escaped in Yahweh's name, intend to conquer in that same name:

> Whenever the ark set out, Moses would say, "Arise, O Lord, let your enemies be scattered, and your foes flee before you." And whenever it came to rest, he would say, "Return, O Lord of the ten thousand thousands of Israel (Num 10:35-36).

The ark, by the time David brings it to Jerusalem, is so imbued with nearly mystical power for destruction against friend (2 Sam 6:6-7) and foe (1 Sam 5) alike, and equally fantastic power for blessing (2 Sam 6:11-12), that David can brilliantly make it the centerpiece of his establishment of Jerusalem as his capital. Although other peoples, including the Egyptians and the Hittites, possessed similar religious objects that contained their covenants with their gods, the Hebrew people believed their ark to be the repository of the law of the God who had personally chosen them out of all other peoples. It, or more exactly the law it contained, set them apart from all other nations because Yahweh was present with them (Exod. 33:12). David is drawing on that tradition in this episode. If Yahweh's ark is with David, Yahweh is with David.

Homecoming Parade and Dance

David uses a victory procession to assure the Israelites that he comes in Yahweh's name. This was a common and effective form used by conquerors to install themselves and introduce their deity to a defeated city. More than one foreign conqueror had accomplished this in Israel's history. In the hands of Samuel's editors the holy parade becomes high political and religious ritual signaling the beginning of a new day—the day of David and Yahweh. The procession is attended

---

Reflections
Sacred Objects and Faithful Living

1. What is the proper role of sacred objects, times, and places in faithful living?
2. What help do these offer?
3. What might be some inherent dangers?

by sacrifices through which David purifies and sanctifies Jerusalem itself. It may be remembered that it was Saul's inappropriate participation in sacrifices at Gilgal after waiting "seven days" that initiated his undoing. No mention of any such violation is made here, and indeed it may be that David's status or the significance of the ark's relocation, or both, mean that David has already eclipsed limits for which Saul paid dearly.

David's dance, whether or not his linen ephod was a sacerdotal sign proclaiming that he was now a priest/king, symbolically reinforces David's close association with the authority implied in Yahweh's ark. The feast that follows (2 Sam 6:19), described in delicious detail, is reminiscent of Yahweh's provision in the wilderness, and is a tangible and symbolic indication of the "good times" to come. We are pointedly told that "all the people went back to their homes," that is, they were satisfied—with Yahweh and with David!

And there is a final point. With the ark properly placed in the tent that David has provided, a tent that recalls the days of the tabernacle, and nothing but crumbs left after the great feast, David heads home, the happy husband. But, Michal, Saul's daughter and one of David's wives, is furious. She did not appreciate her husband's exuberant and scantily clad dancing before Yahweh's ark. The marital row that ensues provides the proverbial "icing on the cake" for the day. Not only has David identified himself completely with Yahweh's favor and future, but using the account of his conflict with Michal to provide a setting, we are informed by the historians/theologians/crafters of the story that the union between Saul's daughter and David never produces children.

In other words, as the day fades into night on the kingdom of David, as the last lamp is doused in the homes of those stuffed with bread, meat and raisin cakes from the king's own table, we are assured that there will be no challenge to David's monopoly on the throne. For the house of Saul, the dance is over. David has indeed "danced with all his might," and in Israel none has been his equal.

Study Bible

On Saul, David, and sacrificial offerings, see *NISB*, 411-12 note on 1 Sam 13:8-15a (Saul) and *NISB*, 450 note on 2 Sam 6:17-19 (David).

Study Bible

On David and Michal, see note on 2 Sam 6: 20-23, *NISB*, 450.

Lectionary Loop

Fourth Sunday in Advent, 2 Samuel 7:1-11, 16 and Sixth Sunday after Pentecost or Proper 11, 2 Samuel 7:1-14a, Year B

David, Jerusalem, and Temple! Forevermore?

Your house and your kingdom shall be made sure forever before me; your throne shall be established forever (2 Samuel 7:16).

The Temple and Royal Messianism

After David transfers the ark to Jerusalem, the prophet Nathan shows up with a dynastic oracle to end all dynastic oracles. His pronouncement contains the good news that David is the recipient of Yahweh's special affection and favor. Yahweh is establishing a unique covenant with David and with his descendants. Nathan's speech represents the epicenter of a powerful theological movement, known by various names such as royal theology or royal messianism or the David-Zion tradition. This theology combined the ideas of a Davidic king, the royal city of Jerusalem, and the presence of Yahweh's temple there in a tripartite nexus that made these three entities—king, city, and temple—the tangible, irreplaceable and eternal signs of Yahweh's unfailing and unending presence and protection.

Royal messianism was an attractive political and religious idea that offered much, and therefore had many adherents. It was also riddled with problems, not the least of which were the possibility of the corruption and disruption of the Davidic line, loss of power to those who were not invited to the royal "feast," and the destruction of Jerusalem and the temple. It therefore had many detractors.

Nathan's oracle itself bears signs of the tension between those who subscribed to the royal theology of the David-Zion school of thought and its primary opponent, a more ethical-legal tradition centering around Moses-Sinai events. This earlier tradition privileged Moses and the wilderness epic as norms for Yahweh's people, and looked for behaviors and practices mandated in Mosaic law far more than for eternal guarantees based on royal pedigrees.

As his message to the king unfolds, we learn from Nathan that David wants to build Yahweh a "house," that is, an abode. But Yahweh will not have it. Rather, Yahweh will build David a "house," that is, a dynasty. The term "house," in Hebrew, baît, is here used in a multivalent word play to suture closely together the idea of David's dynasty (baît) and Yahweh's temple (baît). There will indeed be a house, a temple, built for Yahweh, but David will not construct it. Looking back later, editors needed to address the question of how it came about that God's most beloved king did not actually build the temple. The oracle's answer is that David did not build the temple because God already had another contractor in mind, albeit a Davidic one (vv. 12-13). This resolution of the problem does not harmonize with 1 Kings 5:3, which indicates that David was too busy subduing Israel's enemies, a worthy endeavor indeed, to take time out for a building project. The chronicler states that David has shed too much blood to build a house for Yahweh (1 Chron 22:8-10; 28:3). These different answers imply that the question of why David did not build the temple was a significant one.

There is also a strain of anti-temple sentiment contained in the oracle. For the anti-temple party, the building of a permanent residence for Yahweh raised important theological and political concerns. First, how could the God of all creation and history "fit," so to speak, in any temple? The answer to that concern is found in 2 Samuel 7:13. The temple will be able to hold Yahweh's "name," not Yahweh. Only that dimension of Yahweh chosen by Yahweh for Israel will have the temple as its domicile. But no earthly abode can contain Yahweh's "holiness," that ineffable aspect of God that Moses' himself was not allowed to see (Exod 34:12-23), sometimes called God's "face." Second, it was not lost on the anti-temple party that the centralization of power, naturally arising from the move to a monarchial form of government, found its corollary in a loss of power on the local, tribal level.

The original idea of a reliable and accessible entry to Yahweh had begun with the sense that what Yahweh offered was a temporary meeting place, a "tent of meeting" (Exod 33:9-11; Num 11:16, 24-25), where Yahweh, when Yahweh chose, could be consulted. That idea had grown into one of a tent or tabernacle in which the presence of Yahweh might not only visit, but also choose to dwell. Yahweh's presence, and the security offered by it, remained in this arrangement at the service of Yahweh's sovereign freedom but within reasonable proximity to *all* tribes, at least in theory. A temple, on the other hand, would more permanently connect Yahweh to a certain place with the assumption made that Yahweh was not in other places (*NISB*, 2275-78). In David's theocracy, it would symbolize and facilitate a consolidation of authority in Jerusalem under the king that, while it encouraged the blessing of unity, also brought with it demands for conformity to Jerusalem's dictates. The tabernacle had meant Yahweh went wherever the pilgrim people went (Exod 40:34-38). The temple meant the people would make pilgrimage to come to Yahweh, and, of course, to Yahweh's king, (Cf. 2 Kgs 23:21-23; Deut 16:5-6).

What Temple?

There was finally a more profound, prophetic critique leveled against the temple. Jeremiah, speaking and weeping at the prospect of land, temple, monarchy, and political independence that were wrenched away by war and exile, is perhaps the best representative of this attack on temple theology:

> Thus says the Lord of hosts, the God of Israel: Amend your ways and your doings, and let me dwell with you in this place. Do not trust in these deceptive words: 'This is the temple of the Lord, the temple of the Lord, the temple of the Lord'. . . . do not oppress the alien, the orphan, and the widow . . . or shed innocent blood . . . then I will dwell with you in this place . . ." (Jer 7:4; 6-7a).

Study Bible

On tent of meeting and tabernacle, see note on 2 Samuel 7:6, *NISB*, 450. See also "Excursus: Temples," *NISB*, 122 and "Special Note," *NISB*, 123.

Reflections

Sacred Spaces

1. What "sacred spaces" or "sacred times" are meaningful in our lives?
2. What do they contribute?
3. What are the possible dangers of "sacred space" or a sacred idea?
4. What is our response when something we hold to be sacred turns out to be less than sacred, is lost to us, or changes altogether?

In the searing light cast by the fires of destruction, with David-Zion theology in disrepair, Jeremiah goes on to dream of and proclaim a time when, for the sake of the life of the community, Yahweh finds no shrine, however beautiful or well-constructed, to be adequate lodging for the life-sustaining blessing of the divine presence. Yet, Yahweh will be with Yahweh's people, but in a "temple" from which they cannot be separated (cf. 1 Cor 3:16-17; 6:19; 12:31b–13:13; 2 Cor 6:16). Jeremiah says:

> The days are surely coming, says the Lord . . . [when] I will put my law within them, and I will write it on their hearts; and I will be their God, and they shall be my people. . . . No longer shall they teach one another . . . for they shall all know me . . . (Jer 31:31a, 33-34).

Is it any wonder that the evangelist Mark, clearly framing Jesus of Nazareth in the prophetic tradition of the Hebrews, juxtaposes the story of the widow's relatively meager but whole-hearted temple offering (Mark 12:41-44) with Jesus' warning that the grandeur of the temple will not spare it destruction (13:1-2)?

David's Deal (and Its Faithful Detractors)

Two aspects of the original and unique covenant offered to David stand out. First, it is not contingent on David's obedience. It is based, rather, on Yahweh's sovereign choice and affection. Legal language is conspicuously absent from the oracle. Instead, familial language is heard. Echoing terms often used to relate king and deity in surrounding cultures, Yahweh promises to be a "father" to David and to his line and to adopt the Davidic dynasty as a "son."

Based on this relationship, as David himself in his model prayer later in the chapter will put it, "Because of your promise, and according to your own heart" (7:21), God will punish David's house for wrongdoing, but will not do so to the degree that God's "steadfast love," ḥesed, is removed from the house of David. In other words, David will not be different from Saul. He does not escape being a flawed person and king. The basic differences between Saul and David pertain to

> **Resource**
>
> For more discussion on the widow's offering in Mark 12:41-44, see session 11 of Mark's Gospel in this volume of the *Pastor's Bible Study*.

their standing before Yahweh, their destiny with respect to guiding Yahweh's people, and Yahweh's different response to their failings. These factors will have tremendous meaning during the exilic period and will be a theme of possible renewal despite devastating loss (judgment?) that Ezekiel will richly employ (cf. Ezek 18; 34:10-20).

Exile may not mean, under this promise, that God's love has been utterly and finally withdrawn. Whatever guilt may be assessed to the people, properly or improperly for that matter, does not mean that Yahweh's *ḥesed* is forfeit. In other words, there can be a future in Yahweh even after Yahweh has not spared the people or individuals from "the worst," even after the original promises are a smoldering heap, a haunt for jackals.

Second, the covenant Yahweh establishes with David is an *'ad ōlam* covenant, a "forever" covenant. In contrast to Saul, whose reign lasted one generation and failed to establish stability for the people when it did not continue on through his descendants, the Davidic dynasty is guaranteed forever. The offer is one of political security, self-rule, and independence through David for Israel, without end. It is a word full of promise and fraught with problems during times of foreign occupation and exile. But it will, during a traumatic future far from the banks of the Jordan, create a platform from which to yearn and hope (and design a polity) for the restoration of the Davidic line as a means of restoring the people as a whole.

The King and Royal Messianism

Within royal messianism, the king is identified as the primary agent of Yahweh's salvation. As will be noted, who this king is, how he will function as Yahweh's primary agent of salvation, and just exactly what that salvation will entail became key questions for this line of hope and received various answers. It was axiomatic in the Hebrew tradition by the time of the compilation of the texts before us that Yahweh was a god aggressively active in history on behalf of the chosen people. The natural order itself could be used by Yahweh to fight for Israel (cf. Exod 14; Judg 5).

Yahweh could also raise up leaders such as Moses, Joshua, Deborah, Samuel and David. With David's ascension to the throne, however, we have the first instance of the claim that Yahweh's salvation is to be permanently linked to the institution of Israel's monarchy. The promise, though the exact names of David's successors are not mentioned specifically, is that the Davidic line will continue to rule in history so that the political life and identity of the nation may be preserved forever.

Some of the royal psalms also reflect this idea, opining that the king, Yahweh's "anointed one," is to reign "while the sun endures . . . until the moon is no more" (Ps 72:5,7). Psalm 132 offers perhaps the most explicit expression of this theology outside of the dynastic oracle of Nathan. The presence of this theme in the psalter, Israel's pre-eminent book of worship, indicates its importance in the tradition:

> The Lord swore to David a sure oath from which he will not turn back; "One of the sons of your body I will set on throne. If your sons keep my covenant and my decrees that I shall teach them, their sons also, forevermore, shall sit on your throne (Ps 132:12).

Note that by the time this psalm achieves its canonical form, the unconditional covenant between Yahweh and David has quite emphatically picked up a divine condition! The perpetuity of the Davidic dynasty is now contingent on "keeping my covenant and my decrees." It is also that a future-tense verb, "I shall teach them," is employed with reference to the "decrees" to be observed, and perhaps with reference to the covenant itself. What is conserved and brought forward is the idea of Yahweh's promise to David's house as the reliable locus of God's presence among the people and the tangible token of the security this implies. These continue their distinctly political flavor. What is introduced is that remembering, and counting on the past alone, is insufficient grounds for the preservation of the community. There must be, here expressed within the idea of the king as representative of the people, an obedience that, in particular, includes

Study Bible

See "Excursus: Royal Psalms," 767.

openness to what new demands any new situations might evoke as Yahweh guides and preserves the faithful into their future.

The idea that Yahweh has settled on the office of the Davidic monarchy as the structure through which to preserve the chosen people works well as long as: (a) there is a throne, (b) David or one of his heirs is on the throne, and (c) Israel enjoys the political independence implied in having its own monarch. The emergence of rogue kings, such as the infamous Ahaz, who was of the house of David, but who "did not do what was right in the sight of the Lord" (2 Kings 16:2), however, applied pressure to royal messianism. This pressure was increased in the eighth century B.C.E. when the Mesopotamian military dashed hopes of an enduring peace for both Israel and Judah. Royal messianism, its faith in the Davidic king as the recipient of divine providence and the inviolability of both the temple and the holy city, came under searing attack from the prophet Micah:

> Hear this, you rulers of the house of Jacob and chiefs of the house of Israel, who abhor justice and pervert all equity, who build Zion with blood and Jerusalem with wrong! Its rulers give judgment for a bribe, its priests teach for a price, its prophets give oracles for money; yet they lean upon the Lord and say, "Surely the Lord is with us! No harm will come upon us." Therefore because of you Zion shall be plowed as a field; Jerusalem shall become a heap of ruins, and the mountain of the house a wooded height (Mic 3:9-12).

Under these pressures, royal messianism made an important adaptation. In short, it expanded. The historical possibility of the continuation of the line of David had become tenuous at best. Therefore, in remembrance of the divine promise, it came to be held that Yahweh would personally intervene and restore the Davidic dynasty. The ethical disrepair into which David's line of descent had been driven could not be overcome by merely material means. Yahweh alone could and would revive the house of David by calling out a monarch with royal *qualities* reminiscent and

---

Reflections
Is God with Us?

1. How do we discern when a practice or purpose of a cause is right or good?
2. How do we discern when it is not?
3. Can we be so right we are wrong?

---

worthy of the glory of Israel's first shepherd king. He would have the name, Immanuel, literally "God with us," and his reign would meet and surpass that of his "father" David (cf. Isa 7:14-17; 9:1-7).

The second expansion royal messianism undergoes in this era is a transition from a primarily political hope to a hope with cosmic scope. Israel's peace and security are still important, but they cease to be royal messianism's only goal. The reign of the ideal Davidic king will now be universal. It will include other nations (Isa 42:6-9) and will usher in a return to the conditions of paradise itself (Isa 11:6-9; 55:12-13; 65:25). At this juncture in messianic thought, a question arises: How did exposure to other peoples, even in the disadvantaged condition of exile, alter the way the Hebrews saw Yahweh as their God alone rather than the God of *all* peoples?

The ideal messianic king was to rule with equity and with justice and was to offer protection against all foes (Isa 11:3-5). The foundation of the peace that this king would keep would not be the sword. Fantastically, the knowledge of Yahweh, given only to the people of Israel through the Mosaic law, and the indisputable proof of their special election, would no longer be their exclusive possession. Rather, the people of Yahweh were to become the means, the witnesses, through which the very law that set them apart would became known to *all* nations, and hence Yahweh would be revealed to the nations (Isa 43:8-13; 56:1-7) as the only true God. The time of the messianic king would indeed usher in the unprecedented era in which "the earth will be full of the knowledge of the Lord as the waters cover the sea" (Isa 11:9). The "un-creation" of the original chaos of water (Gen 1:1-2) that smothered the earth would be recreated by and in the "knowledge" of the God of all life.

Post-exilic messianic theology also shows signs that the expectation of an ideal king of David's lineage began to move toward a hope placed in a perhaps historically distant figure, not necessarily physically tied to David. This king would not bring about so much the sequential restoration of David's line as the final, essential expression of that line, Yahweh's last and suf-

Reflections
Persistent Faith in God's Reign

Reflect upon a people in exile, far from the familiar hills of Judah, in a foreign land, the broad plains of Babylon, subjugated and humiliated (Ps 137).

Next, reflect on the bold claims made by these people that Yahweh's glory will be revealed to all people (Isa 40:3-5; 43:8-13; 56:1-7). Yahweh calls them as a covenant people to be a light to the nations and to open the eyes of the blind, to bring out the prisoners from the dungeon (Isa 42:5-9)!

Then discuss:

1. How do we account for such bold and universal faith claims in the midst of captivity and despair?

2. What might have happened to bring about this change? Renewal of faith? The rise of Cyrus, who will overcome their captors (Isa 44:28; 45:1,13)?

3. Despite external factors (Cyrus) why would this prompt Israel to proclaim Yahweh as the God of *all* peoples?

4. Read Isaiah 7:14-17; 9:1-7; 11:6-9 and note that most of these bold faith claims were made *before* the exile, but in the midst of dashed hopes for a Davidic succession of kings.

5. Jesus and his followers also had a persistent faith in God's rule, despite death, discouragement, and despair (Matt 6:9-10, 33; 12:28; 21:31; Acts 8:12; 19:8; 28:31; Rom 14:17; 1 Cor 15:50).

ficient act of salvation. It is unclear whether or not this person would be a completely historical figure, or would somehow figure in the eschatological demise of everything opposed to God's will and the replacement of history with a new age forged in apocalyptic flames. These ambiguities, traceable back to the early questions of Israel's monarchy and to Nathan's dynastic oracle, would remain unresolved, and raise burning issues for years to come—issues faced by the eccentric prophet John the Baptizer centuries later, and to the one who "baptized" after him (Mark 1:1-8; 6:14-16; 8:27-30).

Study Bible

See "III. David's Personal Failures" in the outline of 2 Samuel, *NISB*, 440.

"The Sword Devours Now One and Now Another"

When Kings Go out to Battle, Some Don't

The saga of the Davidic monarchy takes a decided downturn beginning in 2 Samuel 11, and by chapter 18 has spiraled out of control. Most scholars place this chapter within the larger literary unit known as the "Court History" or "Succession Narrative," which begins a few chapters earlier and runs through 1 Kings 2. These materials reflect the community wrestling with the question of how royal power will be transferred from David to one of his heirs. It will be remembered that that was not the case with Saul, so there was no precedent for this question. With stunning frankness, chapter 11 begins to focus on the decline of David. Read as a morality play the chapter is shameful. Seen in the light of Deuteronomistic expectations for the status and function of Israel's king, it is damning.

Bathsheba

It's spring. The rains have ceased. The roads are passable. So it's the time of year when "kings go out to battle." But not David. Once known for his martial prowess, "Saul has killed his thousands, and David his ten thousands" (1 Sam 21:11c), David lingers behind in his capital while the army of Israel engages the enemies of the chosen people. Is he no longer the divinely appointed protector of the people? We learn quickly that David may be lingering behind, but he is not idle. Though the idealized account of David's reign in Chronicles will make no mention of the affair, David, in violation of the Mosaic law (Deut 5:18), and in violation of the trust vouched in the king as Israel's fore-

Lectionary Loop

Seventh Sunday after Pentecost or Proper 12, Year B, 2 Samuel 11:1-15

Eighth Sunday after Pentecost or Proper 13, Year B, 2 Samuel 11:26—12:13a

Proper 6, Year C, 2 Samuel 11:26-12:10, 13–15

Reflections

Political Promises and Broken Vows

1. How have marital infidelities by modern political leaders affected their credibility in the eyes of their constituents and their ability to govern?
2. How do the (inevitable) lies and cover-up lead to more trouble?
3. Who, besides Bathsheba and David, helped make their deadly affair happen (2 Sam 11)?

most guardian of that law (Deut 17), commits adultery with the lovely Bathsheba.

His plan to hide his act is foiled by Bathsheba's fertility (2 Sam 11:4-5). But fertility is at the heart of the one original command of Yahweh (Gen 1:28) and the covenant promises to Israel's ancestors (Gen 15:5; 17:6). Has David turned blessing into curse? The divinely ordained fecundity of the natural order has made things inconvenient for Yahweh's king, not to mention the incredible violation of Bathsheba, passed over in the text in silence, and the dangerous situation into which David has forced her. So, David now considers other means to cover up his deeds. He raises the stakes. He will call Bathsheba's husband home from the war and send him home for rest and recuperation. Sending soldiers home for R & R is in direct violation of Mosaic law when they are engaged in a military campaign (Deut 23:9-14). David is now fomenting sedition against Yahweh by encouraging Uriah to violate that law (2 Sam 11:11).

By now there aren't that many commandments left to break, but David manages to find another one. He conspires with his military commander to have Uriah, loyal soldier of Israel, slain. David's order and a foreign sword accomplish the deed (2 Sam 11:22-24). The act parallels Saul's worst moment, when he ordered Yahweh's own priests slain at Nob by the hand of Doeg the Edomite, a foreigner obeying the command of Yahweh's king to slay fellow Yahwists (cf. 1 Sam 22:18). Can it get any worse? Yes.

Told of Uriah's death, David as much as assures his military commander that everything will be just fine: David said to the messenger, "Thus you shall say to Joab, 'Do not let this matter [David's treachery? Joab's complicity? Uriah's death?] trouble you, for the sword devours now one and now another; press your attack on the city, and overthrow it. . . .' encourage him" (2 Sam 11:25).

David is right, far beyond what he can yet see. A sword, as the following chapters will show, has indeed been unleashed. David cannot foresee or control its appetite. Where will David's wrong lead his house? Where will it lead his people? What does Yahweh think?

"Absalom . . . Absalom!"

The king was deeply moved, and went up to the chamber over the gate, and wept; and as he went, he said, "O my son Absalom, my son, my son Absalom! Would I had died instead of you, O Absalom, my son, my son!" (2 Sam 18:33).

Yahweh's Displeasure

The silence of Yahweh reaches deafening proportions. In chapter 11, one hears commandment after commandment crack and crash, but nothing is heard from Yahweh. Not once does God speak. There is only one oblique reference to the God of Israel. It comes, ironically, poignantly, from faithful, betrayed, doomed Uriah (v. 11). But even Uriah's orthodoxy and honor elicit only silence from heaven. There is no "amen," for Uriah, let alone divine protection.

Then, right at the end of chapter 11, there is heard the following shattering, terse clause: "But the thing that David had done displeased the Lord" (11:27c). Everything changes. David might not have heard it, but at these words a bell tolled somewhere in the kingdom.

Baiting a Trap

Nathan returns. He has brought with him an oracle of judgment disguised as a tale of social injustice. He is introduced carefully in the text, with the narrative threshold of his speech being the formulaic expression that Yahweh was displeased with "the thing" (Hebrew *hadābār*) that David had done. The ambiguity of the reference to whatever "thing" it is that David has done is deliberate. The word *dābār* in Hebrew can refer to a wide range of events, activities, or deeds. It is used here as an invitation to the reader to reflect on the wicked cascade of actions that David has just undertaken and to come away baffled at how anyone could pick out any one "thing" as worse than another.

Was "the thing" that displeased Yahweh David's desertion of his duty to lead Yahweh's army? Was it lust? Was it adultery? Was it violating Bathsheba? Was it abuse of royal power? Was it trying to deceive Bathsheba's husband? Was it ignoring the protocols of holy war and trying to get faithful Uriah to set them aside, too? Was it conspiracy to commit murder? Was it arrogantly dismissing all the above? The point is that it is difficult to know exactly what "the thing" is, yet.

The strategy Nathan employs is deception, just as the king's strategy has been deception. He presents to David—the former shepherd boy who is now shepherd of Yahweh's lambs, including Bathsheba and her late husband—a vivid and detailed account of abuse of power. The prophet tells the tale as if it were a contemporary legal case. (One may recall that hearing legal cases justly and fairly is at the very heart of the Deuteronomistic polity for what makes a moral monarch.) David responds vigorously to the reported abuse, condemning the imaginary injustice of one of his subjects in a fit of indignation. Asserting that the wrongdoer deserves to perish for his abuse offers the reader the opportunity to consider how much more, then, should David perish for the life of Uriah. David actually, suddenly (and surprisingly) gets one part of the sacred law right. He declares that repayment for the lamb will be fourfold, a judgment in accordance with the penalty stipulated in Exodus 22:1. The oldest manuscripts for this portion of 2 Samuel actually have an even stronger sentence issue from David's busy lips. They indicate that he vowed there would be sevenfold (!) repayment, a favorite number of the priestly editors who considered seven to correspond with perfection or completeness (cf. Prov 6:31).

Snap

Nathan springs the trap. In Hebrew, it's actually only two words long: *'attāh hā' îš*. "You are the man (2 Sam 12:7)." Nathan's response, in addition to its brave accuracy, reveals the heart of the prophetic office. The Hebrew prophet proclaims Yahweh's moral will to powers and norms having rejected that will. Prophetic discourse is hopeful in essence even if it is sometimes brutal in form. It believes things are bad but can be salvaged despite great loss suffered and great loss still to come. Whereas the essential spirit of apocalyptic thought is that the time for amending one's ways has passed, God is breaking in, the end (regarding evil) is here, and the reign of the divine will is here, in force and in person.

Consequences?

David learns that, because of his sin, the child in Bathsheba's womb will not survive. This idea is rightfully repugnant to us. We do not share the universal sense of divine causation (everything that happens is finally ordained by the will of Yahweh) of this period, nor was it the Hebrew Scriptures' only or last word on the matter (cf. Jer 31:29-30; Ezek 18:1-4). We also do not accept a view of God that we find ethically grotesque (NISB 457). Children do suffer. Some perish. They suffer and perish, at times, at the hands of their parents or as a consequence of parental behavior. And God's heart breaks every time, for the child and for the parents. They suffer and perish, sometimes, despite every loving thing their parents do. And God's heart breaks every time, for the child and for the parents.

The question raised previously as to just what "the thing" David has done is, is now answered. David, and very strong language is used, has "utterly despised the word [moral and practical law of Yahweh as codified in Israel's sacred texts] of the Lord" (2 Sam 12:9a, a.t.), specifically through adultery and murder (v. 9bc). While we appear to live in an age that encourages the ignoring of God's standards or in a socioeconomic setting that offers the luxury of insulating ourselves from most of the negative consequences that arise from destructive actions, David does not.

Yahweh will not cancel the promise. Yahweh will not abandon David or his house. But Yahweh will not rearrange reality to spare David the outcomes of what

Study Bible
See Excursuses on "Retribution," 1460, and "Suffering," 1686 in *NISB*.

Teaching Tips
Pastoral Care
without Theologizing
Share with the class your concerns as a pastor when visiting a family who has just lost a child by either illness or accident. Explain why listening, caring, and helping are much more important at this time than any of our (feeble) attempts at articulating a theology or theodicy of suffering.

Reflections
David's domestic troubles are recorded in 2 Samuel 11-20 and 1 Kings 1–2. The account is so realistic (e.g., family intrigues) that many scholars believe that a member of David's court wrote these sections of the Bible. In contrast to the chronicler's history (which idealizes David), this court history portrays the king in both his strength and weakness, avoiding any attempts to distort the facts in the interests of theological bias (pro-Davidic spin). Discuss the significance of this realistic record for understanding David and Israel's history. What histories or biographies of great leaders have impressed you with their honest account of the person and the times?

the tradition knows as deliberate, intentional, willful, destructive conduct. Though these verses (vv. 9-15) are written from a later perspective looking back on the bloody history of the all-too-human struggle to succeed David, they bear the lesson of the glory and the tragedy of human responsibility. Yahweh has indeed "put away," that is, removed the legally required penalty, death (v. 13), from David. But David has in fact broken the first commandment. When he destroyed those whom Yahweh created and used them for his own ends, he also "despised" (v. 10b) and "utterly scorned" (v. 14) Yahweh, their creator. Therefore, there will be consequences. The sword David so cavalierly told Joab could not be controlled, will now visit David's own house, out of control, with no end in sight (v. 10a).

Spiral

From Nathan's oracle, preceded immediately by the formula statement of Yahweh's displeasure (11:27c), the Samuel narrative will derive enough literary and theological energy to drive it through the next seven chapters. It is a fierce energy from which great destruction spirals outward in ever-widening, crimson circles. David and Bathsheba will lose a child and have another child who is not first in line for the throne but who will, with some plotting and a nod from Yahweh, end up sitting on it. There will be incestuous rape and vicious psychological abuse in David's own household. His misplaced sympathy in response to the destructive power of lust will add outrage to outrage and will be used by the editors to signal that what David could not control in himself he does not know how to discipline in another. Hatred, revenge, murder, sedition, treason, duplicity, enmity, and civil war will swirl around the throne, seeking David's crown and at times his very life.

Solomon

The question lurking in these chapters, and reaching beyond them through 2 Kings 2, is who will be Yahweh's next king and how will he surface? That this monarch will not be Absalom could not be more clear-

---

Reflections

Read 2 Samuel 12:15-25 and focus on David's actions and attitudes after the prophetic denouncement.
1. What actions and attitudes are commendable in your opinion?
2. How are David's relationships with God, his dying child, the servants, and Bathsheba portrayed?
3. Does David appear remorseful over his wrongful actions?

Study Bible

Read the notes on 1 Kings 2:1-9, David's instruction to Solomon, in *NISB*, 485. Note the Deuteronomic qualities of a just king reemphasized here.

ly answered. It will, in fact, emerge from the mayhem that Solomon is the one who will be able to declare that Yahweh "has established me and placed me on the throne of my father David," and "has made me a house as he promised" (1 Kgs 2:24). The power of Yahweh's promise to shape history and the shape of Yahweh's promise in history is resolved momentarily, both for how the "chosen" relate to each other and for how they relate to "the nations." At the end of the "Succession Narrative" that makes up so much of 2 Samuel, Solomon and his glory are on the rise. The first king is dead. The second king is dead. Long live the king.

Are You the One?

But the Solomonic center will not hold. Forces within will rend the throne from Yahweh's king and tear Yahweh's nation asunder. Forces without will march from the north and across history and dash the divided thrones of Israel and Judah into shards reminiscent of the shattered commandments on the slopes of Mt. Sinai. Jerusalem, for all its strength and despite being Yahweh's home, will be breached and reduced to rubble. The beautiful temple turns out not to be flameproof, as seems to be the case with so much beauty. Has Yahweh fled? Has Yahweh retreated? Has Yahweh abandoned history and those who would be Yahweh's people? If not, what shape will Yahweh's promises and purposes now take? Will there really ever be a sovereign of the line of David whose reign is Yahweh's reign, whose reign is endless, and whose reign is peace?

The crowds that went ahead of [Jesus] and that followed were shouting, Hosanna to the Son of David! Blessed is the one who comes in the name of the Lord! Hosanna in the highest heaven!" When he entered Jerusalem, the whole city was in turmoil, asking, "Who is this?" (Matt 21:9-10).

Teaching Tips

Read the following paragraph to the class:

In conclusion, we see that the life and faith of ancient Israel provide us with a rich understanding of God, God's people, and their expectations of a king like David. Drawing on many favorite Old Testament themes and images, the New Testament writers give us the following dynamic portrait.

"In Jesus the promise is confirmed, the covenant renewed, the prophecies are fulfilled, the law is vindicated, salvation is brought near ... the Son of David reigns, the Kingdom of God has been inaugurated, the Son of Man has received dominion from the Ancient of Days, the Servant of the Lord ... has accomplished the divine purpose." Quoted from F.F. Bruce, *New Testament Development of Old Testament Themes* (Grand Rapids: Eerdmans, 1968), 21.

Reflections
Views on Suffering

Although ancient Israel viewed most human suffering as divine retribution for sin (Job 4:8; 11:20), it was also regarded as inevitable (Job 5:7), disciplinary (Prov 3:11-12; Job 5:17), temporary (Job 5:18-19), mysterious (Job 11:7-10), meaningless (Eccl 2:23; 3:19) and even vicarious (Isa 53:5). See R. B. Y. Scott, *The Way of Wisdom* (New York: Macmillan, 1971); L. G. Perdue and W. C. Gilpin, eds., *The Voice from the Whirlwind: Interpreting the Book of Job* (Nashville: Abingdon, 1992).

THE
TEN COMMANDMENTS

A STUDY BY
THOMAS M^CDANIEL

*Thomas McDaniel is Professor Emeritus of Old Testament Studies
at Eastern Baptist Theological Seminary in Philadelphia, Pennsylvania.*

THE TEN COMMANDMENTS
Outline

Introduction

Exodus 20 and Deuteronomy 5

Displaying the Commandments

Any mention of the Decalogue during the last half of the twentieth century would have triggered recollections of Cecil B. DeMille's three-and-a-half-hour movie, *The Ten Commandments*, filmed in 1956, featuring Charlton Heston (as Moses), Yul Brunner (as Ramases) and Anne Baxter (as Nefretiri). Some older Americans remember when Ten Commandments granite monuments were donated to many municipalities across America in the 1950s and 1960s by the Fraternal Order of Eagles, with the support and sponsorship of Cecil B. DeMille, who wrote from Mount Sinai while filming on site, ". . . we need the Divine Code of Guidance which was given to the world. That is why I am so enthusiastic about the Fraternal Order of Eagles' project of circulating and erecting copies of the Ten Commandments everywhere the Order's widespread influence reaches".

But the gifts of those Ten Commandments monuments erected mid-century on public property and courthouse lawns became, by the end of the century, the basis for lawsuits and legal battles. Any mention of the Ten Commandments now, at the start of the twenty-first century, triggers a religio-political debate about the display of the Decalogue on government or public properties. The best example of this happened on August 1, 2001, when attention shifted from Hollywood and DeMille's film, available on DVD, to the Alabama State Judicial Building in Montgomery, Alabama, where the Alabama Supreme Court Chief Justice Roy Moore had authorized the placement of a

Teaching Tips

Divide the class into two groups. Have one group support the posting or displaying of the Ten Commandments in government and public places (Justice Roy Moore's view) and the other group take the position that these actions violate our separation of church and state and the civil liberties of those who don't adhere to the religious beliefs connected with the Ten Commandments. Make available periodicals or Internet resources that discuss this legal issue (e.g., Elsie Soukup, "Monuments: Thou Shalt Display," *Newseek,* March 1, 2004; http://atheism.about.com/library/decisions/ten/bldec_GlassrothMoore.htm. Allow the class at least fifteen minutes to brainstorm. Have each group select a person to present the findings of the group (five to seven minutes each). Allow additional time for class discussion.

Source

DeMille, Cecil B, "Why We Need the Ten Commandments." *The Eagle Magazine,* September, 5-6, 2001.

5,280-pound granite monument of the Ten Commandments in the building's rotunda. Two months later, on October 31, 2001, two lawsuits seeking the removal of the monument were filed against Chief Justice Moore by plaintiffs represented by the American Civil Liberties Union, Americans United for Separation of Church and State, and the Southern Poverty Law Center. A three-judge panel of the U.S. Court of Appeals for the 11th Circuit ruled unanimously against Chief Justice Moore, resulting in Moore's suspension from office on August 22, 2003, for ignoring a court order to remove the monument. It was finally removed from the rotunda on November 14, 2003, and placed in storage. The fate of Justice Moore now rests with the Alabama electorate, and the fate of the monument rests with the men whose names were chiseled into the granite at its copyright sign: Justice Roy Moore, Richard Hahnemann, the sculptor, and Moore's attorney, Stephen Melchoir.

The Los Lunas Decalogue

While much attention has been given to the legal battles in cities and counties of Alabama, Indiana, Kentucky, Maryland, Pennsylvania, Texas, and Wisconsin over the presence of monuments and plaques of the Decalogue on public property, little attention has been given to the world's oldest Hebrew inscription of the Ten Commandments, which turned up in New Mexico in the nineteenth century. The Decalogue was inscribed in Hebrew (using a quasi-Phoenician script) on the flat face of a large basalt boulder on a mesa now known as "Mystery Mountain" and "Hidden Mountain," three miles west of Los Lunas. Given its antiquity, the monumental boulder is of some significance for early American history. Photographs of it should be in American history textbooks, if not replicas of it placed in schools or on courthouse lawns. In 1949, Robert H. Pfeiffer of Harvard University recognized that the inscription was an abbreviated form of the Decalogue; and since then a number of other scholars, including Harvard Professor Barry Fell (1976: 310), have confirmed the identification.

Resources

Los Lunas Decalogue

http://www.ebts.edu/tmcdaniel/LosLunas.html
http://www.ebts.edu/tmcdaniel/LosLunasRock-4.jpg
http://www.ebts.edu/tmcdaniel/LosLunasRock-5.jpg

Reflections

Lessons on Los Lunas

The displaying of the Ten Commandments by the Los Lunas community, perhaps crypto-Jews among the Spanish conquistadors, did not ensure the survival of this religious community. What lesson is to be learned here for those who feel that taking away the Ten Commandments from our public schools and government places will reduce the number of those who adhere to God's moral law in the Ten Commandments?

My inspection of the inscription, on site, in 1983 and a comparison of the script used on the boulder Decalogue with other early northwest Semitic scripts, led me to conclude that the "Mystery Mountain" inscription is not just centuries old but could possibly be pre-Columbian or even pre-Christian. The most compelling bit of evidence is the unique shape of the letter *q* in the word *lĕqăddĕšô* "to hallow it," referring to the Sabbath. It was written resembling a tall angular number eight in our English script. The letter *q* written this way appears elsewhere only in Phoenician inscriptions found in northern Spain from 200 B.C.E. to 200 C.E. In addition to the unusual shape of the *q*, the use in the "Mystery Mountain" Decalogue of the consonants *'aleph* and *hē* as internal vowel letters parallels the same use of these letters in other Phoenician inscriptions. The content of the Decalogue in this Los Lunas inscription, aside from its being abbreviated and having several spelling errors, which suggest that it was inscribed from memory—such as confusing the sound of a *qoph* (*q*) with the sound of a *kaph* (*k*) so that *šeker* "drunkenness" or *śakar* "hire, wages" was written for *šeqer* "falsehood, lie"—varies little from the received Hebrew texts of Exodus 20 and Deuteronomy 5.

Although some scholars have conjectured that the "Mystery Mountain" Decalogue dates from Solomonic times, the odd shape of the letter *q* precludes that possibility since that script is unattested that early. Others would date the inscription to the first century B.C.E., based upon a petroglyph of a sky-map allegedly depicting a solar eclipse that is said to have occurred on September 15, 107 B.C.E., which would have been the Rosh Hashanah of that year. In my opinion a more likely scenario to account for this Decalogue is that some "Crypto Jews" or Marranos—those Jews of Spain who converted to Christianity upon penalty of death but secretly practiced their Jewish faith—were among the Spaniards who reached (New) Mexico. Once in the New World, some Marranos separated themselves from their Spanish Christian comrades and established an isolated Jewish community on what became known as "Hidden Mountain." An inscription

> ## Study Bible
>
> On the Ten Commandments, see: *NISB*, 115-16 (Exod 20); see also "Special Note" on the Decalogue; and 252-53 (Deut 5).

of the Decalogue in ordinary Hebrew letters would have exposed their true religious identity and have subjected them to persecution or execution. But by writing their Decalogue with rare and archaic Phoenician style letters, the "Mystery Mountain" Marranos hoped to hide their identity as practicing Jews. If so, their security scheme failed them. Once recognized as Jews, the Marranos could have been wiped out like other Jews in the pogroms throughout Europe. On the other hand, a deadly disease could have caused the demise of the community. Either way, destroyed by a virus or by violence, the "Mystery Mountain" worshipers of Yahweh perished without a trace, except for their indestructible basalt Decalogue and assorted petroglyphs.

What makes the Los Lunas Decalogue important for the contemporary religio-political debate over the public display of the Ten Commandments is the obvious fact that the conspicuous display of the Decalogue at the base of the "Mystery Mountain" did not guarantee the survival of that religious community which, no doubt, lived obediently to Yahweh's commandments.

Different Ways to Number the Commandments

Sixteen verbs in Exodus 20:1-17 have an imperative force, whereas in Deuteronomy 5:6-21 there are seventeen such verbs. Different Christian and Jewish traditions reflect several ways to divide these verbs with imperative force so as to come up with exactly ten commandments or ten "words," (Greek, Decalogue) as they were so designated in Exodus 20:1 and Deuteronomy 4:13; 10:4. The rabbinic tradition recognized "I am Yahweh your God" (a verbless statement in Hebrew) as the first of the ten words and then listed and clustered the sixteen or seventeen verbs in such a way to end up with exactly ten commandments. As a result, the commands not to covet a neighbor's wife and not to covet anything of one's neighbor were made into the single tenth commandment. But Roman Catholic and Lutheran tradition followed Origen, Clement of Alexandria, and Augustine who joined together "You shall have no other gods before me" and "You shall not make for yourself a graven image" to make the first of

Teaching Tips

How Is Your Decalogue Numbered?

Discuss the similarities and differences of the following. Can you detect the theological assumptions behind the different arrangements? Note A, 1-3; B, 5, 9-10; C, 2.

A. The Jewish faith:

1. I am the Lord your God 2. No other gods 3. Lord's name in vain 4. Remember the Sabbath 5. Honor your parents 6. No killing 7. No adultery, 8. No stealing 9. No bearing false witness 10. no coveting.

B. Catholics and Lutherans:

1. No other gods 2. Lord's name in vain 3. Remember the Sabbath 4. Honor your parents 5. No killing 6. No adultery 7. No stealing 8. No false witness 9. No coveting your neighbor's property 10. No coveting your neighbor's wife.

C. Protestants (Reformed):

1. No other gods 2. No graven images 3. Lord's name in vain, 4. Remember the Sabbath 5. Honor your parents 6. No killing 7. No adultery 8. No stealing 9. No false witness 10. No coveting. Note: the last arrangement [C] will be followed in this lesson.

the ten commandments. As a result, the prohibition about coveting a neighbor's wife was separated from the one about coveting a neighbor's property, making them commandments nine and ten, respectively. Orthodox, Protestant, and Reformed traditions recognized "I am Yahweh your God" as an introductory statement and made "You shall have no other gods" the first commandment, with the prohibition of graven images becoming the second commandment. And, as in the rabbinic tradition, the two prohibitions about coveting were joined together to form the tenth commandment. In terms of the religio-political debate over the display of the Ten Commandments in America, even the way the commandments are numbered on the plaques and monuments, is a significant indicator of which theological tradition or institution is recognized as normative and authoritative. We will follow the arrangement presented by the Reformed tradition.

The words of Exodus 20:1, "And God spoke all these words, saying" is in Christian tradition an editorial introduction to the entire Decalogue which follows in 20:2-17. The Decalogue itself was an independent literary unit that was inserted into the middle of a separate theophany narrative, now found in the divided texts of Exodus 19:7-25 and 20:18-26. The Decalogue is presented as having been spoken directly by God to the Israelites (who were addressed by the collective singular pronoun "you," as in the *Shema* of Deut 6:5), *without* Moses being a mediator. Thus, the Decalogue in the book of Exodus became revered as a special revelation from Yahweh to the Israelites. They heard Yahweh speak but did not die! But, according to the twenty-eight verses of theophany narrative into which the Decalogue was inserted, Yahweh wanted the people of Israel to hear him but not to see him, saying, "Lo, I am coming to you in a thick cloud that the people may hear when I speak with you" (Exod 19:9). However, the Israelites were so fearful of actually hearing Yahweh ("let not God speak to us, lest we die") that Yahweh reversed himself and made Moses the mediator who would convey the divine words to the fearful tribes (Exod 20:20-22).

> ## Study Bible
> See "Special Note" on theophany and also the revelation of God's mercy in *NISB*, 136.

> ## Reflections
> ### Thoughts on Theophany
> God appears at decisive points in Israel's history: the promises to the patriarchs (Gen 17; 18; 28), the call of Moses (Exod 3), the exodus and Sinai tradtions (Exod 13; 16; 19-20; 24), entry to the promised land (Josh 5), and the call of the prophets (Isa 6; Ezek 1). God's self-manifestations are mostly audible and only partially visible (Exod 33:18-23). How do you experience God's presence today? How is it similar to or different from the biblical accounts back then?

In Deuteronomy 5:4-5, when Moses on the slopes of Pisgah repeated the Decalogue given at Mount Sinai, the Deuteronomist conflated the Exodus 20 variants by having (1) Yahweh speak to the Israelites *directly* ("Yahweh spoke with you face to face at the mountain out of the midst of the fire") and (2) by having Moses mediating the message ("I stood between Yahweh and you at that time to declare to you the word of Yahweh"). For the Israelites, the hearing of Yahweh's voice once was enough. The tribal chiefs and elders acknowledged "we have heard his voice out of the midst of the fire, we have this day seen God speak with people and the people still live." But, terrified that additional hearings of God's voice could be fatal, they petitioned Moses, "Hear all that Yahweh our God will say; and speak to us all that Yahweh our God will speak to you; and we will hear and do it" (Deut 5:23-27).

Lectionary Loop
(For all Ten Commandments)

Twentieth Sunday after Pentecost or Proper 22, Year A, Exodus 20:1-4, 7-9, 12-20

Third Sunday in Lent, Year B, Exodus 20:1-17

Prologue to the Decalogue

Jewish tradition notwithstanding, the identical words in Exodus 20:2 and Deuteronomy 5:6, "I am Yahweh your God, who brought you out of the land of Egypt, out of the house of bondage" (used often in the Old Testament) serve as the prologue to the entire Decalogue. Anthony Phillips and numerous scholars have recognized that this brief prologue parallels the use in Hittite suzerainty treaties of a historical prologue proclaiming the suzerain's prior achievements before the enumeration of the treaty stipulations placed upon the vassals. Here Yahweh is seen as a benevolent overlord who reminds Israel of the accomplishments made on her behalf just before a covenant is initiated. When Exodus 20:2 and Deuteronomy 5:6 are read in a similar manner—as the prologue to the entire Decalogue—it precludes isolating the verse as the introduction to the first prohibition only.

The Decalogue and the Death Penalty

Anthony Phillips presented the case for the Decalogue's having been Israel's criminal law code, over against her civil code, stating:

From the point of view of Yahweh, the Decalogue was Israel's constitution, and any breach of it amounted to an act of apostasy which could lead to divine action against the individual offender and the community. . . . thus breach of a commandment was regarded not only as an offense against Yahweh, but also, since it endangered the community, as an offense against the latter, in other words a crime, for which prosecution must be undertaken in the community's name. . . . Following the conviction of the criminal, immediate exe-

---

Reflections

Absolute and Universal

According to Albrecht Alt, the Ten Commandments are apodictic or unconditional, divine laws, in contrast to the secular, casuistic or conditional laws of Canaan. Apodictic laws are a distinct form of Israelite law, according to Alt. They are characterized by the second personal negative imperative, "Thou shalt not . . ." or as a participial phrase "whoever strikes his father or mother shall be put to death" (Exod 21:15) or a curse, such as "Cursed is he who dishonors his father or mother" (Deut 20:16). Casuistic law is applicable only in certain cases; its basic form being "If . . . 'then . . .'" to which further clauses can be added to make the application more precise (e.g., Exod 21-23; Deut 22:23-29). See: A. Alt, *Essays on Old Testament History and Religion* (Oxford: Basil Blackwell, 1934, 1966) 81-132; W. J. Harrelson, "Law in the OT," *IDB* 3:80-83; Dale Patrick, *Old Testament Law* (Atlanta: John Knox, 1985).

cution was inflicted by the community, for the criminal could no longer be regarded as part of the covenant people. Outside the breach of the Decalogue, the death penalty was never exacted. (1970: 11)

Moshe Weinfeld (1991: 248), in disagreement with Phillips, asserted, "the commandments are not intended to be concrete legislation, rather a formulation of conditions for membership in the community. Anyone who does not observe these commandments excludes himself from the community of the faithful." Ronald Clements (1994: 328-329), in agreement with Weinfeld and in obvious disagreement with Phillips, stated that "exclusion from the covenant community would be the inevitable and appropriate punishment" for any violation of the Decalogue. Clements concluded, "The attempt to elevate all ten of the commandments to cover capital crimes involving the death penalty must be set aside as highly implausible." But what seemed "implausible" for Clements was essential for the Deuteronomist. The death penalty was clearly stipulated for nine identical criminal offenses cited in the Book of the Covenant (Exodus 21:12–22:16) and elsewhere in Exodus, Leviticus, and Deuteronomy. These other texts dealing with identical criminal offenses, examined below, would have to be either subsequent reiterations based on the Decalogue or earlier statutes about capital crimes that eventuated into the Decalogue. Sixteen canonical texts, one deutero-canonical text, and an extra-biblical passage (to be cited under each commandment in this lesson) support the claim that the Decalogue's focus was definitely on capital crimes, much like the deadly curses pronounced in Deuteronomy 28:20-27.

In these sixteen canonical texts, only three of them specify death by stoning. The stoning would have been done by all of the men of the community, with perhaps the prosecuting witnesses initiating the stoning. Phillips noted that stoning was the preferred method of execution because it required the full participation of all members of the community, "and so both individually and corporately propitiate Yahweh" (1970: 24).

Source

For Exodus 20:2 and Deuteronomy 5:6 as a historical prologue proclaiming the sovereign's prior accomplishments before initiating a treaty with his subjects, see two titles by Anthony Phillips: *Ancient Israel's Criminal Law* (Oxford: Basil Blackwell, 1970) 3-11 and *Essays on Biblical Law* JSOTSup 344 (Sheffield: Sheffield Academic Press, 2002) 2-24.

Another reason may well go back to the covenant with Noah, where it was stipulated, "Whoever sheds the blood of human, by a human shall that person's blood be shed; for in his own image God made humankind" (Genesis 9:6, NRSV). Whereas a single executioner would himself become guilty of killing another person in the act of executing a criminal, no one person could be held responsible for the death of a criminal from a communal stoning, for it was impossible to determine which particular stone or stone-thrower actually caused the victim's death. An analogy would be execution by a firing squad when one of the rifles fires only a blank; but those who shoot do not know which rifle has the blank, thereby precluding any individual soldier being held accountable for a killing.

However, it cannot be assumed that death by stoning was always the method of execution. In Exodus 19:12-13, it was stated that "any who touch the mountain [Sinai] shall be put to death. No hand shall touch them, but they shall be stoned or shot; whether animal or human being, they shall not live." According to Exodus 32:27, when Moses came down from Mount Sinai with the tablets of the law and learned that the Israelites had worshiped the golden calf, he quoted God as saying, "Thus says Yahweh, the God of Israel, 'Put your sword on your side, each of you! Go back and forth from gate to gate throughout the camp, and each of you kill your brother, your kith, and your kin.'" In obedience the Levites killed about three thousand kinsmen that day, after which Moses announced, "Today you have ordained yourselves for the service of Yahweh, each one at the cost of a son or a brother, and so have brought a blessing on yourselves this day." The blessing and the ordination of the Levites upon the slaughtering of their kinfolk initiated, idealized, and institutionalized the zealots' motto: "Death to the infidels!" Thus, it is quite clear that, be it either pre-Decalogue or post-Decalogue, the execution of infidels was carried out by several methods: stone them; shoot them; stab them, just so they die—the covenant with Noah notwithstanding.

Teaching Tips

Law Codes Past and Present

1. Have someone in the class read Exodus 19:7-25 and 20:18-26 as a literary unit.
2. Select two members of the class seated at opposite ends of the table or room and have each one read alternately, sentence by sentence, from the same translation of Exodus 20:1-17 and Deuteronomy 5:6-21.
3. Have other members raise their hand when the hear something different from either reader.
4. Make a list on the blackboard of all the verbs as the texts are read and have class members decide ones they would use to make up a "decalogue."

Teaching Tips

Capital Punishment

Read from the "Book of the Covenant," as found in Exodus 21:12–22:16, and list the crimes which carried the death penalty.

Teaching Tips

Religious Tolerance

Recommend that all class members visit the web page of Religious Tolerance.org which deals with the Ten Commandments, available at http://www.religioustolerance.org/chr_10co.htm, and especially the sub-link http://www.religioustolerance.org/chr_10c6.htm, which deals with constitutional issues in the religio-political debate over the commandments.

Recognition that the Decalogue was Israel's code of capital offenses came not only from post-enlightenment scholars, but it was recognized by others like William Cowper (1731–1768) who penned many hymns and poems including the following lines.

> Marshaling all his terrors as he came;
> Thunder, and earthquake, and devouring flame;
> From Sinai's top Jehovah gave the law—
> Life for obedience—death for ev'ry flaw.
> When the great Sov'reign would his will
>   express,
> He gives a perfect rule; what can he less?
> And guards it with a sanction as severe.
> As vengeance can inflict, or sinners fear.
>
> "Truth" 547-554

Death to infidels for violating the commandments of Tablet One, and death to criminals for violating the laws of Tablet Two became normative and routine, with most executions being so insignificant they warranted no historical notice. The stoning of the nameless woman caught in adultery (John 8:3-9) would have taken place without any historical record had it not been for the attempt of the scribes and Pharisees to have Jesus come to the woman's defense and thereby contradict Moses, so that then they could have stoned Jesus along with the adulteress. Similarly, Stephen's being stoned as an infidel (Acts 7:54–8:3; 9:1-2) was just routine business for Saul of Tarsus who, having consented to Stephen's death, proceeded "to lay waste to the church, and entering house after house he dragged off men and women and committed them to prison . . . still breathing threats and murder against the disciples of the Lord." The number of and the names of Saul's victims were, for the most part, not worth any historical recognition or record.

The infamous *Malleus Malificarum* ("The Witches' Hammer"), published in 1486 by the Dominican monks Heinrich Kramer and James Sprenger, became the vilest extension of the Decalogue's demand for the death of infidels. The document was a manual of operations for the inquisitors and the Inquisition to ferret

Teaching Tips

Criminal Code or Covenant?

Divide the class into two groups, one supporting the thesis of the Decalogue as Israel's criminal code (Anthony Phillips and McDaniel in this session) and the other group advocating the Decalogue as conditions for membership in Yahweh's covenant community. For the covenant position, see: Clements, Weinfeld, and G. E. Mendenhall, "Covenant" in the *Interpreter's Dictionary of the Bible*, ed. G. A. Buttrick (Nashville: Abingdon, 1962) 1:714-21. Allow both groups about fifteen minutes to prepare. Have one person from each group present its position (five to seven minutes each). For class discussion: How are the Ten Commandments viewed differently in each position? How does each position impact our understanding of the Ten Commandments in a different way?

Teaching Tips

Death to the Infidels!

Discuss Moses' call for Levites to kill their brothers and sons (Exodus 32:27-28) with the terrorism of today that calls for "death to the infidel!" See also *NISB*, 132-33.

Study Bible

On Exodus 32:27-28, see *NISB*, 132-33, for discussion of Exodus 327-28. On Holy War see Excursus in *NISB*, 314.

out and execute witches. Wicasta Lovelace estimates "the death toll during the Inquisition worldwide ranged from 600,000 to as high as 9,000,000 (over its 250-years-long course)."

Saul's having early Christians "committed" to prison should not be misunderstood to mean that Christians would simply receive a jail sentence. Prisons (for Rome and ancient Israel) were holding pens, so to speak, for people awaiting trial. At trial a prisoner could be (1) found innocent and released, or (2) found guilty of a capital offense and executed (Numbers 15:32-36; Leviticus 24:10-23), or (3) found guilty of a lesser offense and sentenced to some form of corporal punishment, like the forty stripes spelled out in Deuteronomy 25:1-3, or in later times having one's head, hands and feet placed in the stocks. A *prison sentence,* defined as confinement in a penitentiary for a crime, is a relatively modern legal option invented in America by William Penn and the Quakers of Pennsylvania, who opposed all bloodshed, including the execution of criminals. Quakers assumed that prisoners who were held for an extended period of time in silent solitary confinement would become penitent, thus the name "penitentiary."

Where there was no Quaker influence, the Decalogue, as the code of capital offenses, was not only idealized and perpetuated by religious communities in England and America but expanded to include a much wider range of capital offenses. While the northern colonies were more lenient with crimes against property, crimes against morality were more harsh in the north, with blasphemy, idolatry, sodomy, and bestiality having become capital offenses in Connecticut, Massachusetts, and New Hampshire. In Virginia, capital crimes came to include the smuggling or embezzling of tobacco, the fraudulent delivery of tobacco, or the altering of inspected tobacco. Banner noted, "As the New England colonies lost their original sense of a religious mission, they abandoned the death sentence for some of these moral crimes." For example, "Massachusetts decapitalized blasphemy, adultery, and incest in the late seventeenth century, and New Hampshire decapitalized blasphemy in the early eighteenth centu-

Resources

Wicasta, Lovelace. *Malleus Maleficarum: Introduction to the 1948 edition with Translation and Notes by Montague Summers,* 2003. Available online at http:// www.malleusmaleficarum.org.

Source

Stuart, Banner. *The Death Penalty: An American History*. Cambridge, Mass.: Harvard University Press, 2002.

Reflections

Legislating Morality

In our recent history conservative movements like Christian Reconstructionism or Theonomy (R. Rushdoony; G. North), the Moral Majority (Jerry Falwell), and the Christian Coalition (Ralph Reed) have advocated a return to the moral and (many) civil laws of the Bible.

1. How do you feel about legislating biblical morality in America in the twenty-first century?
2. How does our First Amendment to the Constitution influence this question?

ry." But while the some of the colonies were decapitalizing some offenses, in England the "Ten Commandments" (i.e., a code of capital crimes) were expanded twenty-fold to about two hundred crimes which had become capital offenses.

Lectionary Loop

(for all Ten Commandments)
Twentieth Sunday after Pentecost or Proper 22, Year A, Exodus 20:1-4, 7-9, 12-20
Third Sunday in Lent, Year B, Exodus 20:1-17

Session 2   Exodus 20:3 and Deuteronomy 5:7

The First Commandment

"There shall not be to you other gods contrary to my will"

"Before Me," or "Besides Me," or "Against My Will"

The exact meaning of the Hebrew 'al pānāy, generally translated as "before besides me" or "in my face presence," has been difficult to determine. The suggestion here is to follow an insight by Mitchell Dahood (1966: 125), who translated Psalm 19:15 as "May the words of my mouth be . . . according to your will, O Yahweh . . . ." Dahood cited Albright, Johnson, and Speiser, all of whom translated *pānîm* in some texts not as "face" (the primary meaning) but as a homograph meaning "favor, will, intention." The latter word occurs in the opinion of these scholars in Phoenician, in Ugaritic, and in the following biblical texts (with the corresponding word italicized, a.t.)

1. Genesis 10:9 "he was a mighty hunter by the *will* of Yahweh"
2. Genesis 17:18 "Let but Ishmael thrive if you so *will* it"
3. Genesis 27:7 "that I may eat it and bless you with Yahweh's *approval* before I die"
4. Genesis 43:33 "and as the men took their seats at his *direction*"
5. 2 Chronicles 32:2 "his *intention* was war."

Several years later Gunther Plaut (1974: 159) concurred in his commentary on Genesis and translated:

Teaching Tips

In Walter Harrelson, *The Ten Commandments and Human Rights, Overtures in Biblical Theology* (Philadelphia: Fortress Press, 1980), 192, Dr. Harrelson updated the biblical Decalogue with the following contemporary moral code:

1. Do not have more than a single ultimate allegiance.
2. Do not give ultimate loyalty to any earthly reality.
3. Do not use the power of religion to harm others.
4. Do not treat with contempt the times set aside for rest.
5. Do not treat with contempt members of the family.
6. Do not do violence against fellow human beings.
7. Do not violate the commitment of sexual love.
8. Do not claim the life or goods of others.
9. Do not damage others through misuse of human speech.
10. Do not lust after the life or goods of others.

Class Project: For each of the Ten Commandments in Sessions 2–11, a "Reflection" box should be given suggesting that the reader compare Harrelson's *(Continued on Page 172)*

6. Genesis 10:9 as "by the *grace* of the Lord;"
7. Genesis 17:18 as "Oh that Ishmael might live *by Your favor*"
8. Genesis 27:7 as " to eat that I may bless you, with the *Lord's approval*, before I die"
9. Genesis 43:33 as "they were seated by his *direction*" Similarly, the 'al pānǎy "upon my face" in the Decalogue should be repointed and read as 'al pānî.

The prohibition of Israel's having any god other than the Creator addressed the issue of power. The root meaning of 'ēl ("God") is "power," even when the noun is spelled as 'elôhîm or as the frequently used honorific plural 'ĕlôhîm. The expression "God be with you" carried a meaning analogous to the science-fiction salutation "may the Force be with you"—with the difference being that in the former "God" is personal and masculine, whereas "the Force" is an impersonal neuter. The Islamic affirmation (which was added to the flag of Iraq in 1991), "Allahu Akbar," meaning "God is Great," has its parallel in Job 36:5, 'ēl kabbîr "God is Great," which was immediately modified by the phrase *kabbîr koah lēb* "Great, powerful of heart." The modifiers "great" and "powerful" describe the word "God."

The Will to Power

The attraction of the forbidden fruit of Eden for Eve and Adam was that by eating the fruit they would "become like God," which was to say that they would get *power*. The temptation was not about the acquisition of knowledge or holiness; it was about the acquisition of power. The building of the Tower of Babel was about power, the power used for self-defense. But God terminated its construction because "nothing that they propose to do will now be impossible for them" (Gen 11:6). Israel's attraction to the fertility cults of Canaan was not about sex per se, it was about power—the power to perpetuate life and to produce food to sustain life. Israelites were as human as everyone else. They gravitated toward winners with power. Consequently, when the gods of Israel's neighbors won wars

(Continued from Page 172) paraphrase (1980: 192) of that particular commandment and invite the reader to offer an alternative paraphrase for our time.

Source

See Patrick D. Miller, *The God You Have: Politics and the First Commandment* (Philadelphia: Augsburg Fortress, 2004).

Reflections

The Power Source

The attraction to power and the desire to have power are strong human instincts: e.g., the power to influence, command, subdue, dominate, and control. Power, as we know, can be abused: the damaging control and manipulation of human relationships, the tyranny of abusive misrule in unjust governments. Power can be seized or awarded. Power can often corrupt. Read Exodus 15:2; 1 Chronicles 29:12; Psalm 28:8; 73:26; Mark 10:27; 14:36.

1. How does the first commandment relate to God as the only source of power?
2. In what ways can we be empowered by submitting to God as our true source of strength? See also Acts 1:8; 4:33.
3. What can God's power accomplish in our lives today?

for their people and provided lands that really flowed with milk and honey, many Israelites who thought Yahweh was powerless transferred their loyalty to where the *power* seemed to be, to a winner like Babylon's Queen of Heaven (Jer 44:17-19).

The first commandment addressed the deceptive deification of power which would prove to be destructive and deadly. The Creator with cosmic power had initiated a covenant with a powerless people through whom all the families on earth would be blessed. As vassals of a benevolent Lord their absolute allegiance was required. There was no need for Israel as the Creator's royal priesthood and holy nation to seek power from any force or source in nature. Having a covenant relationship with the Creator of the sun, moon, and stars, there was no need to worship any of the the heavenly hosts. Even the death sentence imposed for violating this commandment was a declaration of the power of the Creator. An Israelite's death would not be determined by the deity of the underworld named *Mot* ("Death"), whom the Canaanites worshiped. Israelites would live and die according to the loving-kindness and justice of the Creator. As noted above, "God is Great" and "powerful of heart" and it was the divine will that Israel rely solely upon the Creator.

Mandate or Monotheism

DeMille's statement, cited in the Introduction to this study, that the Ten Commandments were "the Divine Code of Guidance which was given to the world" echos a sentiment shared by a number of biblical commentators, as reflected in the title of Edwin Poteat's 1953 commentary *Mandate to Humanity*. However, for the Deuteronomist, if not for Moses, the Decalogue was Yahweh's unique present to Israel, not a gift to the nations nor a mandate for humanity. The Deuteronomist presented God and Moses from an ethnocentric viewpoint. According to Genesis 12, Yahweh made a covenant with Abraham promising that through him and his seed *all* the families of the earth would be blessed. But from the perspective of the Deuteronomist, Abraham's descendants through Ishmael and Esau were excluded from the covenant. The "thou" of

Sources

Dahood, Mitchell, "Psalms 1-50," vol. 16, *Anchor Bible* (Garden City, N.Y.: Doubleday), 1966.

Plaut, W. Gunther, "Genesis," in *The Torah: A Modern Commentary* (New York: Union of American Hebrew Congregations), 1974.

Teaching Tips

The Queen of Heaven

Have members of the class read from Jeremiah 44:1-10, 15-18. Then have some members of the class role-play the men and women who worshiped the Queen of Heaven because she was a winner, whereas the God of Israel was a loser, incapable of saving his people from their enemies. Another member of the class can role-play Jeremiah as he attempts to make it clear that the people of Israel have violated the first commandment and the defeat of Judah and Israel is a punishment from God for their sin, not a sign of Yahweh's weakness.

Reflections

Ronald E. Clements (*NISB*, 252) stated that "The first commandment identified God as Israel's deliverer and *reveals* the basis of the special relationship that made this nation the means of a revelation given for all humankind. The commandments are thereby shown as *universally relevant* (italics are mine)." Discuss when and how the Decalogue became universal. Since Israelites did not evangelize, how could the first commandment have been made universal? See, e.g., Isaiah 42:1-4, 6; 49:6.

the Decalogue was the same as the "thou" of the *Shema*: "Hear, O Israel, Yahweh is our God, Yahweh alone, and thou [Israel] shalt love Yahweh *thy* God . . ." (Deut 6:5, a.t.). The Song of Moses in Deuteronomy 32 included a stanza affirming emphatically, "When the Most High apportioned the nations, when he divided humankind, he fixed the boundaries of the peoples according to the number of the sons of God; for Yahweh's portion is God's people, Jacob his allotted heritage" (32:8-9, a.t.). The RSV and NRSV follow the texts of the Dead Sea Scrolls and the Septuagint (the Greek translation of the Hebrew) which read here *ʾel* "God" ("sons of God") instead of *yisrāʾēl* "Israel," which appears in the KJV and NIV ("sons of Israel").

The gods which Yahweh assigned for *non-Israelites* to worship were designated in Deuteronomy 4:19, in a warning to Israel (addressed with the singular "you" as in the Decalogue and the *Shema*): "And when you [Israel] look up to the heavens and see the sun, the moon, and the stars, all the host of heaven, do not be led astray and bow down to them and serve them which Yahweh your God has allotted to all the peoples everywhere under heaven." Thus, the Deuteronomist understood that Yahweh through Moses had ordained *monolatry* (i.e., the worship of only one god) for Israel, not a *monotheism* for the entire world. Israel's monolatry would require the worship of the Creator Yahweh only; but all *other people* would have to worship something from the creation—the sun or moon or an astral deity assigned to each nation by Yahweh. Thus, while polytheism and henotheism were prohibited for Israel, they were viewed as legitimate religious options to be tolerated *outside* of Israel. See Ephesians 2:11-12, "Remember that at one time you Gentiles in the flesh . . . were at that time . . . separated from the commonwealth of Israel, and strangers to the covenant of promise, having no hope and without God (*atheoi*, "atheist" or "God rejected") in the world."

Absent from Deuteronomy was any declaration of absolute monotheism (only one god exists) as found in Isaiah 45:5-7, "I am Yahweh, and there is no other; besides me there is no God . . . I am Yahweh and there

Teaching Tips

God and the World

Have members of the class read Deut 4:9-19 and Ephesians 2:11-22, and then discuss the different theological affirmations found in these texts in light of John 3:16, "God so loved the world . . . ."

is no other. I form light and create darkness, I make peace and I create evil—I Yahweh, do all these things." For example, the "greatest" commandment in Deuteronomy 6:4, "Hear, O Israel, Yahweh is our God, Yahweh alone . . . " is not really an affirmation of monotheism but of monolatry, for the phrase *Yahweh 'ehad* cannot mean "Yahweh One." Proper names in Hebrew cannot be modified by numerals; therefore it must mean "Yahweh alone" or "Yahweh only" (not the other gods). The final demise of polytheism, henotheism, and monolatry was envisioned by the psalmist, who, with Deuteronomy 32:8 in mind, penned Psalm 82. In eight verses the psalmist presented the reader with a scene of heaven's Supreme Court when God, as the Chief Justice, indicted *the other gods* for dereliction of duty in adjudicating justice for the poor in their respective jurisdictions. The gods were convicted and sentenced to death ("You are gods, sons of the Most High, all of you, But you shall die like men, and fall like one of the princes"). With the gods of the nations doomed to death, the psalm closed with a spectator in heaven's courtroom pleading with the Chief Justice: "Rise up, O God, judge the earth for all the nations belong to you!" Here, in the last verse of Psalm 82 is both monotheism and universalism. But such a view of God will not be found in the Decalogue of Exodus 20 or Deuteronomy 5.

The Penalty for Violating the First Commandment

Reinforcing this commandment as absolute, unconditional law for Israel is the penalty for breaking it.

- "Whoever sacrifices to any god, save to Yahweh only, shall be utterly destroyed"(Exod 22:20)
- "If a prophet arises among you . . . and if he says, 'Let us go after other gods . . . and let us worship them,' . . . that prophet . . . shall be put to death" (Deut 13:1-5, a.t.)
- "If your brother . . . or your son, or your daughter, or your wife . . . or your friend who is as your own soul entices you secretly, saying, 'let us go and worship other gods,' . . . you shall kill him, your

hand shall be the first against him to put him to death . . . you shall stone him to death with stones" (Deut 13:6-10)

- "But the prophet who presumes to speak a word in my name which I have not commanded him to speak, or who speaks in the name of other gods, that same prophet shall die" (Deut 18:20, RSV).

The Second Commandment

"You shall not make for yourself a graven image . . ."
Exodus 20:4; Deuteronomy 5:8
(cf. Deuteronomy 27:15)

Cain and Graven Images

This prohibition against the crafting of graven images by Israelites may well be grounded in the story about Cain's killing Abel. The name Cain means "smith," with the Hebrew word *qāyin* being the cognate of the Arabic *qain* "smith." In Genesis 4:2 Cain was identified as the "one working the land," which, in light of his name, no doubt referred to mining for metals. By contrast, the name Abel means either (1) a "skilled shepherd," being the cognate of the Arabic *'abil*, which Lane (1863:8) defined as being "skilled in the good management of camels and of sheep or goats," or (2) "farmer," with the name *Hebel* being a by-form of *yĕbûl* "producer of the soil."

For Cain the "fruit of the land" mentioned in Genesis 4:3 would have been *minerals or metals*, rather than grain or grapes. For Abel the "fruit of the ground" would have been either the fruit of the *field or flock*. Consequently, the present which Cain labored over for some time before offering it to Yahweh would have been something of *metal* from the "fruit of the soil," perhaps some sort of image or engraving. Abel, on the other hand, offered to Yahweh "from the firstborn of his flock." Unfortunately for Abel, Cain's gift was rejected by Yahweh, while Abel's lambs were accepted. Depressed, jealous, and angry over God's rejection of his gift, Cain killed Abel. As a consequence, he was cursed by God and told that the land would no longer

> **Study Bible**
>
> For other interpretations see notes on Genesis 4 and "Excursus: Sibling Rivalry in Genesis," in *NISB*, 13.

yield its *koah* "power" to him. Although most exegetes interpret this "power" to refer to "produce" (fruit and vegetables) it was more likely a reference to *metals* and *minerals*. The story about Cain and Abel reflects the tensions in antiquity between sedentary urban craftsmen on the one hand and rustic agrarians or pastoral Bedouins on the other hand. For the purpose of interpreting the second of the Ten Commandments, the Cain and Abel story makes it quite clear that Yahweh's dislike of graven images went way back in legend and tradition—his disdain of images did not begin with golden calf at Sinai (Exod 32).

The Image that God Favors

Once the meaning of the name "Yahweh" comes into focus, the contempt of Yahweh for graven images becomes transparent. As we will see in the next session, the word "Yahweh" denotes the English word "Creator." Nothing in creation—with one exception—can do justice to the Creator. The earth's most pure gold and silver are but paltry products by which to represent the Creator of the cosmos (Exod 20:23; Lev 19:4; Deut 27:15). Freedman (2000: 35-36), after quoting Isaiah 40:18-25 as a commentary on the Second Commandment, stated:

> Nothing of human invention could ever be adequate to capture all that Yahweh is. The one who has made everything and sits as king over the whole earth and its inhabitants could never be comprehended by the human mind, let alone constructed into an image . . . How could a mere creature ever hope to accurately represent the Creator?

Also, because no one had ever seen Yahweh, it was impossible for any image made by mortals to reflect the truth about the eternal. It is true that Numbers 12:8 quoted Yahweh as saying with reference to Moses, "With him I speak face to face—clearly, not in riddles; and he beholds the form of Yahweh." But a commentary on this verse in Exodus 33:20-23, quoted Yahweh as having said, "You [Moses] cannot see my face; for man shall not see me and live. . . . you will see my

---

Teaching Tip

The Image that God Loves

Bring several small mirrors to the classroom and pass them around the class with this instruction: "Take a good look at the image which God made and God loves." Graven images of God are forbidden, but God is so pleased with the men and women, the boys and girls, created as images of the divine that there are billions of them in production.

Reflections

In God's Image

1. What does it mean to be created in God's image?
2. How does embracing this conviction affect your understanding of God, your relationship with others, and yourself?

---

back; but my face will not be seen." Thus, Moses was granted the same courtesy which Yahweh had earlier extended to Hagar, after which she called Yahweh 'el rŏ'î, "the seeing God," and confessed, "Here have I seen the hinder parts of him that seeth me."(Douay Rheims, 1899, Gen 16:13). But neither Hagar nor Moses provided a description of the "back" of God which could have benefited artisans or artists. In the words of John 4:24, "God is spirit, and those who worship him must worship in spirit and truth."

The one image in *creation* which can do justice to the *Creator* is the one image made by the *Creator*. As stated in Genesis 1:26, "God said, 'Let us make humankind ('ādām) in our image, after our likeness'. . . ." In the covenant with Noah the sacredness of human beings ('ādām) as those in God's image was reiterated, "Whoever sheds the blood of 'ādām by 'ādām his blood shall be shed; for in the image of God he made 'ādām" (Gen 9:6). As Freedman noted (2000: 36), "Any attempt to make another image of God, especially from an inanimate object such as wood or metal, is to degrade both God and humankind." Poteat (1953) astutely observed, "Because man is made in God's image, he thinks man is as worthy of worship as God. This is image worship on its subtlest . . . and its most disappointing level."

A Jealous God or a Creator God

The first words of the prologue, "I am Yahweh your God," are repeated in the second commandment in Exodus 20:5 and Deuteronomy 5:9, where they are followed by the title 'l qn', which was read as 'ēl qannā' "a jealous God" (in most translations). It is stated that Yahweh claimed this title because, even though he showed steadfast love to thousands of those who loved him (cf. Exod 34:7a; Neh 9:17, 31; Jon 4:2; and Ps 108:4), he visited the iniquity of the fathers upon the children, unto the third and fourth generation of them that hated him (cf. Exod 34:6-7b; Num 14:18; and Jer 32:18). However, the title 'l qn' could *also* be read as 'ēl qōnē' "creator God," with the participle qōne' being a variant spelling of qōnēh "creator," as in "El Elyon, creator of heaven and earth" (Gen 14:19, 22, a.t.). The verb qānāh "to create" is found in Proverbs 8:22, as

Teaching Tips

Creator of Heaven and Earth

Have class members look up and read the following texts on God the Creator, Genesis 1:1-3, 26-27; 2:4-7; Exodus 20:11; Nehemiah 9:6; Job 12:9; 26:7; Psalms 102:25; 104:5-6; Isaiah 40:28; 45:12; 48:13; Acts 4:24; 14:15; 17:24; John 1:1-3; Hebrew 11:3.

Discuss:
1. Why is it important to understand God as the Creator of heaven and earth?
2. How does this understanding distinguish God from creation?
3. Is it wrong to exalt creation above its Creator?
4. Why is the constructing of images and idols symbolic of this confusion between creation and its Creator?

Teaching Tips

God is Great and Good

Before dealing with the meaning of the Hebrew words for "god/God" find out how the class members define the English word "god/God." For the etymology of the English word "God" check online at http://www.newadvent.org/cathen/06608x.htm and share the information with the class (preferably as a printed handout). Note how grace before meals taught to children, "God is great, God is good . . ." begins with an etymologically correct definition of the noun "God."

translated in the Septuagint and many contemporary English translations (e.g., RSV, NRSV, NJB, NIV, NLT). David Freedman proposed (1986: 515) that the phrase *yahweh qannā' šemû* of Exodus 34:14a, means "He creates zeal in his name," and the *''ēl qannā' hû* of Exodus 34:14b means "he is a zealous God." But in Exodus 34:10, the verb *nibrē'* "they had been created (v. 10b)" and the phrase *ma' seh yĕhowāh* "the work of Yahweh (v. 10d)" suggests that the repeated "jealous" *qannā'* in our verse 14 could well have been the by-form of *qānāh* "to create" (as in Gen 14:19, 22; Prov 8:22) permitting the translation in Exodus 34:14 "Yahweh Creator is his name" and "Yahweh is a creator God." Precisely because Israelites have the *Creator* as their God they must not worship any *thing* which was *created*, be it astral or earthly.

Jeremiah appears to have had both definitions of *'l qn'* in focus when he prayed (32:18-19), "Ah, my Lord Yahweh, you have made the heavens and the earth by your great *na dby* your outstretched arm" (which reflects the idea of *'ēl qannā'* creator God"), and then followed the affirmation with, "You requite the guilt of the fathers to their children after them" (which reflects the idea of *'el qannā'*, "a jealous God"). But, surprisingly, Jeremiah continued, "O great and mighty God whose name is Yahweh Sabaoth, great in counsel and mighty in deed; whose eyes are open to all the ways of mortals, *rewarding all according to their ways* and *according to the fruit of their doings*." These italicized words reinforce Jeremiah's prediction found in 31:29-30, "In those days they shall no longer say: 'The parents have eaten sour grapes, and the children's teeth are set on edge.' But all shall die for their own sins; the teeth of everyone who eats sour grapes shall be set on edge."

Ezekiel was even more emphatic in challenging the statements in Exodus 20:5b and Deuteronomy 5:9b that Yahweh "visited the iniquity of the fathers upon the children, unto the third and fourth generation" of them that hated him. However, he did not challenge Moses or the Decalogue directly. Rather, like Jeremiah, he challenged the veracity of the well-known

Study Bible

See Excursus: The Character of Israel's God," *NISB,* 134-35. It calls attention to Numbers 14:18, Nehemiah 9:17, 31; Psalms 103:8; Jonah 4:2-3; Nahum 1:2-3; 2 Esdra 7:132-140; and 8:19-36.

proverb that, "The parents have eaten sour grapes, and the children's teeth are set on edge" (Ezek 18:2). The justice of Yahweh, as expressed in Exodus 20:5b and Deuteronomy 5:9b, led many Israelites to assert, "the way of the Lord is not just!" (Ezek 18:25). As a result, thirty verses in Ezekiel 18—cited as a direct quotation of Yahweh—affirm emphatically, "The soul that sins shall die;" "the righteous shall surely live;" "the son shall not suffer for the iniquity of the father, nor the father suffer for the iniquity of the son" (18:4, 9, 20).

It is most unlikely that Yahweh changed his mind and message sometime between the time of Moses and the time of Jeremiah and Ezekiel. It is more likely that the ambiguous *'l qn'* in Exodus 20:5 and Deuteronomy 5:9 originally meant "a creating God" but was mistakenly read as *'ēl qannā'*, "a jealous God." Once the misinterpretation of the *'l qn'* occurred, an explanatory gloss was added to explain why Yahweh became known as a "jealous God." Subsequently, both Jeremiah and Ezekiel presented Yahweh as correcting the error in perfectly clear statements about the workings of Yahweh's justice and love of life. Thus, in disagreement with Exodus 20:5b and Deuteronomy 5:9b, Yahweh is quoted by Ezekiel as saying, "'Why will you die, O house of Israel? For I have no pleasure in the death of anyone, . . . so turn and live!' (Ezek 18:32). For Ezekiel this was the true "oracle of my Lord Yahweh," not Exodus 20:5b or Deuteronomy 5:9b.

The Penalty for Violating the Second Commandment

"If there is found among you . . . a man or woman who . . . has gone and served other gods and worshiped them, or the sun or the moon or any of the host of heaven, which I have forbidden, . . . you shall stone that man or woman to death with stones . . . the hand of the witnesses shall be first against him to put him to death" (Deut 17:2, RSV).

- A death sentence for the idolater lies behind (1) "I will destroy your high places, and cut down your sun-images, and cast your dead bodies upon the bodies of your idols" (Lev 26:30, RSV) and (2) "I

Teaching Tips
Sins of the Fathers
In light of the reality of HIV- and drug-infected babies, discuss the tension between Exodus 20:5b and Deuteronomy 5:9b, on the one hand, and Jeremiah 31:29 and Ezekiel 18, on the other hand. What does it mean to be free from the sins of your parents?

181

will lay the corpses of the people of Israel in front of their idols; and I will scatter your bones around your altars . . . And you shall know that I am Yahweh when their slain lie among their idols around their altars" (Ezek 6:5 and 6:13).

The Third Commandment

"You shall not take the name of Yahweh your God in vain"

To Swear or Not to Swear

A second imperative must be read in conjunction with this commandment, namely, Deuteronomy 6:13, "You shall fear Yahweh your God; you shall serve him, and swear by his name." Thus, swearing by Yahweh's name is a mandate for Israelites; but there was to be no *false* swearing, as Leviticus 19:12 makes perfectly clear, "And you shall not swear falsely *(la āqer)* by my name, profaning the name of your God: I am Yahweh." The name "Yahweh" occurs in Genesis over one-hundred-twenty-five times, from the time of Cain and Abel down to the death of Joseph. It is therefore surprising to read in Exodus 6:2-3 (a.t.), "I appeared to Abraham, to Isaac, and to Jacob, as *ēl šadday* 'God Almighty,' but by my name Yahweh I did not make myself known to them." It is all the more surprising because *El Shaddai* appears only six times in Genesis. The disparity disappears once (1) the disjunctive "but" is read as the conjunctive "and," and (2) the negative particle *lo'* "not" is read as the emphatic affirmative *lu'* "indeed." Thus, by simply changing one vowel, Genesis 6:3 can be read as "I appeared . . . as God Almighty *and* by my name Yahweh I did *indeed* make myself known." The noun *sāw'* "vain, empty" used in this commandment was used in conjunction with the following words:

- *berak* "to bless" with the antithetical meaning "to curse," when used in proximity to the name

Teaching Tips

Names Have Their Meanings

Because names have meanings, ask class members to tell what their names mean and for those who do not know, advise them of the internet site http://www.behindthename.com/. After discussing personal names, see what the class members know already about the meaning of Jehovah, Yahweh, Joshua, Jesus. Knowing the meaning of the divine name is essential if one is to honestly swear by that name as required in Deuteronomy 6:13. Otherwise, the swearing by the very name of God is meaningless and is one form of "taking the name of God in vain." Clarify the meaning of the word "fear" in Deuteronomy 6:13, "You shall fear Yahweh your God; you shall serve him, and swear by his name." The Hebrew word for "fear" is *ya'rē'* (YAH-RAY) and has both positive and negative connotations, like the English word "awe" (with the positive "*awesome*" and the negative "*awe*-full," "awful") and the Latin *terrere* which gives us the English positive "*terrific*" and the negative "*terrible*." Clarify for the class that the command to "fear God" does
(Continued on Page 184)

or person of God, as in Job 1:5, 11; 2:5, 9; Psalms 10:3, and 1 Kings 21:10, 13.

- *nāʾaš,* "to blaspheme," which appears in 2 Samuel 12:14, "you [David] have really blasphemed Yahweh"; Isaiah 52:5, "their masters howl in triumph, declares Yahweh, and my name is blasphemed continually every day"; Ezekiel 35:12, "I, Yahweh, have heard all the blasphemies which you have uttered against the mountains of Israel"; Nehemiah 9:18 "even when they made for themselves a molten calf . . . and committed great blasphemies"; Nehemiah 9:26, ". . . they killed your prophets . . . and committed great blasphemies"; and Psalms 74:10, "Will the enemy blaspheme Your name forever?"

- *qālal,* which appears in Exodus 22:28, "Do not blaspheme God or curse the ruler of your people" (NIB); Leviticus 24:15, "Those who blaspheme God will suffer the consequences of their guilt and be punished" (NLT); 1 Samuel 3:13 ". . . because his [Eli's] sons were blaspheming God, and he did not restrain them" (RSV, NRSV).

- *nāqab,* "to blaspheme," which occurs only in Leviticus 24:10-17, which tells of an Egypto-Israelite who blasphemed and cursed "the Name," and as a result was stoned to death.

In Leviticus 24:10-17, the name "Yahweh" does not appear, only the noun with the definite article, *haššēm* "the Name." This substitute for *ʾădōnāy* is consistently used by Jews so as not to profane the ineffable name. The care taken to refrain from pronouncing the name resulted in the meaning and pronunciation of the name "Yahweh" being forgotten—with "Yahweh," meaning "Creator" (see below), being a scholarly reconstruction. Many pious Jews extend their reverence for the holy name to include the noun "God" by spelling it as "G-d."

Sura 2:224-225 in the *Quran* also provides a commentary on this commandment. It reads,

Use not Allah's name for your vain oaths, making them an excuse for refraining from doing

(Continued from Page 183)
not mean "to be terrified by an awful God," but to "hold God in *awe*," for God is *"terrific/awesome."*

Teaching Tips
"I Swear to God"
Highlight for the class participants the ways in which

1. A *profession* of faith in Jesus Christ or a *confirmation* of one's faith in Jesus Christ parallels the practice in ancient Israel of "swearing by the name of Yahweh."
2. A denial of the divine, analogous to Peter's denial of Jesus (Matt 26:69-75), is to "take the name of God in vain."

good and working righteous and promoting public welfare. . . . Allah will not call you to account
for that which is unintentional in your oaths, but
he will call you to account for the evil to which
you have deliberately assented.

In the context of the current American religio-political debate much more is involved than just the prohibition against the profane use of divine names and
nouns. In an article on the Pledge of Allegiance,
(*Philadelphia Inquirer*, March 28, 2004), Jane Eisner
called attention to the prevalent "ceremonial deism" by
which some argue that the phrase "one nation under
God" in the Pledge of Allegiance is "so conventional
and uncontroversial as to be constitutional," leading
some Christian and Jewish clergy to file a legal brief
"contending if *under God* isn't to be taken seriously,
'then every day, government asks millions of school-
children to take the name of the Lord in vain.'"

Yahweh as the Creator

Edgar Park (1962: 980) stated in his exposition of
Exodus 20:2, "The LORD does not at the moment name
himself as 'Creator of the universe,' 'Lord of the whole
world,' but as the liberator of Israel from the foreign
yoke." However, the *creative* power of God is actually
reflected in the name *Yahweh*. Before *Yahweh* became
an ineffable name it was pronounced and spelled in a
number of different ways. The early church fathers
pronounced it as *Iaô* or *Iao* or *Yahô*, all of which point
to the holy trigrammaton *YHW* used in personal names
like *Yĕhônātān* or *Yônātān* for Jonathan, meaning
"Yahweh has given." In Greek sources it was pronounced as *Iabe* or *Iae* or *Iaôue* or *Iaôuai*, all of which
reflect the more familiar tetragrammaton *YHWH* and
point to its original pronunciation as the verb *yahweh*
"he caused to be, he caused to exist."

David Freedman (1986: 500, 513) in agreement
with his mentor, William F. Albright, stated, "*yahweh*
must be causative . . . . The name *yahweh* must therefore be a hiphil [causative]. Although the causative of
hwy is otherwise unknown in Northwest Semitic it
seems to be attested in the name of the God of Israel."

Source

David, Freedman N., M. P. O'Connor,
and H. Ringgren, 1986. "YHWH" in
*The Theological Dictionary of the Old
Testament* (Grand Rapids: Eerdmans)
5: 500-521.

Reflections

What's in a Name?

What's in a name? We have brand
names that sell products (e.g., Pepsi
Cola, RCA, Cadillac). We have
famous names that obtain some popular support (e.g., Disney, Buffalo Bills,
major Hollywood films). Certain
names convey authority (e.g., Presi-
dent of U. S., the Vatican). Emissaries
and ambassadors make negotiations
and agreements "in the name of" the
leader or official whom they represent.
The name of God tells us who God is
and what God does for us. It also con-
veys divine authority, prestige, and
power. God's name is to be revered
and respected by those who serve God.
God/God's name is honored and
revered in thought, word and deed, in
prayer, divine worship, and service to
others (Mark 12:29-31). See *Catechism
of the Catholic Church* (New York: Doubleday, 1994) 575-79; *An Explanation of
Luther's Catechism*, ed., J. Stump, 2nd
rev ed. (Philadelphia: Fortress, 1960) 37-
40; *The Westminster Shorter Catechism*,
2nd ed., G. I. Williamson (Phillipsburg,
N.J.: P & R Publishing Co., 2003), Questions 53-56.

Freedman also suggested (1986: 515-516) that the statement *'ehyeh 'ăšer 'ehyeh*, "I am who I am," in Exodus 3:14 could be read as a causative meaning "I create whatever I create," to be interpreted as "I am the creator par excellence." (Shifting from "I am" to "I create" requires the verb *'hyh* to be read as *'ahyeh* rather than *'ehyeh*, with the *a* vowel in the first syllable being needed to make it a causative form.) So as not to profane the holy name of God, the Jewish scribes deliberately mispronounced and misspelled the name of Yahweh by combining the consonants *YHWH* with either the vowels of the substitute title *'ădōnāy* "my Lords" (an honorific plural) or the vowels of *'ĕlōhîm* "God" (an honorific plural). Similarly, by vocalizing *'hyh 'šr 'hyh,* as *'ehyeh 'ăšer 'ehyeh*, meaning "I am who I am," rather than as *'ahyeh 'ăšer 'ahyeh*, meaning "I create what I create," the scribes out of piety also deliberately mispronounced the phrase and thereby obscured its true meaning.

The evidence in support of reading *YHWH* as "Creator" and *'HYH* as "I create" is compelling. Most of the six thousand-plus occurrences in the Bible of the verb-based name *Yahweh* could be paraphrased in English by using the noun *Creator*. Consequently, the prologue to the Decalogue could be read as "I, the Creator, am your God who brought you out of the land of Egypt, out of the house of bondage." Israel would be the holy people of the Creator alone—upon pain of death.

The Penalty for Violating the Third Commandment

"He who blasphemes the name of Yahweh shall be put to death; all the congregation shall stone him. The sojourner as well as the native, when he blasphemes the name, shall be put to death" (Lev 24:16).

Exodus 20:8; Deuteronomy 5:12

The Fourth Commandment

"Remember the Sabbath day, to keep it holy . . .
[Yahweh] rested the seventh day, therefore
Yahweh blessed the Sabbath . . ."

Exodus 20:8

"Remember the Sabbath day, to keep it holy . . .
you shall remember that you were a servant in the land
of Egypt . . . and Yahweh your God brought you out
from there . . . ."

Deuteronomy 5:12

According to Deuteronomy 5:15, Yahweh commanded the observance of the Sabbath because of the Exodus, saying in his pronouncement, "Remember that you were once a slave in Egypt, and that Yahweh your God brought you out of there with mighty hand and outstretched arm; this is why Yahweh your God has commanded you to keep the Sabbath day (a.t.)." However, some of the Israelite tribes had never gone down to Egypt. The tribes which became enslaved in Egypt included the Joseph tribes, the Levites, and perhaps Simeon. The other tribes, with Judah being the strongest and largest, were located in the Negeb and the territory of the Kenites; and the concubine tribes (Dan and Naphtali, Gad, Asher, Issachar, Zebulun) evidently remained in the highlands of the north and central hill country. So with about half of the tribes having never been enslaved in Egypt, the reason for observing the Sabbath, as given in Deuteronomy, did not reflect the historical reality of those tribes. In the attempt to give a reason for the Sabbath observance that would embrace all tribal histories,

Teaching Tips

Sabbath or Sunday?

Provide information for a discussion about the debate among some Christians as to the legitimacy of the shift from the Saturday "Sabbath" to the "Lord's Day" on Sunday. The following Internet links provide the opinions of some who wrestled with the issue:

http://www.megspace.com/religion/museltof/sabbath.html
http://www.religioustolerance.org/sabbath.htm

Discuss how the issue of keeping the "Sabbath" or "Lord's Day" holy (i.e., requiring a day of rest for everyone) is related to the issue of eliminating sweatshops around the world. Do Christians who rigorously observe a Sabbath (be it a Saturday or Sunday), nevertheless violate the intent of the fourth commandment when they purchase products crafted the sweatshops which are then sold in boutiques? Raise this question in class, "Is the particular day of rest important or is the rest itself what is important?"

the Exodus 20 Decalogue grounded the Sabbath commandment in the creation story.

Genesis 2:2a can be translated as "And God was *fatigued* on the seventh day [from] his work which he had done (a.t.)." This weariness of God is noted in Exodus 31:17, which speaks of God's taking a breather: "Yahweh made the heavens and the earth, and on the seventh day he stopped and refreshed himself." The theme of fatigue among the gods is dominant in the *Atra-Hasis* creation myth, which includes the following lines (I:1-4; III:162-163) as translated by Lambert and Millard (1969:43, 49):

When the gods like men
Bore the work and suffered the toil—
The toil of the gods was great,
The work was heavy, the distress was much—
. . . they suffered the work day and night
. . . Excessive [toil] has killed us;
Our work [was heavy], the distress much.

The threat of a revolt by the work-wearied lesser gods against the high gods of leisure eventuated in the creation of the *lulu*, "human beings," whose labor would permit all the gods to stop work and rest. The Genesis and Babylonian traditions were in agreement that the *work* of God/gods led to divine *fatigue*, followed by divine decision(s) to give *rest* to the weary. In the myth only the gods were granted rest. But in Exodus 20 not only had God rested, but also those created in his image were gifted with a Sabbath rest, precluding the exploitation through endless labor of anyone in Israel.

A key phrase in the Exodus account is "Yahweh blessed the Sabbath day and made it holy," which led Weinfeld (1991: 302-303) to point out that in Exodus 20 "the Sabbath belongs to the *divine* sphere and not originally a social-humanistic institution as the Deuteronomic version of the Decalogue seems to present it (Deut 5:15)." Weinfeld further noted

The day of the Sabbath is marked not only by cessation of work but by its sacred character: "to keep the Sabbath holy" means to preserve its dis-

Source

W. G. Lambert and A. R. Millard, *Atra-Hasis: The Babylonian Story of the Flood* (Oxford: Clarendon Press, 1969).

Teaching Tips

"True Blue" Laws

The ambiguity of language, addressed already in previous sessions, is well illustrated by the English adjective "blue" (as used in the term "Blue Laws") which can mean (1) having the color of the clear sky or the deep sea, (2) livid (of skin), (3) sad and gloomy; depressed or depressing, (4) balefully murky, (5) puritanical, rigorous, (6) wearing blue garments (Union soliders) and (6) indecent; risqué, suggestive. Moreover, the terms "blue blood," "blue nose," "blue beard," and "blue devils" cannot be taken literally. The observance of the Sabbath in America brings into focus the "blue laws." Ask the class members to explain why such laws were modified by the word "blue." If there is no knowledge of why, refer to the following internet sites

http://www.snopes.com/language/colors/bluelaws.htm
http://www.museumofhoaxes.com/bluelaws.html

Discuss the history and current status of the blue laws in your local community. The following internet links cover recent court decisions:

http://www.csmonitor.com/2003/1205/p01s02-usju.html
http://www.eckhausolson.com/bluelaws4.htm

tinctive features by positive actions, such as visiting holy places (Ezek 46:3; Isa 66:23), consulting the prophet (2 Kings 4:23), and performing special sacrificial and ceremonial rites (Lev 24:8-9; Num 28:9-10; 2 Kings 11:9).

Jesus' statement, "the Sabbath was made for man, not man for the Sabbath" (Mark 2:27), suggests that Jesus followed the Deuteronomic version of the Decalogue, giving priority to the social-humanistic institution of the Sabbath.

The Penalty for Violating the Fourth Commandment

- "You shall keep the Sabbath, because it is holy for you; every one who profanes it shall be put to death; whoever does any work on it, that soul shall be cut off from among his people. . . whosoever does any work on the Sabbath day, he shall surely be put to death" (Exod 31:14-16,)
- "Six days shall work be done, but on the seventh day you shall have a holy Sabbath of solemn rest to Yahweh; whoever does any work on it shall be put to death" (Exod 35:2).

Sources

Radical Kingdom Ethics?

On the reversal of human values and conventions with the dawning of God's reign proclaimed by Jesus, see: N. Perrin, *Rediscovering the Teaching of Jesus* (New York: Harper & Row, 1976) 54-206; M. Hengel, *The Charismatic Leader and His Followers* (New York: Crossroad, 1981) 13; G. Theissen and A. Merz, *The Historical Jesus: A Comprehensive Guide.* Trans. J. Bowden (Minneapolis: Fortress, 1998). See also "Eschatology of the NT," *IDBS*, 273.

Session 6   Exodus 20:12; Deuteronomy 5:16

The Fifth Commandment

"Honor your father and your mother"
Exodus 20:12; Deuteronomy 5:16 (cf. Deut 27:16)

Honor or Hate?

For many Christians the statement by Jesus (Mark 2:27) about the Sabbath has provided the key for the command's proper interpretation. By contrast, one statement by Jesus about child-parent and family relationships appears to turn the fifth commandment upside down. According to Luke 14:26 Jesus said, "If any one comes to me and does not hate his own father and mother and wife and children and brothers and sisters, yes, and even his own life, he cannot be my disciple." According to Moses, God said "Honor!" but, according to Luke, Jesus said "Hate!" Many Christians simply ignore Luke 14:26, preferring to live by Matthew's agreeable version, "Anyone who loves his father or mother more than me is not worthy of me (Matt 10:37)." But others, believing that the kingdom of God proclaimed by Jesus would require a complete reversal of human values (Matt 5:39-41; Mark 8:35; 10:23, 25; Luke 9:60; 14:11, 26; 16:13) set the teachings of Jesus against Moses (e.g., "You have heard it said [by Moses] 'but I say to you that'" Matt 5:21-41).

The clarity of the fifth commandment, coupled with a biblical litany of love which is traceable *from* Leviticus 19:17 to "love your kinfolk" (and its quotations in Matt 19:19, 22:39; Mark 12:31; Luke 10:27; Rom 13:9; and James 2:8) *through* 1 Corinthians 13:13, "the greatest of these is love," and *culminating* in 1 John 4:21, "this commandment

Teaching Tips

Love and Hate

Have members of the class create "A Litany of Love" by reading the following texts dealing with the commandments to love one another, including kith and kin:

    Leviticus 19:17-18 *
    Matthew 19:19; 22:39*
    Mark 12:31*
    Luke 10:27*
    Romans 13:9*
    James 2:8*
    Leviticus 19:34*
    Matthew 5:44*
    Luke 6:35*
    John 13:34-35*
    John 15:12-13, 17*
    Romans 13:10*
    1 John 3:11-4:21*
    1 Corinthians 13:13.*

After reading each of these Scriptures—marked with the asterisk—the teacher will interject the reading of Luke 14:26, which calls for would-be disciples of Jesus "to hate themselves and their families." (See also Jesus and the sword in Matt 10:34; 26:51-52). Following this litany, solicit the opinions of the class members about the apparent contradiction between Luke 14:26 (cf.,) and the fifth commandment and the Scriptures read as a litany of love.

191

we have from him, that he who loves God should love his brother also," makes the plain meaning of Luke 14:26 questionable.

A misreading of just one consonant or vowel could have created this disparity about *honoring* or *hating* one's parents. Luke may have used Hebrew and Aramaic sources when writing his Gospel (sources which would have had no vowel signs or vowel points). If so, the Hebrew word *l'* could have been read as either *lō'* "not" or as *lu'* "truly." Thus, the phrase in Hebrew or Aramaic could have meant "if you *truly* hate . . . " rather than "if you do *not* hate . . . ." Moreover, Hebrew spelling in Jesus's day did not distinguish the *s* sound from the *sh* sound. A verb spelled *snh* or *sn'* could have been read either as *śānē'* "to hate" or as *šānāh'*, "to forsake" or *śānā'* "to give one his rightful due." The question then becomes, did Luke's source mean (1) "if you do not forsake" or (2) "if you do not hate," or (3) "if you do not do right?" The disparity between the Decalogue's demand and Jesus' command might be explained by the ambiguities of Hebrew and Aramaic spelling.

Another position regards the meaning of the Greek *miseo* ("hate") in Luke 14:26 to mean, "to be disinclined to" or "to disregard" in contrast to showing preferential treatment (e.g., Matt 6:24; Luke 16:13; John 12:25; Rom 9:13) rather than "to hate" or "detest" (Matt 5:43; 24:10; Luke 1:71; 6:22, 27; 19:14; John 15:18-19, 23-25; Rev 17:16; *BDAG* 652-53).

In Hebrew the verb *kābēd* "to honor" comes from the stem meaning "to be heavy, weighty, serious." Its Arabic cognate includes the idea of "struggling, contending with difficulties or troubles." In a healthy, functional family filial piety would naturally be expressed by *kābôd* "respect and honor" being given by children to parents. But in dysfunctional families where child abuse is systemic—with the World Health Organization estimating that millions of children in the world today are abused—the *kābôd* "honor" must shift its meaning to "difficulty, distress, affliction, trouble," like its Arabic cognate *kabad* (Lane 1885: 2584). Dysfunctional, HIV-infected, and drug addicted parents *must be taken seriously*, if not honorably. In the words

Sources

On *miseo* "hate" relating to Luke 14:26, see W. F. Bauer, F. W. Danker, et al. *Greek-English Lexicon of the New Testament and Other Early Christian Literature*, 3rd ed. (Chicago: University of Chicago Press, 2000) 652–53. The Coptic *Gospel of Thomas*, Sayings 55, 101, also reflect the strong language of *miseo* "hate" in Luke 14:26. See also *NIB* 9:292.

of Poteat (1953: 141), "One must take one's father and mother seriously even if they are altogether dishonorable. It is quite possible that the most valuable lessons for our mature guidance are to be found as much in the failures and vices of our parents as in their success and virtues."

In Ephesians 6:1-4, Paul recognized that the fifth commandment cuts both ways and added the admonition, "Fathers, do not exasperate your children; instead, bring them up in the training and instruction of the Lord." Wisdom literature provided good advice on how, in a healthy, functional family, to honor one's parents, including

Proverbs 1:8 "Listen, my son, to your father's instruction and do not forsake your mother's teaching."

Proverbs 19:26 "He who robs his father and drives out his mother is a son who brings shame and disgrace."

Proverbs 23:22 "Listen to your father, who gave you life, and do not despise your mother when she is old."

Sirach 3:1-16 is an extended commentary on Exodus 20:12 and Deuteronomy 5:16, including the promise in 3:3 that "those who honor their father atone for sins" (cf., Proverbs 16:6). The admonition in Sirach 3:12, "O son, help your father in his old age" is also found in the *Quran* (Sura 17:23-25):

The Lord has commanded that ye worship none but Him and has enjoined benevolence towards parents. Should either or both of them attain old age in thy lifetime, never say 'Ugh' to them or chide them, but always speak gently to them. Be humbly tender with them and pray: 'Lord have mercy on them, even as they nurtured me when I was little' . . . . Render to the kinsman his due and to the needy and the wayfarer.

The Penalty for Violating the fifth commandment

- "Whoever strikes his father or his mother shall be put to death (Exod 21:15)
- "Whoever curses his father or his mother shall be put to death (Exod 21:17)

- "All who curse father or mother shall be put to death; having cursed father or mother, their blood is upon them (Lev 20:9)
- "Cursed be anyone who dishonors father or mother." All the people shall say, "Amen!" (Deut 27:16).

The Sixth Commandment

"You shall not murder"
Exodus 20:13; Deuteronomy 5:17 (cf. Deut 27:24-25)

In Genesis 4 reference was made to two killings: Cain killed Abel, and five generations later his namesake, Tubal-Cain, killed an unidentified attacker for striking him. But such scattered violence accelerated when, according to Genesis 6, the extra-terrestrial "sons of God" impregnated the terrestrial "daughters of men," resulting in the birth of the Nephalim, who became known in tradition as "the mighty men that were of old, the men of renown." But in the rabbinic work *Genesis Rabbah* 26, a certain rabbi named Aha interpreted the *ʾanšê haššêm* "men of the name" to mean "they laid desolate the world, were driven in desolation from the world, and caused the world to be made desolate." He associated the word translated "renown" with the *šāmēm* verb "to ravage, to terrify." Rabbi Aha was correct in concluding that the *hšm* in Genesis 6:4 did *not* mean either "the name" or "renown." For Rabbi Aha they were *infamous*, not famous. (Rabbi Aha missed, though, the proper derivation of the *hšm*, which is the cognate of Arabic *hašama* "to destroy, smash, shatter"). Thus, "the mighty men of yore" were actually *ʾanšê hāšām* "men of violence." And, according to Genesis 6:11-13, the violence of this mixed breed of warriors led to the flood, as Yahweh indicated, "the earth was corrupt in God's sight and the earth was filled with violence . . . I have determined to make an end of all flesh, for the earth is filled with violence." The rampant violence and

Teaching Tips
Study War No More I
Begin the class with a pop-quiz dealing with God's covenant with Noah. Reserve the "A" for those in the class who remember not only the rainbow, but (1) God's prohibition of people killing other people, (2) the institution of capital punishment as a deterrent against people killing people, and (3) God's affirmation of all people being in the divine image (Gen 9:3-6).

Teaching Tips
Study War No More II
Solicit from class members their opinions as to why God's covenant with Noah was abrogated by Moses and Joshua, so that killing fellow humans for religious reasons was promoted rather than being prohibited. Have a member of the class read Psalms 46:8-11. Then follow the reading with a discussion about the "hawks" and the "doves" in ancient Israel, calling attention to (1) the dovish passages like Micah 4:24 and Zechariah 2:4-5; 9:9 and to (2) the hawkish texts like Micah 4:13, 5:7 and Zechariah 9:13 and 10:5.
(Continued on Page 196)

195

killings cited in Genesis 6 are reflected in later interpretations of the text, as in

Enoch 9:10, "and the women have born *giants*, and the whole earth has thereby been filled with blood and unrighteousness

Enoch 15:11, "And the spirits of the giants afflict, oppress, destroy, attack, do battle, and work destruction on the earth and cause trouble."

Jubilees 5:1-2, "the angels of God saw them [the daughters of men] . . . and they bare unto them sons and they were *giants*. . . and they began to devour each other."

The Covenant with Noah

It was the pervasiveness of the killings in the pre-flood era that led Yahweh to stipulate after the flood in his covenant with Noah, "And for your lifeblood I will surely demand an accounting. . . . And from each man, too, I will demand an accounting for the life of his fellow man. Whoever sheds the blood of man, by man shall his blood be shed; for in the image of God has God made man" (Gen 9:5-6). In this scheme of governance, capital punishment was to be a deterrent against all killing. From the accounts of Noah's time until after Israel's exodus from Egypt, Yahweh never violated the covenant with Noah by requiring Hebrews or Israelites to kill anyone. Whenever killing was required Yahweh retained the prerogative to do it. At the first Passover, "at midnight Yahweh struck down all the firstborn in the land of Egypt (Exod 12:29)" and at the Sea of Reeds "Yahweh routed the Egyptians in the midst of the sea (14:27)." Thus, the Israelite slaves walked away in freedom from Egypt without a single Israelite having killed a single Egyptian. The covenant with Noah was honored by both parties. Yahweh required no one to kill anyone, and not a single Israelite was put to death for violating the prohibition against shedding the blood of fellow humans who were in the image of God.

But in the wilderness of Sin the covenant with Noah was abrogated. When the Amalekites attacked the Israelites Moses authorized Joshua to marshal a

(Continued from Page 195)
Call attention to the statistics from World War I (at thirty-two million [dead, wounded and missing civilian and military] casualties) and World War II (at least fifty-eight million [dead, wounded, and missing civilian and military] casualties). Then invite the class members to estimate the casualty figures for World War III. Then direct the discussion to this question: "Why would God, who prohibited all killing of humans by humans—with a penalty of death—in the covenant with Noah, prohibit only *murder* in the covenant with Israel—and, at the same time, allegedly instigate and promote religious warfare and ethnic cleansing?"

Reflections

Moses, Jesus, Mohammed, and Holy War

Read the following text from the *Quran* (*Sura* 9:111), "Lo! Allah has bought from the believers their lives and their wealth—because the Garden shall be theirs! *They shall fight in the way of Allah and shall slay and be slain. It is a promise that is binding on Him in the Torah and the Gospel and the Quran*" (italics mine). It seems that the *Quran* built the case for *jihad* and the killing of infidels on the model of Moses, who, according to the Torah (Exod 32:25-29), commanded the Levites to kill in a single day three thousand of their own sons and brothers—immediately after he received and delivered the tablets that stated in part, "You shall not murder!" See also *Sura* II:216 "Warfare is ordained for you although it is hateful unto you,"

(Continued on Page 197)

militia. As a result, "Joshua mowed down Amalek and his people with the edge of the sword" (Exod 17:13) with Yahweh's approval, apparently because the war was in self-defense. Shortly thereafter, at the foot of Sinai, obedient Levites killed three thousand of their own family members in a single day at the behest of Moses upon orders from Yahweh. These Levites were then rewarded with ordination into the priesthood (Exod 32:27-29). Whereas killing of another human had been an offense against God, at Sinai it had become a favor *for* God and was said to be favored *by* God. Warfare and ethnic cleansing became normative in Israel and the belief that God would drive out the Canaanites by hornets rather than by sword (Deut 7:20-23; Jos 24:12-13) faded away. Killing for religious reasons was not prohibited.

Twelve words in biblical Hebrew can be translated into English by the verb "to kill," but only one of those twelve words appears in the Decalogue, *rāṣaḥ* ("murder, slay"). It was not a general term for killing but a technical word for "murder," either *with premeditation* (as in Num 35:16-21, 30-31; Hos 4:2; and Jer 7:9) or *without intention* (as in Deut 4:42; 19:3-6; Num 35:6, 11, 12, 25-28; Jos 20:3-6 and 21:13, 21-26). Childs (1974: 420-421) summarized the scholarly debate about the meaning of *rāṣaḥ*, including the opinions that it was used for (1) "illegal killing inimical to the community," or (2) killing which was related to blood vengeance and the role of the avenger, or (3) killing out of personal malice, hatred, or deceit, which came to include murder and assassination. This verb did not deal with killing for religious reasons. Therefore, Moses was free to command the Levites to kill idolatrous Israelites, Joshua was free to kill pagan Canaanites indiscriminately, and King Pekah of Israel felt free to kill one hundred twenty thousand Jews in a single day (2 Chron 28:6). Holy war, crusades, and *jihad* were not prohibited by the sixth commandment as they had been in the covenant God made with Noah. Noah's dove was devoured by the hawks.

(Continued from Page 196)
and *Sura* IV:74, "Whoso fighteth in the way of Allah, on him we shall bestow a vast reward." The opponents in holy war are identified as oppressors of the faithful and idolators. See *The Meaning of the Glorious Koran*, expl. and trans., M. M. Pickthall (New York: Mentor, 1953) 52, 155. Support from the Gospel for holy war (according to *Sura* 9:111) may derive from Matthew 10:34 and Revelation 19:11-16 (Christ on white horse as returning conqueror).

Study Bible

On the massacre by the sons of Levi (Exod 32:27-28), see *NISB* 132-33.

Reflections

Jesus and the Sword

The statement of Jesus in Matthew 10:34-36, "I have not come to bring peace but a sword" (which may be the basis for the Gospel being mentioned in *Sura* 9:111, cited in Reflections: Moses, Jesus, Mohammed, Holy War) may go back to a misunderstood Hebrew text meaning, "I have not come to bring the end but a change." See also what Jesus says about the sword in Matthew 26:51-52 and notes in *NISB*, 1795. Finally, see the study on this saying available online at http://www.ebts.edu/tmcdaniel/cbbp-chapter30.pdf.

The Penalty for Violating the Sixth Commandment
- "Whoever strikes a man so that he dies shall be put to death (Exodus 21:12)
- "He who kills a man shall be put to death" (Lev 24:17 and 24:21)
- "But anyone who strikes another with an iron object, and death ensues, is a murderer; the murderer shall be put to death. . . . ." (Num 35:16, 17, 18, and 21).
- "Do not accept a ransom for the life of a murderer, who deserves to die. He must surely be put to death" (Num 35:31).

Sources
Brevard S. Childs, *The Book of Exodus: A Critical Theological Commentary*, OTL (Philadelphia: Westminster, 1974) 420-21. See also: Susan Niditch, *War in the Hebrew Bible: A Study in the Ethics of Violence* (New York: Oxford University Press, 1993).

Source
On Exodus 17:8-16, see W. Brueggemann, "Exodus," *NIB*, 819-23.

Session 8   Exodus 20:14; Deuteronomy 5:18

The Seventh Commandment

"You shall not commit adultery"
Exodus 20:14; Deuteronomy 5:18 (cf. Deut 27:20-23)

The Need to Know *Who* the Child's Father Was

According to Exodus 22:16-17, the seduction of a virgin was not an act of adultery, nor was it a capital crime. The penalty for such a seduction was a marriage or a monetary settlement equivalent to the marriage present for a virgin. Detailed lists of sexual sins, which were viewed in Israel as capital crimes, appear in Leviticus 18 and 20. Adultery is sexual intercourse between a betrothed or married woman and any man who is not her betrothed or husband. The sin of adultery heads the list in Leviticus 20:10-16. In comparing adultery with the other sins in the lists, Phillips (1970: 117) noted the prohibition of adultery was "to protect the husband's name by assuring him that his children would be his own. This explains why the law of adultery is restricted to sexual intercourse with a married woman, but does not seek to impose sexual fidelity on the husband." In agreement with Phillips, Freedman (2000: 26) added, "One reason for the emphasis placed on virgin brides, along with the harsh punishments toward unfaithful wives, is a grievous fear of mistaken paternity."

Moreover, in early Israel there was no belief in a life after death in a heavenly kingdom. Sheol was the abode of the dead, the realm of the netherworld, where the deceased slept with their fathers in eternal repose. A kind of personal salvation and eternal life was achieved through one's *progeny*. All of one's ancestors

Study Bible

See discussion on adultery under Leviticus 20:10-16, *NISB*, 175.

Teaching Tips

Sex for Eternal Life

For the ancient Israelite the only available "eternal life" was that which came from being remembered by one's progeny. Were the progeny ever to end, so too would the "living memory" of all the deceased in that family's ancestry perish forever. This understanding of "eternal life" to a large degree controlled the sexual mores of the Israelites. It was imperative to know who was the father of the child, for through that child a particular ancestral family would live on in the newborn and, in time, through the newborn's progeny. This idea that ancestors "lived on forever" through the perpetual memory of their progeny

1. Required a woman to have only one sexual partner once married so that paternity of her children could never be in doubt. It was a matter of fidelity to the husband's ancestors, not just fidelity to the husband.

(Continued on Page 200)

199

lived on in the memories of their offspring, generation after generation. Every birth perpetuated a particular line of ancestral memory. Without progeny there would be no memory; and without memory the last vestige of life would vanish into oblivion, taking with it the newly deceased and all those in the ancestral family. Thus, progeny provided a degree of life after death. Consequently, there was the social pressure to "be fruitful and multiply (Gen 1:28)," and there could be *no uncertainty* about who was the father of the child and whose ancestral family would be perpetuated through the memory of the newborn. Similarly, the levirate marriage (Gen 38:6-11 and Deut 25:5-10) was instituted to provide progeny for the man who died *without a male heir* so that the deceased and his ancestors might live on in family and tribal memory. It allowed a brother of a man who died without a son to impregnate the widow of the deceased, and "the first son she bears shall carry on the name of the dead brother so that his name will not be blotted out from Israel" (Deut 25:6).

Adultery and Idolatry

In Jeremiah 3:8 Yahweh is quoted by Jeremiah as saying "She [Judah] saw that for all the adulteries of that faithless one, Israel, I had sent her away with a decree of divorce; yet her false sister Judah did not fear, but she too went and played the harlot." Reference here to a *divorce* being Yahweh's punishment for Israel's adultery may indicate that adultery was *not always* a capital crime. But even in Hosea 2:3 there is a death threat from Hosea to Gomer when he states, "Plead with your mother . . . that she put away . . . her adultery from her breasts lest I strip her naked . . . and slay her with thirst."

The fact that neither David nor Bathsheba were stoned to death for their adultery (nor David for his murder of Uriah) indicates that the crime of adultery had not yet been codified or that the law was applied selectively. Childs' statement (1974: 422), "Even the king, David, falls under the death sentence for his adultery with Bathsheba," is really a misstatement. So also is Freedman's statement (2000:134), "And so

(Continued from Page 199)

2. Contributed to the profound guilt experienced by barren wives whose "infertility" would be responsible for the "ultimate death" of every ancestor.
3. Legitimated a man's multiple marriages and sexual liberties in the noble effort to keep the ancestors alive in multiple lines of memory.
4. Made homosexual relations an abomination since there could be no progeny by which the family line could be continued and the ancestors could live on in the family memory.

Teaching Tips
Sex and the Bible

1. To put the prohibition against adultery in context, a review of the major elements in ancient Israel's sexual laws and mores as recorded in Leviticus 18 and 20 and Deuteronomy 22 may prove helpful—though for some it may be a bit embarrassing.
2. The tangential issues of polygamy and prostitution in biblical literature may come up for discussion. Be prepared to answer questions like "Why did Solomon need a thousand women (1 Kings 11:3, seven hundred wives and three hundred concubines)?" The answer must include the fact that those women needed Solomon—not for sex but for security! So many upper class young Israelite males were killed off fighting King David's wars that thousands of upper class Israelite young women could not

(Continued on Page 201)

David is punished tenfold for his action." Despite the stipulation in Numbers 35:31, "Do not accept a ransom for the life of a murderer, who deserves to die. He must surely be put to death," Nathan immediately assured David, "you shall not die." Instead of being stoned, a *substitutionary atonement* was provided for the king through the death of the infant conceived in adultery and the announcement that unnamed members of his family would be slain by the sword (2 Sam 12:13-23). But the sword never touched David, who, according to 1 Kings 2:10, died of old age. When Nathan told David of Yahweh's decree, "I will take your wives and give them to one who is close to you, and he will lie with your wives in broad daylight," ten innocent women were punished, but not David. When Absalom forced David's ten women into adultery, Absalom paid for the adultery with his life—but by hanging rather than by stoning (2 Sam 12:11-12; 18:10).

In the NIV translation "adultery" appears twenty-two times in each testament. In the Old it translates not only the technical term *nā'ap* but also (1) *bā''el* "he went into (Bathsheba)" in the superscription of Psalm 51, (2) *zûr*, "strange" in Proverbs 22:14, and (3) *zānāh*, "to be a harlot" in Jeremiah 3:6-9 and Hosea 1:2, 2:4, 4:15. The NRSV and others use "adultery" to translate the *nākĕrîyāh* "stranger" in Proverbs 2:16; 7:5. The expression in Isaiah 57:3, "you sons of a sorceress, you offspring of an adulterer and a prostitute," clearly equated the "adulteress" with the "prostitute."

In addition to *nā'ap* being the technical term for "adultery," it was used as a metaphor for idolatry, as in Ezekiel 23:37, "for they have committed *adultery* and blood is on their hands; they committed *adultery* with their idols (a.t.)." It was used along with *zûr*, for idolatrous worship in:

Jeremiah 3:8-9, "I gave faithless Israel her certificate of divorce . . . because of all her adulteries. . . . she also went out and played the harlot."

(Continued from Page 200)
find a living male to marry. Solomon provided welfare for these upper class young women by bringing them into the royal household—thereby maintaining the support of the upper class Judahites for the Davidic dynasty. It was for political reasons, domestic and international, that he had a thousand women—not for sexual reasons. Solomon taxed the poor so heavily to pay for this welfare for the rich that the ten northern tribes of Israel rebelled against Rehoboam, Solomon's son and successor, when Rehoboam followed his father's tax policies benefiting the rich at the expense of the poor.

Jeremiah 5:7, "Your children have forsaken me and sworn by gods that are not gods. . . . they committed adultery and thronged to the houses of prostitutes.

Jeremiah 13:27, "your adulteries and lustful neighings, your shameless prostitution."

Hosea 2:4, "Let her remove her whorings (*zĕn ûnêhā*) from her face and her adulteries (*na'ăpûpêhā*) from between her breasts."

The reason "prostitution" was used as a metaphor for idolatry could have been that Canaanite fertility cults made use of cultic prostitutes, and the gods and goddesses of the cult were represented by idols. On the other hand, the association could also come from the coincidence that one of the Semitic words for "idols" was *zun*, which survived in Arabic where the masculine *zûn* and the feminine *zûnat* meant "an ornament, idol, or anything taken as a deity and worshiped beside God" (Lane, 1867: 1273). This *zônat* would have been spelled in Hebrew as *zĕnah*, which was by coincidence the same spelling as the Hebrew word for "prostitute." The coincidence in speech and spelling made for a powerful *double entendre*.

The Penalty for Violating the Seventh Commandment

- "If a man commits adultery with the wife of his neighbor, both the adulterer and the adulteress shall be put to death" (Leviticus 20:10)
- "If a man lies with his father's wife . . . . daughter-in-law . . . . with a male . . . . both shall be put to death (20:11-16).

The prohibition of illicit sex in the Decalogue finds a parallel in Maxim 9 of the *Wisdom of Ani*, which warns against adultery even with a foreign woman. As translated by John Wilson (1955, 420), it reads:

Beware of the woman from abroad whom nobody knows in the town . . .

A woman whose husband is far away, says every day to you:

Sources

E. W. Lane, ed., *Arabic-English Lexicon*. eight volumes. (Edinburgh: Williams and Norgate, 1863–1893; Reprinted 1956. New York: Unger, 1956).

John Wilson, 1955. "The Instruction of the Vizier Ptah-Hotep," 412-414 and "The Instruction of Ani" 420-21 in *Ancient Near Eastern Tetxs Relating to the Old Testament* (Princeton: Princeton University Press, 1955).

"I am beautiful" when she has no witnesses . . .
This is a crime worthy of death.

Similar advice appears in *The Instructions of Vizier Ptah-Hotep*, dating from about 2450 B.C.E, which is here quoted from Pritchard's *Ancient Near Eastern Texts* (1955: 413):

If thou desirest to make friendship last in a home to which thou hast access as master, as a brother, or as a friend, into any place where thou mightest enter, beware of approaching the women. . . . One is made a fool by limbs of fayence, as she stands (there), . . . A mere trifle, the likeness of a dream—and one attains death through knowing her. . . . Do not do it—it is really an abomination.

Session 9   Exodus 20:15; Deuteronomy 5:19

The Eighth Commandment

"You shall not steal"
Exodus 20:15; Deuteronomy 5:19 (cf. Deut 27:17)

Martin Luther, in his reflection on the Decalogue in his *Larger Catechism* cited by Paul Lehmann (1995: 179), stated,

A person steals not only when he robs a man's strong box or his pocket, but also when he takes advantage of his neighbor at the market, in a grocery shop, butcher stall, wine and beer cellar, workshop, and, in short, wherever business is transacted and money exchanged for goods or labor . . . Daily the poor are defrauded, new burdens and high prices are imposed. Everyone misuses the market in his own willful, conceited, arrogant way as if it were his right and privilege to sell his goods as dearly as he pleases without a word of criticism.

Luther's recognition that defrauding the poor is one form of robbery echoes the prophets: Ezekiel 22:29, "The people of the land practice extortion and commit robbery; they oppress the poor and needy and ill-treat the alien, denying them justice," and Isaiah 1:23, "Your rulers are rebels, companions of thieves; they all love bribes and chase after gifts. They do not defend the cause of the fatherless; the widow's case does not come before them."

Two verses from the Torah that are crucial for the interpretation of the eighth commandment are: Exodus 21:16, "Anyone who kidnaps another and either sells him or still has him when he is caught must be put to

Sources

Freedman, H. 1935. *Sanhedrin: Translated into English with Notes, Glossary, and Indices* (New York; Soncino Press, 1935) II: 569, sec. 86a. Albrecht Alt, 1953. "Das Verbot des Diebstahls im Dekalog," in *Kleine Schriften zur Geschichte des Volkes Israel (*Munich: C. H. Beck, 1953) 333-40.

See also A. Alt, *Essays on Old Testament History and Religion*, (New York: Doubleday, 1966, 1989). Brevard S. Childs, *The Book of Exodus: A Critical Theological Commentary*. OTL (Philadelphia: Westminster, 1974), 424.

Moshe Weinfeld, *Deuteronomy 1–11: A New Translation with Introduction and Commentary*, AB 5. (New York: Doubleday, 1991) 314. See Anthony Phillips, *Ancient Israel's Criminal Law* (Oxford: Basil Blackwell, 1970), 130-31.

On "you shall not steal," see *Dr. Martin Luther's Larger Catechism*. Translated by J. N. Lenske (Minneapolis: Augsburg Publishing House, 1935), 179. It is located under the 7th not 8th commandment, following the Catholic/Lutheran order. See also: http://www.ccel.org/l/luther/large_catechism/large_catechism.html. This text was converted to ascii format for Project Wittenberg by Allen Mulvey and is in the public domain.

death," and Deuteronomy 25:7, "If a man is caught kidnapping one of his brother Israelites and treats him as a slave or sells him, the kidnapper must die. You must purge the evil from among you."

According to the Talmud (Sanhedrin 86a) the rabbis debated the meaning of the eighth commandment, which included the question, "Where do we find the law against kidnapping?" Rabbi Josiah, repeating what he had been taught, said it was spelled out in the eighth commandment; but he was challenged by another rabbi who argued that the eighth commandment dealt with the theft of money. Arguing back, Rabbi Josiah commanded: "Go forth and learn from the thirteen principles whereby the Torah is interpreted"—knowing that one of the thirteen principles was that a law is to be interpreted by its general context. Rabbi Josiah then pointed out that the context of the Decalogue was a code of capital crimes, concluding, "Hence this too refers [to a crime involving] capital punishment."

Albrecht Alt (1953: 333-340), independent of rabbinic tradition, came to the same conclusion, arguing that the three short commandments (Exod 20:13-15; Deut 5:17-19) originally must have had an object following the verb just like the other commandments. Therefore, the eighth commandment should be reconstructed to read, "You shall not steal a person." Childs (1974: 424) was not fully convinced by Rabbi Josiah nor by Alt's arguments, stating, "The sharp distinction suggested by Alt between stealing a man and stealing his property cannot be easily sustained." But he concurred in part by concluding, "It does seem clear that the shortened form of the eighth commandment without an explicit object had the effect of expanding the scope of the prohibition beyond its initial object." On the other hand, Weinfeld (1991: 314) disagreed emphatically with Rabbi Josiah and Alt, stating, "The absolute categorical nature of the commandments of the Decalogue should, therefore, be applied to this commandment too: 'You shall not steal' includes all possible objects, people as well as goods."

However, Phillips (1970: 130-131) offered the most helpful insight about Israel's prohibition of theft when

Teaching Tips

Stealing Property and People

To put the eighth commandment into context, prepare a responsive or antiphonal reading of Exodus 22:1-14, 21-29, and conclude with the teacher reading Malachi 3:5-10 in an authoritative voice. Follow the Scripture reading with an opportunity for class members to share any experiences of when they were robbed or cheated, or cases of significant recent thefts in the community. Ask if anyone has been subjected to identity theft. Then shift the discussion to the subject of stealing people, i.e., hostage-taking and kidnapping as a terrorist tactic in Latin America, the Philippines, and most recently in Iraq and Saudi Arabia. Show how the eighth commandment covers everything from the collapse of Enron and WorldCom, to shoplifting at Wal-Mart and Kmart, and the enforced prostitution in today's sex market (as reported and tracked by Johns Hopkins University's *Protection Project*).

he noted that "theft of property in Israel was not a crime, but a tort [a civil offence] resulting in an action for damages by the injured party. . . . the injured party being restored as far as possible to the position he was in before the damage of which he claims occurred." The civil offense of theft called only for a compensatory penalty rather than punishment. *Restitution* and *deterrence* were the key issues, with enslavement only for those who did not make restitution—as spelled out in Exodus 22:1-3:

> If a man steals an ox or a sheep and slaughters it or sells it, he must pay back five head of cattle for the ox and four sheep for the sheep. If the stolen animal is found alive in his possession—whether ox or donkey or sheep—he must pay back double. A thief must certainly make restitution, but if he has nothing, he must be sold to pay for his theft.

The punitive damages requiring *double restitution* were widely extended beyond just livestock, so that:

> If a man gives his neighbor silver or goods for safekeeping and they are stolen from the neighbor's house, the thief, if he is caught, must pay back double. . . . In all cases of illegal possession of an ox, a donkey, a sheep, a garment, or any other lost property about which somebody says, "This is mine," both parties are to bring their cases before the judges (*hā 'ĕlōhîm "God"*). The one whom the judges (*hā 'ĕlōhîm*) declare guilty must pay back double to his neighbor (Exod 22:7-9, a.t.).

Proverbs 6:30-31 called for a seven-fold payback, and Numbers 5:7 required full restitution, plus a twenty percent penalty.

However, there is a hint of a death penalty for stealing property in Ezekiel 33:15, "if the wicked gives back what he took in pledge for a loan, returns what he has stolen, follows the decrees that give life, and does no evil, he will surely live; he will not die." An even stronger reference to a death sentence for a common thief appears in the Septuagint text of Zechariah 5:3-4.

The NIV translates the Hebrew text as:

> This is the curse that is going out over the whole
> land; for according to what it says on one side,
> every thief will be banished, and according to
> what it says on the other, everyone who swears
> falsely will be banished. . . . I will send it out, and
> it will enter the house of the thief and the house
> of him who swears falsely by my name. It will
> remain in his house and destroy it, both its tim-
> bers and its stones.

But the repeated verb "will be banished" was rendered into Greek meaning "will be punished to death"
(Greek Septuagint, *thanatou 'ekdikēthēsetai*).

Mass Murder, Kidnapping, and Theft—All for God!

The greatest case of murder, theft, and kidnapping
in Israelite tradition is recorded in 2 Chronicles 28:5-
8, and alluded to in 2 Kings 16:1 and Isaiah 7:1. For
the chronicler, because of the gross idolatry of and
child sacrifices by King Ahaz of Judah, Yahweh gave
him into the hands of King Rezin of Damascus (Syria)
and King Pekah of Samaria (Israel), in what became
known as the Syro-Ephraimite War (734–733 B.C.).
Though unable to defeat Ahaz, King Rezin "took cap-
tive" (i.e., he kidnapped, with the intent to enslave) a
large but unspecified number of Jews and took them to
Damascus. Then King Pekah, seeing Rezin's booty,
proceeded to attack Jerusalem also. In Isaiah's words,
"but they could not overpower her." Nevertheless,
Pekah decimated Jerusalem even though he did not
capture and occupy the city. The chronicler reported (2
Chron 28:6-8):

> In one day Pekah . . . killed a hundred and twen-
> ty thousand soldiers in Judah—because Judah
> had forsaken the LORD, the God of their fathers.
> Zicri, an Ephraimite warrior, killed Maaseiah the
> king's son, Azrikam the officer in charge of the
> palace, and Elkanah, second to the king. The
> Israelites took captive from their kinsmen two
> hundred thousand wives, sons and daughters.

They also took a great deal of plunder, which they carried back to Samaria.

Though King Ahaz violated *all five* of the commandments on tablet one of the Decalogue, he survived and died a natural death, at age thirty-six, and was buried in Jerusalem. But one-hundred-twenty-thousand allegedly idolatrous Jewish soldiers loyal to Ahaz were killed by the sword and the killings were done by fellow Israelites—reminiscent of the Levites' slaughtering their sons and brothers at Sinai (Exod 32:27-29) at Moses' behest for their dancing before the golden calf. Moreover, two hundred thousand Jews were kidnapped and destined for slavery in Samaria and Northern Israel.

Had it not been for the Samaritan prophet Oded, who protested the slaughter of Jerusalem's soldiers ("you have slain them in a rage which has reached up to heaven") and a "peace party" of fellow Samaritans who protested the kidnappings and the intended enslavement of their fellow Israelites from Judah (2 Chron 28:9-15), all of Samaria would have consummated their violation of the tenth commandment, "You shall not covet," as well as the eighth commandment, "You shall not steal." Though disguised as doing God's will, Pekah and his people coveted what Ahaz had and whatever wealth there was in Jerusalem. Thus, they used a religious alibi to legitimate their slaughter and pillage to seize what they *coveted*. Thankfully for the kidnapped Jews, Oded and his colleagues secured their freedom and escorted them safely home as far as Jericho. Oded obviously understood the entire Decalogue and recognized that Pekah's coveting had cause countless deaths of the innocent. Coveting caused Pekah's own death, for he was slain by a rival who coveted his throne—and as Pekah sowed, Pekah reaped.

The kidnapping of two-hundred-thousand women and children by Pekah's troops finds many parallels throughout the histories of warfare and of slavery. To this day the kidnappings continue, though not for any religious reason or alibi. A 2001 report by Protection Project, based at the Johns Hopkins University School

> ## Teaching Tips
> ### The Good Samaritan Oded
> Introduce the Prophet Oded to the members of the class by assigning a reading of 2 Chronicles 28:1-15 as homework. F. Scott Spencer presented a good case in the *Westminster Theological Journal* (1984: 317-349) that Oded was the inspiration for Jesus' parable of the Good Samaritan.
>
> Summarize for the class the study about Oded, which is available online at http://www.ebts.edu/tmcdaniel/ cbbp-chapter12.pdf.

of Advanced International Studies in Washington, D.C., has documented the rising trends in the sex slave trade and has provided the following estimates

- ten thousand women from the former Soviet Union have been forced into prostitution in Israel.
- ten thousand children aged between six and fourteen are virtually enslaved in brothels in Sri Lanka.
- fifteen thousand women are trafficked into the United States every year, many from Mexico.
- twenty thousand women and children from Burma have been forced into prostitution in Thailand.
- six thousand Thai children have been sold into prostitution.
- one hundred twenty thousand women are smuggled into Western Europe, mainly from Central and Eastern Europe, and forced into prostitution.
- two hundred thousand young girls from Nepal are working as sex slaves in India.

This slavery mocks all *five commandments* on the second tablet of the Decalogue.

The Penalty for Violating the Eighth Commandment

- "Whoever steals a man, whether he sells him or is found in possession of him, shall be put to death" (Exod 21:16)
- "If a man is found stealing one of his brethren, the people of Israel, and if he treats him as a slave or sells him, then that thief shall die" (Deut 24:7).

Resource

On the Protection Project, see: http://www.protectionproject.org/main1.htm

Session 10 — Exodus 20:16; Deuteronomy 5:20

The Ninth Commandment

"You shall not bear false witness"
Exodus 20:16; Deuteronomy 5:20 (cf. Deut 27:18-19, 25)

Judicial Safeguard for Justice

This prohibition deals with a key element in the judicial process as spelled out in the book of the Covenant in Exodus 23:1-3, "Do not spread false reports. Do not help a wicked man by being a malicious witness. Do not follow the crowd in doing wrong. When you give testimony in a lawsuit, do not pervert justice by siding with the crowd, and do not show favoritism to a poor man in his lawsuit." A second text providing the judicial context of the ninth commandment is Deuteronomy 19:15-21,

> One witness is not enough to convict a man accused of any crime or offence he may have committed. A matter must be established by the testimony of two or three witnesses. If a malicious witness takes the stand to accuse a man of a crime, the two men involved in the dispute must stand in the presence of the LORD before the priests and the judges who are in office at the time. The judges must make a thorough investigation, and if the witness proves to be a liar, giving false testimony against his brother, then do to him as he intended to do to his brother. You must purge the evil from among you. The rest of the people will hear of this and be afraid, and never again will such an evil thing be done among you. Show no pity: life for life, eye for eye, tooth for tooth, hand for hand, foot for foot.

Thus, according to the closing sentence of Deuteronomy 19:21, the sentence for false testimony could even be death. The requirement for two or more witnesses in cases of a capital offense also appears in Deuteronomy 17:6, "On the testimony of two or three witnesses a man shall be put to death, but no-one shall be put to death on the testimony of only one witness," and in Numbers 35:30, "Anyone who kills a person is to be put to death as a murderer only on the testimony of *witnesses*. But no-one is to be put to death on the testimony of a single witness (a.t.)."

The Lies of Ahab, Jezebel, and Jehu

The well-known story of King Ahab's acquisition of Naboth's vineyard in Jezreel (1 Kings 21) provides a commentary on the deadly consequences which *false witnesses* cause. When Naboth politely declined to exchange or sell his ancestral property to King Ahab, Queen Jezebel facilitates the transfer of property from Naboth to the king by having Naboth convicted on a trumped-up charge of blasphemy against God and king—for which he would be executed as the law required. To implement this scheme, she sent a letter, under the king's name and seal, to the elders and nobles of Jezreel, instructing them to "proclaim a day of fasting and seat Naboth in a prominent place among the people. But seat two scoundrels opposite him and have them testify that he has cursed both God and the king, then take him out and stone him to death." The queen's commands were read as the king's commands and were fully obeyed by the officials of Jezreel. Thus, based upon the false testimony of two scoundrels, Naboth was convicted and stoned to death.

Although Ahab had nothing to do with the plot against Naboth, aside from his coveting Naboth's vineyard, when Elijah met the king in Jezreel he was to charge Ahab with a capital offense, saying, "This is what the LORD says: 'Have you not murdered a man and seized his property?' Then say to him, 'This is what the LORD says: In the place where dogs licked up Naboth's blood, dogs will lick up your blood—yes, yours!' (1 Kgs 21:19, NIV)" The two scoundrels who provided the false testimony were never identified or

Teaching Tips

Lie Detectors

Have three members of the class read these relevant texts: (1) Deuteronomy 27:18-19, 25, (2) Deuteronomy 19:15-21, and (3) Exodus 23:1-3.

Share with the class the way in which the technology of the twenty-first century may make the ninth commandment the most widely obeyed of all the commandments. Summarize for the class the four technologies for lie-detection that are replacing the polygraph test, namely,

1. brain "fingerprinting"—the use of an electroencephalograph that measures the shifts in brain activity when one is lying. This method is currently being used by the FBI and is admissible in court (whereas evidence from a polygraph test is inadmissible).

2. MRI—the use of nuclear magnetic resonance imaging to measure the blood flow in the brain. Lying requires thought, telling the truth does not. Thus, activity in the brain's calculation center, requiring an increase in the blood flow there, can be detected.

3. face scanners—the small blood vessels in the face become enlarged when one is lying, emitting heat signatures which can be detected by heat scanners.

4. VSA—voice stress analysis. Sound waves of the voice vary when one is lying, and those variations can be detected. VSA detectors are now on the market for about $100 and they can be plugged into a telephone to let everyone know if the person on the other end is telling the truth.

held accountable, nor were the corrupt elders and nobles of Jezreel—they were all "just following orders." Even Ahab's sentence was commuted when Yahweh said to Elijah, "Have you noticed how Ahab has humbled himself before me? Because he has humbled himself, I will not bring this disaster in his day, but I will bring it on his house in the days of his son" (1 Kgs 21:29, NIV). On the other hand, all participants in Naboth's mock trial and his murder may have been included in the curse of 1 Kings 21:21 (cf., 2 Kgs 9:8), "I will consume your descendants and cut off from Ahab every last male in Israel—slave or free."

Ahab actually died on a battlefield when struck by a random arrow (1 Kgs 22:34-38), and the prediction in 1 Kings 21:19 that dogs would lick up Ahab's blood was reported in 1 Kings 22:38 as having been fulfilled. King Jehu then ascended the throne of Israel and, thanks to a royal commission by an unnamed prophet, he assumed the role of God's chief executioner in the extermination of the house of Ahab (2 Kgs 9:7-10). Jehu first killed Joram, the son of Ahab and Jezebel, leaving his body unburied in Naboth's vineyard (2 Kgs 9:25-27). Jezebel then paid for her capital crimes when, on Jehu's command, she was tossed out of a window and, as predicted, was devoured by dogs (2 Kgs 9:30-37).

But the story about Naboth's mock trial and the scoundrels who—contra the ninth commandment—falsely testified against Naboth does not end with Jezebel's death. It ends only with the death of the house of Jehu and the fall of the ten-tribe kingdom of Northern Israel. In 2 Kings 10:30 Yahweh tells Jehu, "Because you have done well in accomplishing what is right in my eyes and have done to the house of Ahab all I had in mind to do, your descendants will sit on the throne of Israel to the fourth generation," but the prophet Hosea proclaimed a death sentence upon Jehu and his dynasty for all of his violations of the sixth commandment, "You shall not kill."

When Hosea's first son was born God commanded, "Call him Jezreel, because I will soon punish the house of Jehu for the massacre (*d mi* literally, "the bloods of") at Jezreel, and I will put an end to the kingdom of

Teaching Tips

On Perjury

Define "perjury" for members of the class and illustrate the definition with notorious examples current in the country/county/city at the time of your teaching (like the Martha Stewart and Larry Stewart convictions for perjury in 2004). See if class members can come up with contemporary parallels to the deceit of Ahab, Jezebel, and Jehu. For example, what will be the long-term ill effects of the false information from a few nameless witnesses about Iraq's having weapons of mass destruction? How many will die because of little lies? Or ask these question: "What traits and theological perspectives does Osama bin Laden share with Elisha and Jehu?" Are religious leaders who instigate massacres and bloodbaths in God's name—like Elijah and Jehu—guilty of bearing false testimony about the way and will of God? If so, what is the penalty? For class members struggling with all the violence in the Old Testament, the hermeneutical key available at http://www.ebts.edu/tmcdaniel/HermeneuticalKey.pdf may be helpful.

Israel" (Hos 1:4, a.t.). The plural "bloods of (*d mi*) Jezreel" is significant for Jehu's bloodbaths, according to 2 Kings 10:

- the beheading of Ahab's seventy sons and a presentation of their heads to him in Jezreel;
- after receiving the heads, "Jehu killed everyone in Jezreel who remained in the house of Ahab, as well as all his chief men, his close friends and his priests, leaving him no survivor";
- on his way back to Samaria, via Beth Eked, Jehu killed forty-two Jews who had been visiting Ahab's sons;
- when Jehu came to Samaria, he killed all who were left there of Ahab's family;
- then under false pretenses Jehu orchestrated a mandatory worship service for all Baal worshipers at which he himself offered a sacrifice to Baal— only to follow it with an order to kill all the worshipers once he made his exit at the end of the service.

Jehu's killing spree was inspired by Elijah, and both men obviously thought the Decalogue (or its prototype) permitted religio-political killings. Hosea, in clear disagreement, reported Yahweh's condemnation, "There is no faithfulness, no love, no acknowledgment of God in the land. There is only cursing, lying and murder, stealing and adultery; they break all bounds, and bloodshed follows bloodshed." (Hos 4:1-2). Similar words appear in Hosea 10:7 and 10:13-15 (NIV):

> Samaria's king shall perish, like a chip on the face of the waters. . . But you have planted wickedness, you have reaped evil, you have eaten the fruit of deception. Because you have depended on your own strength and on your many warriors, the roar of battle will rise against your people, so that all your fortresses will be devastated. . . .When that day dawns, the king of Israel will be completely destroyed.

What began simply as (1) Ahab's coveting Naboth's vineyard, eventuated into (2) the death of Ahab, (3) all

Source

Brevard S. Childs, *The Book of Exodus: A Critical Theological Commentary*. OTL, (Philadelphia: Westminster, 1974), 426.

Moshe Weinfeld, *Deuteronomy 1–11: A New Translation with Introduction and Commentary*, AB 5, (New York: Doubleday, 1991), 316.

of his family, friends, and royal associates, as well as (4) the end of Jehu's dynasty and (5) the demise of Northern Israel as an independent kingdom a century later (722 BCE). A major catalyst in the downward spiral was *the false testimony* of two measly witnesses in a minor trial in Jezreel convened by corrupt judges. Who would have believed that one incident of false testimony about old man Naboth would become *so deadly and destructive* with such a long term effect! A false witness can bring death to many and in the end can become self-destructive. What a contrast to Jesus' statement, "you will know the truth, and the truth will set you free (John 8:32)."

The Penalty for Violating the Ninth Commandment

"If the witness is a false witness and has accused his brother falsely, then you shall do to him as he had meant to do to his brother . . . Your eye shall not pity; it shall be life for life, eye for eye, tooth for tooth, hand for hand, foot for foot (Deut 19:21).

The Tenth Commandment

"You shall not covet your neighbor's house.
You shall not covet your neighbor's wife . . .

Exodus 20:17

You shall not covet your neighbor's wife.
You shall not set your desire on your neighbor's
house . . .

Deuteronomy 5:21 (cf. Deut 27:17)

From Bridled Desire to Unbridled Lust

The last commandment in the Decalogue differs slightly in Exodus 20:17 from the one in Deuteronomy 5:21. The word order varies and the former repeats the verb *ḥāmad* "to covet" (Exod; Deut) but the latter shifted the second verb to *hit'awweh* "to desire, to crave (Deut)." The prohibition *'al taḥmod* in Proverbs 6:25 means "do not lust" and differs from the tenth commandment, *lō' taḥmod*, "do not covet," only in the use of a different negative particle. The difference between the "covet/lust" of Exod 20:17 and the "desire/crave" of Deuteronomy 5:21b led Childs (1974: 426) to conclude,

the stress on the emotion of the soul is certainly peculiar to *hit'awweh* in distinction to *ḥāmadô* [but] in closely paralleled passages, *hit'awweh* and *ḥāmad* are used interchangeably without any significant difference in meaning.

Weinfeld (1991: 316) concurred but added, ". . . therefore hmd might sometimes connote more than just intention." He paraphrased the prohibition as "You shall not plan to appropriate the other's wife and the other's property." But the "appropriation" of a neighbor's wife puts the sole focus on the wife as a piece of property. The focus was also on the neighbor's wife as a sexual person, so a better paraphrase might be, "Do not *bring to fruition* fantasies of fornication with your neighbor's wife," comparable to Proverbs 6:25, "Do not lust in your heart after her beauty or let her captivate you with her eyes."

Susanna and the Two Lying, Lecherous Judges

As noted in session eleven, King Pekah and his personnel *coveted* the people and portable possessions of Jews in Judah; and the story in 2 Chronicles 28 provides a commentary on the tragic consequences when kinsmen *covet* their neighbor's house, wife, servants, animals, or anything that belongs to their neighbor. Ahab's *coveting* of Naboth's vineyard (1 Kgs 21; session 11), is a case study of the dynamics and deadly results of simply coveting another's property, with no hint of sexual lust.

The story which best illustrates the fatal consequences of *coveting* a neighbor's wife is the Book of *Susanna* in the Apocrypha. According to this short story, a wealthy and revered gentleman in Babylon, with a beautiful and pious wife named Susanna, frequently invited fellow Jews to his garden home and often hosted two elderly Canaanite judges who would hold court at the rich man's residence. The two judges would linger after their court sessions to watch beautiful Susanna as she strolled in her husband's garden. *Coveting* their rich neighbor's wife, they perverted their minds and turned away their eyes from looking to Heaven or remembering righteous judgments. Both were overwhelmed with passion for her, but they did not tell each other of their distress, for they were ashamed to disclose their lustful desire to possess her. And they watched eagerly, day after day, to see her (9-12).

Once the judges became aware of each other's lust, they conspired to seduce Susanna. If she rejected their invitation for sexual intimacy, the two judges—with the authority of their office—would prosecute her on a trumped-up charge of adultery and have her stoned to death. When Susanna rejected their advances, prefer-

Reflections

Keeping Up with the Joneses

1. How does mass media advertising and our capitalist consumerist culture, which drives the American economy, conflict with the tenth commandment?
2. Does one's "keeping up with the Joneses" demonstrate a disobedience to this commandment?
3. What is the difference between getting what you only need and having whatever you want?

Source

F. H. Colson, *Philo: Volume VII*. Loeb Classical Library 320 (Cambridge: Harvard University Press, 1937; 1998 Reprint) 59-62.

Study Bible

On Susanna, see introductory notes and commentary, *NISB*, 1543-46.

ring death "rather than to sin in the sight of the Lord," the judges proceeded with their threat and publicly announced that they had caught Susanna being intimate with a man who had been hiding in the garden. "The assembly believed them, because they were elders of the people and judges; and they condemned her to death" (41).

But before a stone was thrown a young man named Daniel shouted out, accusing the judges of bearing false witness against Susanna. Daniel called for a retrial in which the judges would be questioned separately. Contradictory testimony by the judges when questioned exposed their treacherous lies and Daniel's verdict was, "You also have lied against your own head, for the angel of God is waiting with his sword to saw you in two, that he may destroy you both." Thus, Susanna was saved and the crowd "rose against the two elders, for out of their own mouths Daniel had convicted them of bearing false witness; and they did to them as they had wickedly planned to do to their neighbor; acting in accordance with the law of Moses, they put them to death" (59-62).

The two old men had crossed the invisible line between bridled desire and unbridled lust. Truth set Susanna free and, in truth, coveting can be deadly for the coveter. Philo of Alexandria (20 B.C.E.–50 C.E.) rightly assessed the purpose of the closing prohibitions of the Decalogue, stating:

> The fifth [commandment of the second tablet] is that which cuts off desire, the fountain of all iniquity, from which flow all the most unlawful actions, whether of individuals or of states, whether important or trivial, whether sacred or profane, whether they relate to one's life and soul, or to what are called external things; for, as I have said before, nothing ever escapes desire, but, like a fire in a wood, it proceeds onward, consuming and destroying everything; and there are a great many subordinate sins, which are prohibited likewise under this commandment, for the sake of correcting those persons who cheerfully receive admonitions, and of chastising those

---

Reflections

How Many?

1. How many times over the ages has an innocent Susanna been falsely charged with a capital offense by lecherous old men?
2. "How many of the six million to nine million women publicly burned at the stake as witches were actually as innocent as Susanna, falsely charged for denying sexual favors to those in positions of authority?

stubborn people who devote their whole lives to the indulgence of passion. (*On the Decalogue* 32: 173-174).

The Penalty for Violating the Tenth Commandment

- "Do not look intently at a virgin . . . Turn away your eyes from a shapely woman, . . . do not look intently at beauty belonging to another . . . by it passion is kindled like a fire. Never dine with another man's wife, nor revel with her at wine; lest your heart turn aside to her, and in blood you be plunged into destruction (Sirach 9:5-9).
- The "Hymn to the Sun-god" from the library of Ashurbanipal (668-627 B.C.) provides an extrabiblical reference to the fate of the one who covets, stating, "a man who covets his neighbor's wife will die before his appointed day. Your weapon will strike him and there will be none to save" (Lambert 1960: 130).

Conclusion

It is impossible to establish with certainty that the Decalogue, or its archetype, was widely recognized as the quintessential criminal code in Israel and enforced consistently. The Decalogue may well have shared the fate of the Passover which, according to 2 Kings 23:21-22, had not been heard of nor observed for more than four hundred years. When and where the Decalogue was recognized in Israel and Judah its goal was to keep people alive on earth ("that your days may be prolonged"). But when the Decalogue came into focus in the New Testament the goal had shifted to the quest for eternal life (Matt 19:17-22; Luke 10:25-28). The Decalogue took third place after the *Shema* of Deuteronomy 6:4-5, "Love the LORD your God with all your heart and with all your soul and with all your strength," and its runner-up in Leviticus 19:18, "Love your neighbor as yourself" (Matt 22:34-40; Mark 12:28-34; Rom 8:10-13). According to John 13:34-35, Jesus said, "A new command I give you: Love one another. As I have loved you, so you must love one another. By this all men will know that you are my disciples, if you love one another" (which is reiterated in

Study Bible

See notes on 2 Kings 23:21-23 in *NISB*, 565.

Source

W. G. Lambert, *Babylonian Wisdom Literature*, (Oxford: Clarendon Press, 1960), 130.

Teaching Tips

The Quest for Eternal Life

Have two members of the class read in tandem Matthew 19:16-22 and Luke 10:25-28, and then discuss Jesus' assurance to the young man,

1. "If thou wilt enter into life (eternal), keep the commandments,"
2. "You have given the right answer; do this, and you will live (eternally)," and
3. "If you wish to be perfect, go, sell your possessions, and give the money to the poor, and you will have treasure in heaven." Then compare Jesus' assurance with James's words in James 2:8-10, 14-18.

John 15:12-13, 17 and 1 John 3:1–14:21). The motivation for obeying the Decalogue had been survival—so that one's life would not be taken away. With Jesus' new commandment, love was dominant and life was to be given away, for "Greater love has no-one than this, that he lay down his life for his friends" (John 15:13).

Teaching Tips

Grounded in Love, Not Fear

Conclude the class and this series on the Ten Commandments with a reminder of the "Litany of Love" (which came into focus in the sixth session), acknowledging that a Christian's obedience to the Ten Commandments is grounded in love, not fear.

"Beloved, let us love one another, because love is from God; everyone who loves is born of God and knows God. Whoever does not love does not know God, for God is love. God's love was revealed among us in this way: God sent his only Son into the world so that we might live through him. In this is love, not that we loved God but that he loved us and sent his Son to be the atoning sacrifice for our sins. Beloved, since God loved us so much, we also ought to love one another. No one has ever seen God; if we love one another, God lives in us, and his love is perfected in us" (1 John 4:7-12).

CULTURAL DIVERSITY AND INCLUSION

A STUDY BY

MARK WILSON

*Mark Wilson is Assistant Professor of Congregational Leadership
at the Pacific School of Religion in Berkeley, California.*

CULTURAL DIVERSITY AND INCLUSION
Outline

Introduction—Diversity and Inclusion: A Pastoral Challenge To Create New Heavens and New Earths, Revelation 7:9-11

    A. The Idealism of Diversity and Inclusion

    B. The Risky Business of Diversity and Inclusion

    C. Definition of Diversity in this Study

I. Session 1—How Did Things Get To Be this Way? Genesis 11:1-9

    A. Why Can't We All Get Along?

    B. Sources of our Division: A Biblical Explanation—Genesis 11:1-9

    C. The Tower of Babel and Social Order

    D. The Conflict Approach—We Are Not the Same

II. Session 2—A Family of Many Colors, Numbers 12:1-15

    A. Formation of Ideas about Black and White

    B. Historical Context—"Moses, Miriam, Aaron, and the Ethiopian Woman"

    C. The Subtleness of Racism and Racial Ideas—the Problem Is Never What It Is

    D. No Pure Types in the House and Family of God—Reversing the Emphasis

III. Session 3—Truth Will Make Us Free, John 4:1-30; 39-42

    A. The Exclusion of Women

    B. Historical Context—"Jesus and the Samaritan Woman"

    C. Freedom From Sexual Hurt and Shame

    D. Freedom From Gender Discrimination

IV. Session 4—Diversity and Inclusion by Any Means Necessary: Making Room for the Disabled, Mark 2:1-12

    A. The Church and Accessibility

    B. Theological Context—"Jesus and the Paralytic"

    C. Self Initiative—Just Do It!

    D. Persistent Faith—"A Little Help From My Friends"

V. Session 5—There's Nothing to Prevent You: Sexual Refugees Are Welcome Too, Acts 8:26-40

    A. Imagine a Different World

    B. Historical Context —"Philip and the Ethiopian Eunuch"

    C. Sit Down and Get to Know Me

    D. Share Some Good News

VI. Session 6—Living at the Margins of Diversity—Reviving Youth Culture, Acts 20:7-12

    A. The Balcony Kids

    B. Historical and Theological Context—"Paul and the Resurrection of Eutychus"

    C. Take Ministry to the Streets

    D. Proclaim Life, Not Death

VII. Session 7—Another Plate at the Table—Wait for the Poor: 1 Corinthians, 11:17-34

    A. What's Communion All About?

    B. Historical and Theological Content: "Abuses at the Lord's Supper"

    C. A New Way to Look at the Bread and Cup

VIII. Session 8—There's A New Day Coming: The Power that Makes Us One, Acts 2:1-21

    A. Finding a Language to Understand

    B. The Day of Pentecost: A Response to the Tower of Babel

    C. Concluding Thought: It Takes Power and Passion to Become One

A Great Multitude from Every Nation: Diversity and Inclusion

When I received my first-year student orientation package from Harvard Divinity School in the summer of 1982, I discovered a word in the Divinity School's promotional literature that would later become a central part of my ministry, my academic research and my journey with Christ. Throughout the orientation package, one word—*"inclusiveness"*—stood out as the Divinity's School's main value, central theme, and its mission for educating future religious leaders, community activists and theologians like myself. At that time, I was a twenty-one-year-old graduate from Howard University, and like many of my friends from the early Hip Hop generation I was more concerned with getting occasional "touch ups" on my Jheri Curl hair style and having the right label on my designer jeans than with really beginning to think about the meaning of *"inclusiveness."*

My journey at the Divinity School would later change this, as issues of race, ethnicity, class, gender, sexual orientation, nationality and religion would be a part of every class discussion and our worship. I remember worship experiences there that changed both my language and my life, as the Holy Spirit revealed to me that my experience and faith journey as an African American, rather sexist male Baptist Christian, did not have to separate me from other children of God whose spiritual lives and social backgrounds were different from my own. In worship, a spiritual space was created where diversity and inclusion became real, as students of African, European, Latino, Asian, and Arab descent; Christians, Jews, Buddhists, Muslims, Hindus, Sikhs, Wiccans, hetero-

Lectionary Loop
Pentecost, All Saints Day, Year A, Revelation 7:9-17

Lectionary Loop
Fourth Sunday of Easter, Year C

225

sexual women, heterosexual men, gay men, lesbian women, bisexuals, and transgenders all found a common language in prayers, music, and ritual. What a blessing it was; yet over the years of my pastoral ministry since then, I reflect differently upon my first experience with *"inclusiveness"* at Harvard and now find that we were a bit too idealistic. Indeed, idealism is necessary for sustaining hope and belief that something greater than our divisions, battles and quarrels with each other is attainable, but the idealism of our "inclusiveness" did not take seriously the risks, sacrifices, and challenges that it takes to make real diversity and inclusion happen in our congregations, social settings and communities of faith.

Risky Business Of Diversity and Inclusion

Many pastors and leaders in congregational settings would take pride in building a diverse and inclusive community, like the community and great multitude of people seen in John's Revelation: *"After this I looked, and there was a great multitude that no one could count, from every nation, from all tribes and people and languages, standing before the throne and before the Lamb, robed in white, with palm branches in their hands. They cried out in a loud voice, saying, 'Salvation belongs to our God who is seated on the throne, and to the Lamb!'"* (Rev 7:9-10) Wow! I don't know too many pastors who wouldn't want to stand before a diverse congregation like this one, or better yet, brag at the next meeting of the pastor's cluster group about the unique cultures, languages, races, and faces of people worshiping God under our leadership. To have an experience or kind of revelation like John's would, indeed, be a true sign of God's work among us, and well it should. But let's not forget. The revelation of a new heaven and new earth, where one inclusive people gathered to worship and cry out to God from diverse nations, tribes, cultures and languages, was not seen by a preacher welcomed as a full-fledged paying member of the pastor's conference. The revelation of John was seen by an outcast, an exile, a prisoner on the isle of Patmos, exiled by the government and left alone as a jail inmate because he took the risk and challenge of

Teaching Tips
Defining Diversity

Before examining the texts in this study, it will be helpful for you to discuss how diversity and inclusion are defined.

1. Diversity is often narrowly defined in racial and ethnic terms that do not take into account the wide range of cultural differences and social identities that clergy and congregation members encounter.

2. Sociologically, race is used to describe social constructions based on skin color, physical and visible appearance, while ethnicity refers more to heritage, language and traditions of racial groups.

3. We often overlook or ignore the voices and concerns of Latinos, Asians, Southeast Asians, Pacific Islanders, Arabs, and other racial/ethnic groups within and between the racial spectrum of black and white.

4. Beyond race and ethnicity, what other aspects of human identity might we recognize as part of our definition of diversity?

Source

Andersen Margaret, and Patricia Hil-Collins, *Race, Class, Gender anthology*, 4th ed. (Belmont, Calif.: Wadsworth, 2001)

not going along with the mainstream when it came to his faith and his religious tradition.

The pastor who has the vision to create and welcome a diverse and inclusive community must first be willing to recognize and admit that building an inclusive ministry is challenging and risky work. Many pastors know all too well the stories of colleagues and friends who were thrown into the ring of a congregational fight by the mere mention of welcoming other racial and ethnic groups into the congregation, or by making changes in music and worship that would reflect other cultural traditions. In my own religious tradition as an African American Baptist, I have watched pastors expelled from ministers' unions by their own friends when they welcomed the ordination of women, or welcomed gay, lesbian, bisexual and transgendered persons. These experiences have made many pastors fear mentioning the words "diversity" and "inclusion."

Make no doubt about it. Creating diverse and inclusive communities of faith involves risks and challenges that some clergy are afraid to take. As a pastor and religious leader, you might find yourself in the shoes of John, exiled for standing up against longtime traditions and beliefs that have created racism, sexism, classism, nationalism and heterosexism. Yet, your role and call as a religious leader and student of the Bible place you in a unique position to transform these traditions and beliefs, because traditions of exclusion are often based on biblical ideas. Behind every act of hate and discrimination lies someone's interpretation of "what the Bible says." Yet, while the Bible can and has been used as an instrument of discrimination in the hands of those who promote exclusion and hate, the Bible is, at the same time, a source of comfort, hope, healing, reconciliation, liberation, equality, freedom, pride and good news to those whose ministries are not confined to maintaining the status quo, but who see the work of God in the biblical witness as an ongoing dynamic process to create, for every generation, a more diverse and inclusive world.

This study on diversity and inclusion challenges

Reflections

Inclusivity and Exclusivity in the Bible

1. Other biblical passages that suggest inclusion of diverse people are Isaiah 56:3-8; 1 Corinthians 12:12-31; and Galatians 3:26-29.
2. However, there are biblical passages that explicitly exclude others, such as Ezra 10:10-12 and Matthew 10: 5-6.
3. What is the basis for exclusion of certain people in Ezra and Matthew? Does this exclusionary attitude ever change? (See Matthew 28:19-20).
4. When has it been dangerous for you to take a stand against a social convention?

you to grapple with questions like these and to think more practically about the role you play as a pastor or leader in either working against diversity and inclusion, or making it happen in your congregation, community and in God's global world. This study moves toward a broad definition of diversity and inclusion, in terms of what sociologists Margaret Andersen and Patricia Hill-Collins identify as a "matrix" of cultural experiences. As a pastor, you may have already considered and attempted to address the web of interrelated, multi-layered and sometimes contradictory cultural differences of class, race, gender, sexual orientation, nationality and generation in one congregation. As you journey through the texts selected for this study, the matrix approach will guide you to see that even the members in your congregation who seem most accepted can and may be excluded and isolated in other ways. Therefore, always keep, within your pastoral call, the compassion to see that everyone in your ministry, at some point, needs the message of God's inclusive love.

The texts for this set of Bible studies were chosen because they have been in seminars and presentations on diversity issues. I find that the texts reflect the personal experiences of many persons, including me, who participate in a conversation about who is to be included and why in the worship and nurture of our congregations. We begin with Genesis 11:1-9, the story of the Tower of Babel, where God scattered the people, and in so-doing, gave them diversity. Session 2 deals with a case of apparent racial prejudice in Numbers 12:1-15 and discusses the ways in which the church disguises racial prejudice behind other issues. Session 3 addresses the inclusion of women in the church with a reflection on Jesus and the Samaritan woman in John 4:1-30; 39-42. The subordination of the needs of disabled people, the topic of Session 4, is illuminated by the story of the paralytic and his friends in Mark 2:1-12. The baptism of the Ethiopian eunuch in Acts 20:7-12 gives us an opportunity to discuss sexuality as a context for diversity and inclusion in the church in Session 5. The risk of losing young people to venues more exciting (and potentially more dangerous) than the church is the focus of Session 6, with the story of Eutychus falling out of the window while Paul preaches in Acts 20:7-12. Paul scolded the Corinthian church for their exclusion of the poor from the common meal (1 Cor 11:17-34); our similar treatment of the poor is the topic of Session 7. Finally, Session 8 focuses on the power of the Holy Spirit to bring diverse peoples together into one church, based on the story of Pentecost in Acts 2:1-21.

Reflections

How Do You Read the Bible?

If given the choice to use the Bible as a source of discrimination or a source promoting cultural diversity and inclusion, what choice would you make as a pastor? What revelation would you see? Would you continue to perpetuate biblically based traditions that hold racial, class, sexual, and gender discrimination in place? Would you question those traditions and biblical beliefs so that you might see new heavens, new earths, and new kinds of people, which no one could categorize "or count," finding welcome in the community of Christ? And if it is the message of diversity and inclusion within the Bible that inspires you, what kind of personal sacrifices would this interpretation call you to make? What kinds of privileges would an inclusive interpretation inspire you to give up?

Genesis 11:1-9

How Did Things Get to Be This Way? The Tower of Babel: A Biblical Definition of the Cultural Divide

Why Can't We All Get Along?

When Rodney King, having himself been brutalized by the police, emerged on national television during the 1992 Los Angeles riots with the question, "Can't we all just get along?" I doubt if he realized what an impact his comment would have upon the general public and popular culture in America. "Can't we all just get along?" has become a punch line in comic acts of entertainers like Chris Rock and has even been used in the business and technology world to describe the conflicts between "network folk and programmers" in the "game of e-commerce." The popularization of King's statement in the media, popular culture and the business community proves that the general population is concerned about the gaps and divisions between different sets of people. But, by mimicking King, some people belittle his comment and don't recognize how severe and violent rifts between cultural groups can become. Should it take the kind of violent outbreak evident in the 1992 Los Angeles rebellion for people of faith to take seriously the question, "Why can't we all just get along?"

Our cultural divisions in congregations may not always erupt in violence; yet congregations and church leaders could also consider King's question when trying to determine the sources of cultural divisions.

Sources Of Our Division: a Biblical Explanation– Genesis 11:1-9

Why can't we all just get along in the family of God? What are the origins of the cultural conflicts we experience and continue to construct in congregations?

Lectionary Loop
Christ the King Sunday, Year B, Genesis 11

Sources
Corey Feldman, "Can't We All Just Get Along," in *Business to Business*, May 15, 2000; "Can we all get along?" Rodney King, May 1, 1992; *Time*: Rodney King Riots Cover, May 11, 1992 (http://www.time.com/time/news-files/rodneyking/#)

Sources
For discussion on priestly tradition in the formation of Genesis, see the *NIB*, Vol. 1, pp. 321-30.
For discussion of Genesis 11:1-9, see *NIB*, Vol. 1, pp. 410-14.

Study Bible
"The Tower of Babel," *NISB*, 24.

To answer these questions, it would seem natural to journey to Genesis, the book of beginnings, where the origins and sources of things are explained. The Hebrew priests and redactors of Genesis who preserved the traditions, ideas, rituals, and narratives of the Old Testament community of faith were as concerned with finding the origins of diversity and cultural differences as we are today. In the book of beginnings, one of their earliest explanations for "why we all just can't get along" is found in the Tower of Babel story, Genesis 11:1-9. This biblical narrative highlights two sociological approaches for understanding cultural conflict that may prove to be helpful in getting at the root of the fusses and fights we encounter in creating diverse and inclusive ministries—the order approach and the conflict approach.

The Tower Of Babel and Social Order

Let's put the Tower of Babel in its historical context. Imagine that you just survived the destruction of a world flood, and it is your task, along with many others, to reconstruct a new community and world. What kind of order would you create? This was the task and dilemma of the Hebrews, as they faced the challenges of building a new community following the exilic period. The flood chronicled in Genesis chapters 7-10 serves as a metaphor for the slavery and oppression that separated people from one another during the exilic period, scattering them to many other parts of the world. Like racial groups during the Los Angeles riots were forced, through violent means, to think about what new community they could build together, the challenge of these early biblical sojourners was to build and construct a new community. How would they go about the task?

The answer finally comes in verse 4: "Let's build a city, and a tower, and make a name for ourselves; otherwise we shall be scattered abroad upon the face of the whole earth again." They could have built a city around a lake, a river, a park or some kind of community development center—a central location that would have made it easier for everyone to gather around and "be equal." Rather, the city they construct-

Sources

For discussion on the order vs. conflict approach, see Max Weber, "Open and Closed Economic Relationships" in *Economy and Society*, Roth, Guenther and Claus Wittich, eds. (Berkeley: UC Berkeley Press, 1978), pp. 341-343.

See Lorenzen Thorwald, "Liberating Discipleship" in *The Pastor's Study Bible*, Vol. 1, pp. 215-250, for discussion on church, social institutions, conflict and authority in social structures.

Laura Edles, "Introduction: What is Culture and How Does it Work?" in *Cultural Sociology in Practice*, (Boston: Blackwell, 2002).

Reflections

Defining Order

One way of interpreting cultural conflict from this passage of Scripture (Gen 11) is to think about how we have constructed and defined "order" within our congregations.

Are the structures of our pastoral ministries open enough to welcome difference, or are they structured in such a way as to assimilate groups of people into only one language, one form of worship and music, and one theological understanding and word?

Congregations that are structured as top-down towers, where no difference is seen between the opportunity of dominant cultural groups and the lesser chances of oppressed and subordinate groups, will probably remain closed to finding hidden gifts and untapped resources that the strict order of these congregations has silenced in diverse groups of people.

ed was built around a tower, a building, or temple, which implied an ordered hierarchy, with levels of power. It was a place where some could "make a name for themselves."

The Order Approach

The order approach views cultural differences as necessary for maintaining the structure, hierarchy and functions of the society, organizations and churches we create. This approach assumes that society and its institutions are ordered, stable, and unproblematic; that groups of people have the same opportunities and chances to climb up the ladder of success and make society work, providing they assimilate and follow the social order. The text assumes this sort of sameness and order, as the writer informs us in verse 1 that the whole earth had "one language and used the same words." Given assumptions about order and sameness in society, it's not that difficult to make the same assumptions in our ministries and churches.

The Conflict Approach

Where the order approach assumes sameness and aims to deny difference, the conflict approach understands cultural difference and conflict as a real, and sometimes necessary, consequence of society and human relationships. This approach emphasizes that one size doesn't fit all and doesn't have to. "Why can't we all just get along?" The conflict perspective's answer to that question has to do with the kind of "confused speech" seen in verses 7-9 of Genesis. Whites and people of color, men and women, the young and old, rich and poor, heterosexual and homosexual people in our faith communities and the world, often find themselves at odds with one another because we have not yet learned to appreciate the different languages and experiences that have characterized other journeys of faith. In sociological and cultural theory, language, verbal or non-verbal, is the primary way that cultural groups communicate ideas, beliefs, and symbols. Language is more than conversation. Language carries meaning and helps us to shape and determine our cultural identity. To change or confuse the language sug-

---

Reflections

The Structure Of My Church

Think about the shape and symbol that best describes your congregation.

1. Is it a tower that grows smaller at the top?
2. Is it a circle that encompasses and embraces everyone?
3. What is the order of your congregation's organizational flow chart?
4. Are diverse cultural groups represented in the leadership?
5. Are diverse members active and involved in the congregation?
6. Are those who make decisions about the program, vision, mission, outreach, worship and music in your church culturally diverse?
7. Does your church fit the order or conflict approach?

gests that many cultural meanings and identities are possible in the church and in the world.

For the God of our Judeo-Christian theological tradition to divide rather than to unite seems pretty cruel. Yet the Tower of Babel narrative is not about creating division, but about the danger of creating "sameness." God sees our towers, our constructed hierarchies, our politically governed and technological cities, our prestigious churches and says, in verse 6: "Look they are one people, and they all have one language. This is only the beginning of what they will do." And since the beginning, look what cultural groups have done in the name of "sameness": Gentiles have been cursed, Africans enslaved, Arabs run underground by the Christian Crusade, African Americans lynched, Native Americans exterminated, Jews put in gas chambers, Latinos dislocated from their lands, Asian Americans put into concentration camps, Muslims slaughtered and erased by Serbs, Palestinians bombed, Iraqis abused and raped as prisoners of war, the poor neglected to lives of squalor, violence, and illness, and women, gays and lesbians brutalized or killed.

The writers of Genesis 11:1-9 don't let us off the hook, but leave things unresolved. At the end of the narrative, we are left in a city called Babel, a community, or congregation, where the babblings and confused languages of a scattered people remain misunderstood. Why? Well, perhaps it's necessary for us first to embrace our conflicts and admit our differences as real before hastily running off to find solutions that might be in the language of a few, but that do not really address the needs of the many in our congregations and world who have yet to speak.

Teaching Tips
Cross the Line

Make a list of twenty categories of people excluded or stigmatized in groups, organizations and churches for various reasons. These reasons may be functions of class, race, body size, gender, income, sexual orientation, disability, etc. (e.g. people of color, people who've been called fat, people who believe they are fat, people from a rural town, people living with chronic illness, etc.) Make an imaginary line in the meeting place where your Bible study is conducted. Have all the class members stand on one side of the line. Explain to them that the side of line where everyone is standing is the majority line. The opposite is the minority side. Call off your categories one by one, asking members who believe they fit into those categories to cross the line. Group members should be quiet as possible during this exercise, and after each time someone crosses have the different sides of the line look at each other. Call each category and for your last category include: People who have not crossed the line. Make sure you communicate the following guidelines:

1. Be confidential and respect the feelings of others,

2. Know what risks you are willing to take, and

3. Don't take risks you aren't willing to take. Process the exercise by asking how it felt to be on the minority or majority side of the line. What made them feel comfortable, what made them feel uncomfortable?

A Family Of Many Colors:
Moses and the Ethiopian Woman

As a child growing up in the Sunday school program in Mt. Zion Missionary Baptist Church in Oakland, Calif., I always enjoyed the flannel-board presentations that our teachers would use to give us a pictorial representation of the characters and lessons of the Bible. One particular presentation had a lasting impact on the development of my racial identity and consciousness.

Our congregation was a large, historic African American church in Oakland. Many of our parents and grandparents had migrated to California from the South to find work and create economic opportunity following World War I. It was now the mid-1960s, and, though members of our congregation were engaged in activism of both the Civil Rights and Black Power movements, our congregation welcomed Christian missionaries of many different racial and ethnic backgrounds as guest speakers. One such missionary was a white woman from the Loyal Temperance League (LTL). We called her "the LTL Lady." Her mission was to educate us young children on the dangers and sins of drinking alcohol. To give us a pictorial definition of sin, her flannel-board presentation would begin with the picture of a black-colored heart, which she would describe in the following way: "You see this black heart? This is what sin does to your heart. It makes it black and dirty." Then she would replace the black heart with a white heart and continue with the following: "But when you let Jesus in, you become clean and he makes your heart white as snow." Surprisingly enough, this was not only her approach to helping young Sunday school children understand "sin" but also the approach of our African American teachers who internalized this way of thinking.

Toni Morrison's novel, *The Bluest Eye,* demonstrates what damaging effects definitions like these can have upon children. In Morrison's novel, images that associate "black" as dirty, sinful and profane, and "white" as clean, lovely, holy and pure, create within the mind of a young black girl the feeling that she is dirty, ugly, and worthless before God, and cannot be pure or pretty without having blue eyes. The cultural critiques and writings of Cornel West also point to the role these ideas and beliefs about black and white play in constructing racism and racial discrimination, particularly when it comes to naming darker-skinned people as immoral and impure and whiter-skinned people as holy, pure and moral. While West has held that these ideas were primarily formed during the Enlightenment period and were expanded upon in scientific thought and in advanced capitalism of the latter 1800s, the biblical witness demonstrates that discrimination based on the ideas about skin color was also a concern in ancient biblical times. The racial conflict that emerged in the family of Moses in Numbers 12:1-15 serves as a prime example.

Historical Context

Suppose you were sitting in church on Sunday morning, when an interracial couple, a black man and a white woman, walked in and sat in the pew across from you. Though you were too open-minded even to notice, you did notice the unspoken tension in the sanctuary that caused others in the church to stare or smile at the couple sheepishly, and gossip about their discomfort. Moses had the same reaction from his sister Miriam and his brother-in-law Aaron in verse 1 of this text, when he walked into the family gathering with his wife, a woman not of Jewish descent but from Cush. Wow! Aaron and Miriam, guess who's coming to the family dinner?

Placing this text in its historical context, biblical commentaries rightfully point to the growing animosity and legal restrictions against intermarriage in the Hebrew community in the postexilic period, yet down-

Sources

1. For discussion on race images of black and white, see Toni Morrison, *The Bluest Eye,* (New York: Plume Books, 1994), and Cornel West, "The Genealogy of Modern Racism" in *Prophesy Deliverance.* See also: "Reading the Bible as African Americans," *NIB* 1:154-60.

2. For discussion on growing concern of interracial marriage in OT, see *NIB* 1:580-81.

3. For discussion on the history of race relations as looking through a different mirror, see Ron Takaki, "In A Different Mirror" in *Race, Class, Gender Anthology,* Andersen, HillCollins, eds., 4th ed. (Belmont, Calif.: Wadsworth, 2001), pp. 52-65.

play the writer's concern about racial difference. With regard to skin color, there is an interesting juxtaposition in the comparison of v. 1 to v. 10. In v. 1 the writer is clear to mention, not once, but twice for special emphasis—and in parentheses—that Moses married a Cushite woman: "for he indeed married a Cushite woman." "Cush" is the Hebrew word for Ethiopia, just south of Egypt in northern Africa. But beyond geographic location, to be Cushite or Ethiopian had just as much to do with one's physical appearance, as it did with one's geographic origin. "Ethiopian" is derived from the Greek word, *aethiops*—a person with dark skin. To be Cushite was to have dark skin, to be African or Arab. In verse 1 a woman with dark skin, possibly from Africa or who could have been Moses' Arab wife, Zipporah from Midian, is targeted and spoken against. Then, ironically, in just a few short verses, in verse 10, her accuser, Miriam, is likewise targeted, spoken out against and put out of the camp, not for having dark skin, but for having white skin, which had turned "white as snow" due to leprosy.

This text highlights two ideas that may prove helpful in revealing racial tensions and creating racial diversity in our congregations:

1. The subtlety of racism and racial ideas
2. No pure types in the household of God.

The Subtlety Of Racism and Racial Ideas—the Problem Is Never What It Really Is

Whenever I lead a workshop on racism and racial inequality, my participants are always quick to mention how racism is much more subtle now than in the 1950s and 1960s. During one workshop, a white male, a friend of mine, commented that racial diversity in the church made him uncomfortable because it would involve the singing of hymns and praise songs with an exclusive theology that he has long rejected. When I responded that communities of color have songs that are theologically inclusive and that not all white congregations sing anthems and hymns that he would accept, he finally admitted the real problem: "I know it's me and the prejudice I learned against other races

Teaching Tips

"Cushan" is used as a parallel to Midian in Habakkuk 3:7. Moses' wife Zipporah was a Midianite (Exod. 2:15-21).

Source: See *NISB*, 208 and *NIB* 2: 108-113.

Sources

1. For reference to Midians and Zipporah, see Exodus 2:16-21.
2. See *Jerome Biblical Commentary*, eds. R. E. Brown, J. A. Fitzmyer, R. E. Murphy (Englewood Cliffs, N.J.: Prentice Hall, 1968), p. 90.
3. For discussion on Ethiopians in classical times, see Frank Snowden, *Blacks in Antiquity: Ethiopians in the Greco-Roman Experience* (Cambridge, Mass.: Harvard University Press, 1970).

as a child." He continued to share his need to change his ideas about race and his perception of African American members who were bringing new traditions into the congregation.

Sometimes our discomfort with racial diversity isn't what it seems at all. In verse 2 of the text, Aaron and Miriam would have faired better if they had taken a big dose of honesty. Some interpreters think that they criticize Moses for his leadership and question if he's the only spokesperson for "the Lord," but perhaps the real problem does not concern his leadership or through whom God speaks, but concerns their tradition of racial prejudice. Yes, God can speak through them, but what words about race will they say? Their real complaint is about the race of Moses' wife; yet it seems to have changed in verse 2. Likewise, people in some congregations may be prone to hide their real thoughts and at one moment talk about how the "quality" of worship, the "sophistication" of music, the length of service, and the content of theology will be negatively affected by the mere welcome of darker skinned people into their churches. The real problem may not be these outward things, however, but their inward prejudices: the learned ideas about white, yellow, red, brown and black that we could, with the help of God, transform and deconstruct.

No Pure Types in the House and Family Of God— Reversing the Emphasis

Ron Takaki, an Ethnic Studies professor at Cal Berkeley, uses the metaphor of a "mirror" to help groups and communities of people create diversity, justice and inclusion where race is concerned. Where many of us looked into the same old mirror of society and describe ideas and beliefs about race that we've inherited through tradition, Takaki encourages us to look into "a different mirror"—one that not only shows us the image of ourselves as we would like to be seen, but one that is honest enough to show us the history of racism that every racial/ethnic group has suffered. That task is easier for my students of color at Cal than for white students whom I teach, who are quick to mention that they have no racial group. But

Reflections

Let's Talk About Race

1. What are your earliest memories of learning about your race and ethnicity?
2. What were you taught about race and ethnicity in your family and church?
3. Why is the evil in the Bible depicted as darkness and white depicted as good?
4. What does that depiction have to do with the way we think of blacker-skinned and whiter-skinned people?
5. What are the reasons that differences between racial and ethnic groups are constructed: class and economic competition or cultural stereotypes and ideas?
6. Is it easy to talk about race and the color of skin?
7. If Moses was your brother, how would you respond to his bringing his Ethiopian wife to the family gathering?

when they look into a different mirror and are reminded of their immigrant history, they begin to realize that things would not have been so lovely and pure for them in America had it not been for the constructed notions of white supremacy and beauty that welcomed them, while excluding others.

Miriam would do well to take a new look into her mirror, when things are reversed: Ironically, she becomes "white as snow" (v. 10). This time the metaphor "white as snow" is not used as a symbol of salvation and purity in God; it is, rather, a sign of her sickness and exclusion. In her mirror, she now sees a different person. When ideas about race empower some and exclude others, it's difficult for those with power to comprehend how those excluded members of the community feel. To create racially inclusive congregations, God's call to us sometimes will be to present before our members different mirrors and different images of who they are. God wants us to reverse the favoritism; to imagine a world where white is no longer dominant, and where "white as snow" is not the spiritual goal to achieve. Maybe then we will find the real goal of our faith and journey: to be one in Christ, a people of many colors in the family of God.

Teaching Tips

Have members of the Bible study write a family history of their racial and ethnic origins, and what their families and churches taught them about race. Have them identify the problems or oppressions, privileges and power they gained for being a member of their racial/ethnic group.

Have members of the Bible study bring a mirror to class, and describe their racial characteristics.

Invite another racial/ethnic group to your Bible study and read the passage together. What feelings emerge from the discussion? Have them create a mission work project they can do to bring them closer together.

Truth Will Make Us Free: Overcoming Gender, Race, and Sexual Discrimination

Jesus and the Samaritan Woman

Clergy colleagues and my seminary students are generally shocked and surprised to find out just how sexist I was as a young college student at Howard University. I was raised in a family of strong, spirit-filled, independent women and understood how my single mother was hurt and discouraged by the theology of black Baptist churches that denied the validity of her own calling to ministry. But not even the strong faith of those influential women in my family would deter me from carrying on the tradition that excluded women, the one that I learned from older preachers like those whom I sought to emulate. As a young, twenty-year-old preacher, I organized the Howard University Ministers' Association, an ecumenical clergy group for undergraduate male preachers. We were young students from Baptist, Methodist, Pentecostal, Episcopalian, and Seventh Day Adventist backgrounds. One can imagine the kind of theological debates we had with one another, particularly when we attempted to worship together. We did not have the same theology about salvation, baptism, speaking in tongues, seminary education or what day to call the Sabbath, but we chose to be inclusive and to agree to disagree about these things. We also strongly agreed that it was a sin for women to preach and "usurp the authority of men." (1 Tim 2:12)

Fortunately for me, anti-discrimination policy at the university, seminary education, some heart-changing encounters with God and with my own closets of fear, and some backroom "come to Jesus meetings" with

Lectionary Loop

Third Sunday in Lent, Year A, John 4:5-42

241

women clergy and friends transformed and rescued me from this practice of gender exclusion and discrimination. Yet there are women, young and old, in many of our congregations who are still negatively impacted by the theology and discriminatory practice of some preacher, and who, therefore, will find it next to impossible to develop fully their God-given potential, to know their own truth and to be free. The story of faith of one such woman, the woman of Samaria, stands out in "Jesus and the Woman of Samaria" (John 4:1-30; 39-42).

John's Gospel appears when the church was forming as a culturally inclusive community of faith, comprised of traditional Jews, Hellenized Jews, Greeks, Africans, Palestinians and many other migrants who shared life and culture in the cities and towns of biblical times. At the well, some of these cultures intersect, and the issues and concerns that emerge between them as they interact with one another in the community and church.

The first issue that emerges from the text is the issue of racial separation in verses 7-9. Jesus surprises the Samaritan woman by asking for a drink of water. That's pretty strange, as we learn from the writer's side comment, "Jews do not share things in common with Samaritans." Samaritans were mixed racial people, of Jewish and Assyrian ancestry, "half-breed" children of the exile when Hebrews were carried off into Assyria. This biracial and mixed cultural identity caused them to be viewed, by their Jewish neighbors, as impure and inferior. They lived on the fringes of Jewish culture and faith and were thought to be a difficult reminder of the oppression the people had endured. Thus, Jews and Samaritans became enemies and not only found it difficult to drink from the same cup, but also to worship together, as verses 20-24 suggest.

The second issue that emerges from the text concerns the nature of true worship. With so much racial diversity, ethnicity and culture joining together in the early church, what kind of worship would be accepted as true: an open form of ancestor worship in the mountains (v. 20a), or a more traditional form of worship

Study Bible

For discussion on John 4, Jesus and the Woman of Samaria, see notes on 4:4-42 in *NISB*, 1914-15. See also *NIB*, 9:561-73.

Sources

See "Samaritans" in *Interpreter's Dictionary of the Bible*, 4: 190-196, and the *Interpreter's Dictionary of the Bible Supplement (1976)*, 776-77.

centered in the temple in Jerusalem (v. 20b)? John gives an answer: "God is spirit, and those who worship must worship in spirit and in truth (v. 24)." That kind of worship would indeed cause many of us in congregations to arrive more quickly at inclusive worship. True inclusive worship is spiritual worship that welcomes many testimonies and stories of faith that have shaped truth—worship that makes all people free. Jesus helps the Samaritan woman to find, in particular, two kinds of freedom that many women today, whom we serve, seek—freedom from sexual hurt and shame and freedom from gender discrimination.

Freedom from Sexual Hurt and Shame

How well do I remember the days in churches when women would be brought before the congregation and made to apologize for sexual and intimate relationships that the pastor declared inappropriate. I also remember the double standard that churches used by making women apologize before the church for having sex outside of marriage, for being unwed mothers, or for divorcing and marrying again; but never making men come before the church to do the same. In some congregations, this double standard was part of church membership. As the policy in one Baptist church in Boston read: "Any unwed mother's membership will be terminated from the church. Any unwed father's membership will be terminated for one year." This policy gave men the grace and possibility to rejoin the church in a year, but didn't allow women to do the same.

Some of these rules and rituals that are practiced by some of our congregations have been based on a misinterpretation of the Samaritan woman's story, particularly in the dialogues between her and Jesus in verses 9-18. Some clergy have characterized her as a prostitute tempting Jesus sexually, or have disparaged her for having more than one husband. Dr. Charles G. Adams, pastor of Hartford Memorial Baptist Church in Detroit, offers an interpretation of the "husband" dialogue that needs further attention. In a sermon entitled, "If You Only Knew," inspired by Dr. James Forbes of Riverside Church in New York, Adams cites Forbes'

Source

Tape of Adams' sermon are available through Hartford Memorial Baptist Church bookstore, 18700 James Couzens Highway, Detroit, MI, 48325.

interpretation of Jesus' words in verse 18, and claims that Jesus' intent was not to disrespect her, but to understand the hurt and shame she experienced in five previous relationships. Forbes and Adams assign fictive identities to the five husbands in order to illustrate the many kinds of pain women might experience in their marital relationships: (1) Husband #1 cheated on her with her best friend (2) Husband #2 could not recover from his drug addiction (3) Husband #3 beat and abused her, (4) Husband #4 was an elderly man and was not sexually compatible with her, and (5) Husband #5 told her he was gay. She thought she could change him but she was wrong. By the time she met potential husband #6, she was too hurt in her previous intimate relationships to even think about marrying again. We too know women in our ministries who have been disempowered by society's sexist ideology that defines them as weak, submissive, and controllable. To be diverse and inclusive, our pastoral concern must involve quenching the spiritual thirst and social needs of women (v. 13), healing the shame, hurt and embarrassment many women have endured in church and society, and helping them find what the Samaritan woman found in Christ—"spiritual waters" gushing into eternal life (v. 14).

Freedom from Gender Discrimination

The other freedom expressed in the text is freedom from gender discrimination that both the disciples and the Samaritan woman experience for themselves. In verse 27, the disciples are astonished to see Jesus speaking to a woman in a public place, a second violation of the community's code and tradition in addition to his first: communicating with a Samaritan, a racial outsider. The disciples are bound by their definitions of gender. They notice Jesus' uncommon gender behavior, yet they say nothing about it, and when it comes to diversity and inclusion in congregations, not everything that seems strange and unusual to us disciples in the church needs to be mentioned and stated. Not everything we think needs to come up and out, particularly when it may work to discriminate against someone, and especially if it will interfere with what God is

Study Bible

See "Misogyny" in *NISB*, 1485-86.

Reflections

Are Women and Men That Different?

1. What makes women and men different? Do gender differences make women more weak, less knowledgeable and less skillful than men?

2. Are these differences natural and biological, or are they constructed by society and the church?

3. Is dialogue between women and men in the church easy or difficult to do?

4. What conversations are needed in our congregations to make women free to find calling and vocation that is not inferior to the vocations of men?

5. What can we say to help men be better listeners like the disciples of Christ? What pots, water jars, positions and limitations can we leave behind to end gender discrimination, so that all gendered people might be free?

doing to bring people together. When we desire to discriminate on the basis of gender, we should do like the disciples: Be silent, think before we speak, listen before we act and see what new calling God has for the Samaritan woman, and for women like her in our churches.

The calling of the Samaritan woman to be free and not limited by the gender definitions of her time was her means of finding her truth and her potential. It was common work for women during that time to make pottery and carry pots of water to conducting their household chores. Though it was uncommon for Jesus to dialogue with her in public, her conversation with Jesus causes her to put down her water jar and leave her pots behind, as she now answers her new calling in ministry, to share the good news of what had been done for her (John 4:28-30).

So, as followers of Christ we are challenged by this text to ask ourselves about the uncommon dialogues across gender lines. We need to end the kind of religious bigotry and discrimination against women characteristic of the all-male clergy group that I organized years ago. We need to know that the living water of Christ quenches the thirst of women and men of all races and genders.

Teaching Tips
Listening to the Voices Of Women

Ask the participants of your Bible study to form a women's group and a men's group. Ask the participants to discuss what "gender" definition means to them (i.e., what "being a woman" means to the women, and what "being a man" means to the men; then what "being a woman" means to men and what "being a man" means to women), and discuss how they think those definitions and gender identities were formed. Ask both groups to make a list of the things that hurt and exclude women, what separates women and men fromone another in the church, and what notions about their gender they can change. Ask members of the group to discuss where their experience of gender fits into the text. Have the group make a list of mission projects women and men can do together to end discrimination, violence, harassment and shame experienced by women.

Diversity and Inclusion by Any Means: Making Room for the Disabled

Jesus and the Paralytic Man

Some years ago I served in a congregation that was inadequately prepared to welcome the disabled. It was 1980, ten years before the 1990 Americans with Disabilities Act (ADA) would be approved. Since there was no legal policy requiring that buildings be handicapped accessible, our church had neither a ramp to assist physically disabled members and visitors to enter the church and get up the outside stairs, nor a chair lift or elevator for them to gain access to Sunday school classrooms that were mostly upstairs.

One Sunday, a man in a wheelchair came to visit our church. That day was the first time in my ministry and life that I would recognize how cruel and severe discrimination of the disabled in congregations could be. He looked like he could have been a man in his sixties, and his clothing and appearance gave me the impression that life for him had been pretty tough. He wore a pullover shirt and a pair of khaki pants, unlike the other men in the congregation, who wore suits and ties. He reminded me of an injured war veteran I'd known in my ministry. Was this man's inability to speak clearly and his paralysis from the waist down a result of mentally disabling post-traumatic stress from war, or some violent act done to him on the streets? We had no way of knowing, and we really didn't seem to care what his journey of faith may have been. As eager Christians, we were more interested in getting him in church, into "the Word," and into a Sunday school class. So, we took his wheel chair, gave him a rather bumpy ride up the stairs to the entrance of the church,

Lectionary Loop

Seventh Sunday after Epiphany, Year B

Teaching Tips

Desperate Need, Desperate Measures

The phrase "By Any Means Necessary" borrows from the ideology for social change and concept coined by Malcolm X.

1. Were the paralytic's friends wrong for destroying property, for removing the roof of the house and digging through the clay and mortar to make the house of Christ more handicapped-accessible as they lowered the paralytic down into the midst of the community of faith?

2. Had they checked to see if Jesus or the homeowner had any insurance to cover the damages they made to the roof? Do desperate needs demand desperate measures? Why does the crowd of members within fail to hear the cries of the disabled and dispossessed without?

and since we had no elevator or chair lift, we took him out of his wheel chair and carried him up two flights of stairs. It still disturbs me to think of the look on his face, as I participated with several other men of the church in this transport. As we carried him, one man, a deacon of the church, fussed with him: "Man, you're heavy. Come on, why can't you use your legs?"

In her theological study entitled, *The Disabled God*, Nancy Eiesland develops a theology of disability and describes the exclusion and "social inhospitality" that disabled people experience in congregations. Eiesland writes that: "For many disabled persons the church has been a "city on a hill"—physically inaccessible and socially inhospitable" (p. 20). Like other people who feel oppressed or who are excluded from the church because of their race, class, gender or sexual orientation, the disabled form yet another cultural group that needs to experience particular theological language, signs, and symbols in order to feel welcome within our congregations.

The narrative of Jesus and the paralytic, in Mark 2:1-12 offers us a model for addressing these needs.

Theological Context

A major theological theme in the Gospel of Mark concerns the meaning of discipleship—what it is, what it isn't, and what it often fails to be. There is no birth narrative in Mark's Gospel. Rather, the Gospel begins with Jesus' mysteriously appearing on the scene, being baptized, and immediately beginning the work of his ministry. Throughout the Gospel, Jesus' mysterious power, authority, purpose and mission are misunderstood by religious authorities, his crowd of followers, and even by his own disciples, the people who perhaps should have understood him best. Sometimes, followers of Christ, both then and now, don't get it. Even where diversity is concerned, disciples often fail to understand what the message and work of Christ are really all about.

In verses 1-2, Jesus' crowd of followers finds him at home, and stop by for a visit. So many people from the crowd were "gathered" there to hear his words that there is no room left for anyone to walk in the front

---

Reflections

Accessibility

1. How *structurally* accessible for the disabled are our congregations?
2. How *theologically* accessible for the disabled are our congregations?
3. What would it take to make the disabled feel completely welcome in the house of God and fellowship of Christ?

Sources

Eiesland, Nancy L., *The Disabled God: Toward a Liberatory Theology of Disability* (Nashville: Abingdon, 1994).

Lorenzen, Thorwald, "The Call of Discipleship" and "No Cheap Grace" in *The Pastor's Bible Study* (v.1), (Nashville: Abingdon, 2004, pp. 221-29.

On Mark 2:1-12, Healing of the Paralytic, see *NIB* 8: 547-51.

door. Like these people who were seeking to get all they could get from Christ, we sometimes fail or refuse to notice that there are others not as physically able as we are who cannot gain access into Christ's house of teaching, healing and worship. A paralyzed man is at the door, and no one makes room for him. However, some unidentified people come along, who are not from the church, and they do what needs to be done. Rather than wait for the crowd or even Jesus to recognize them, they create accessibility for the disabled man, by any means necessary: they literally raised the roof (v. 4). These are questions for us to ponder in our pastoral ministries, and the actions of the paralyzed man's friends may help us to find our response. Two factors of their action stand out as helpful principles and strategies for making our congregations more diverse and inclusive—self-initiative and persistent faith.

Self-initiative—Just Do It!

There's a popular bumper sticker that is being seen more and more in Christian bookstores and on the bumpers of cars parked at churches. It simply reads: WWJD. When I first saw the bumper sticker, I thought it was a promotional, publicity sticker for a radio station called WWJD. I soon learned that the letters represent, "What Would Jesus Do?" This question is asked sometimes during our debates about being diverse and inclusive people. When discussions about creating diversity get heated in congregational settings and denominational meetings, someone is always quick to ask, "What would Jesus do?" This question helps us pray our way out of facing the paralysis of making change.

Good disciples and followers of Christ ought to ask, "What would Jesus do?" Yet, when it comes to the narrative of the paralytic in Mark, the emphasis is as much on what Jesus does as it is on what people, the friends of the paralytic, do. Jesus teaches, Jesus heals, and Jesus confronts religious authorities who would rather argue about the inappropriateness of the day and time of the healing than rejoice and glorify God with others (v. 12). And yes, we also should do the same as Christ

Reflections

There is some debate in the Gospels whether this Peter's home or if Jesus had his own house in Capernaum (see Mark 1:29; Matt. 4:13; John 2:12). Also, see *Interpreter's Bible Commentary*, pp. 668-669. If Jesus is the homeowner, how would it affect our Christology?

Teaching Tips

Have students rewrite the narrative of the paralytic man using their opposite hand (i.e. the left hand for right-handed people, and the right hand for left-handed people). As you begin discussion of the text, dialogue about this experience and how it feels for them to have diminished ability to do a simple task. Have some discussion about what they believe the strengths and weaknesses of both "able" and "disabled" bodies might be.

to accept and heal; but it is the paralytic's supportive friends who take the initiate and make the real difference. They are the ones at front stage and center.

One bumper sticker reads, "What Would Jesus Do?" but the words of another bumper sticker characterize the self-initiative evident in this text: "Just Do It!" To achieve inclusion of those different from ourselves in our congregations, we cannot wait for others to make it happen, but must act in love, take initiative in God, and do the work of justice we know has to be done.

Persistent Faith—"A Little Help from My Friends"

At the beginning of this lesson, I described my own discomfort in how we treated a disabled man in the church. He was physically unable to climb the stairs, and that should have called from within us the compassion to recognize his disability, and to help him, rather than to try to make him like us. It is the disabled church who cannot help disabled people. There are many members in our churches who lack the physical, mental, social and financial ability to help themselves; yet there are forces and beliefs, both in our churches and in the political world, that tend to blame victims for their own oppression rather than find ways to support them and to tear off the roofs and ceilings in society that keep them from having power and opportunity.

A key message from this text calls us to a faith that is not always about what we can get or gain, but a faith that persists in helping others become included and be who they were meant to be. In some healing narratives, Jesus asks about the faith of the person who seeks to be healed, as in the case healing of the woman who had been suffering from hemorrhages for twelve years (Mark 5:34). Jesus tells her, "Daughter, your faith has made you well." In Mark (2:1-12), it is not the faith of the paralytic man that heals him, but what preaching professor Mary Donovan Turner of the Pacific School of Religion calls "a little help" and faith "from his friends." Jesus sees the faith of the people who carried him, and as a result of their faith the man is healed from all that brought about his disability. Their persistent faith, not his own, has made him well.

In our efforts to create diverse and inclusive congregations, there will be times when we will encounter people who have been so disabled by society that they have neither the faith nor the will to speak for and represent themselves. It will then be our task and calling to persist in a faith that represents and speaks out for them.

Reflections

Accessibility and Self-Initiative

Think about what the word "accessibility" means to you.

1. Is there a difference between the definition of accessibility for able and disabled people?
2. How structurally accessible for the disabled is your church?
3. How spiritually and personally accessible to the needs of the disabled is your congregation?
4. When it comes to welcoming disabled persons into the congregation, what initiative could you make on their behalf?

There's Nothing to Prevent You: Sexual Refugees Are Welcome, Too

Philip and the Ethiopian Eunuch

Close your eyes, and imagine for a while that you live in a world where the dominant expression of intimacy and sexual attraction is same-sex, same-gender love and affection. In this world, people who are sexually attracted to the same-sex are considered beautiful, moral, pure, normal in the eyes of society and righteous in the eyes of God. If you're a person who is sexually attracted to someone of the opposite sex, you are considered strange, weird, ugly, immoral, and abnormal in the eyes of society and an abomination in the presence of God. Think about what it might mean for your job, your life goals and dreams, your relationships with family and friends, your faith and your relationship with God. What would it be like to live in a world where you are hated, excluded, stigmatized and put out of your church for being sexually attracted to someone of the opposite sex?

This guided meditation may help those who are heterosexual to begin to understand the kind of discrimination, exclusion, hurt and pain with which lesbian and gay people live on a daily basis and throughout their lives. Diversity that welcomes sexual minorities in congregations is a bridge that we just can't seem to get across. What prevents us, as people of faith, from getting across it? What prevents us from sharing good news with all God's children, and sexual minorities in particular? This question is raised by a representative of a sexual minority in the early church, the Ethiopian eunuch (Acts 8:36), whose journey of faith and dialogue with Philip, in Acts 8:26-40, offers us hope that our congregations

Lectionary Loop

Fifth Sunday of Easter, Year B, Acts 8:26-40

Teaching Tips

Eunuchs were excluded from the assembly (Deut 23:1), but they were promised God's favor and an everlasting name (Isa 56:4-5). Isaiah prophesied that eunuchs, foreigners, and outcasts would be accepted at the house of prayer and the mountain of the Lord (Isa 56:3-8).

Sources

For definition and discussion on "spiritual refugees" (particularly "sexual refugees") who are not welcomed in our ministries, see Archie Smith, "Not Everyone Feels Welcome" in *Navigating the Deep River*, (Cleveland: United Church Press, 1997).

For alternative points of view, see Robert Gagnon, *The Bible and Homosexual Practice* (Nasvhille: Abingdon, 2001); Marion L. Soards, *Scripture and Homosexuality: Biblical Authority and the Church Today* (Louisville: Westminster John Knox, 1995)

can be places of welcome and refuge for the sexually wounded, despised and oppressed.

Historical Context

In verse 36 of the text, the Ethiopian eunuch asks, "What is to prevent me from being baptized?" This is a good question that emerges out of one of the central themes within the Gospel of Luke: the universal history and progress of salvation to all people and nations. In both volumes of Luke's writings, the Gospel of Luke and Acts of the Apostles, Luke has a special concern for the pressed and outcasts of Israel, those whom pastoral counselor and professor Archie Smith, of Pacific School of Religion, calls "spiritual refugees." This concern is most clearly seen at the beginning of Jesus' ministry, in Luke 4:16-19, as he announces the purpose of his work: (1) to bring good news to the poor (2) to release the captives (3) to recover sight to the blind (4) to let the oppressed go free, and (5) "to proclaim the year of the Lord's favor," particularly for the excluded and oppressed. Outreach is not limited to the ministry of Christ, but will continue in the work of the church after the ascension of Christ in Acts 1:8-9, where Jesus promises his disciples, that they will be "witnesses" progressing the history and work of salvation in nearby Jerusalem (Acts 1:12–8:3), in Philip's mission to outcasts in "all Judea and Samaria" (Acts 8:4-40), and to the ends of the earth (Acts 8:26-40). The furthest and most remote places in the world as they knew it included Africa, from which came the Ethiopian eunuch. With every progression and greater development of the church came greater acceptance of many who had been excluded. Why not be baptized, the eunuch wonders. Why not unite with the church and join in with the progression and flow of this spiritual movement? Times were changing; every generation of the church was expanding, becoming more open and inclusive, welcoming ritualistically impure foreigners, Samaritans, Gentiles, and those with certain physical deformities, including sexual abnormalities. The church was opening up even to Ethiopians like the eunuch who were "impure" not only because of racial and ethnic origins, but also because of his sex-

Reflections

In Matthew 19:12, Jesus tells his disciples that there are eunuchs "from birth," eunuchs who "have been made eunuchs by others," and eunuchs who "have made themselves eunuchs for the sake of the kingdom of heaven." Jesus concludes: "Let anyone accept this who can."

In the context of this discussion on diversity, is "becoming a eunuch for the sake of the kingdom" an invitation for church members to take on the role of an outcast?

Teaching Tips

For discussion of the Lukan theme of "salvation for all alike," see *NIB* 9: 21-25. For discussion of Philip's mission to outcasts, including the Ethiopian eunuch, see *NIB* 10: 134-45.

Resources

1. On Deuteronomy 23:1, see *NISB*, 279 and *NIB*, vol. 2, pp. 458-63.
2. For discussion of Isaiah 56:4-8, see *NIB* vol. 6, pp. 483-86.
3. For discussion of a mission to both Jews and Gentiles in Matthew, see *NIB*, vol. 8, pp. 386-87.
4. For an early discussion on eunuchs as sexual outcasts in the Bible, see Tom Horner, *Jonathan Loved David*, (Westminster Press: Philadelphia, 1978), pp. 59-70, 82-83. For a different point of view, see Gagnon, *The Bible and Homosexuality*, 146-54, 188.

ual status. He could not enter the temple and assembly of God for what was considered his defect, his voluntary or involuntary inability to reproduce. Yet, Philip does not condemn or avoid him for being sexually different. Philip is not so tied to rules, doctrinal statements and restrictions that he cannot hear voices of angels (v. 26) and be moved by the progressive and inclusive Holy Spirit in the early church. Rather, he welcomes and affirms this sexual minority person, characteristic of the biblical tradition of love, understanding, openness and acceptance of eunuchs shown by the prophet Isaiah, in Isaiah 56:3-5. When it comes to the welcome and inclusion of lesbians, gay men and other sexual minorities in the church, Philip models two pastoral responses that would help heterosexuals find common ground with sexual minorities:

1. Sit down and get to know me
2. Share some good news

Sit Down and Get to Know Me

In verse 31 of the text, the Ethiopian eunuch challenges Philip with an invitation. Here he not only expresses his need for a spiritual guide and mentor, but also the need for Philip to know him more deeply: "he invited Philip to get in [his chariot] and sit beside him." Many of us who have taken the time to visit and to know our members rarely return without a new perception about them and about our own selves. The same can be true for pastors and church members who are less motivated to judge and condemn lesbian and gay members, and more quick to sit down beside them, discuss Scriptures together with them (v. 32), as they share a common journey with the cross and the suffering (v. 33).

Share Some Good News

In his book of sermons entitled *Good News: Sermons of Hope for Today's Families*, Dr. Jeremiah Wright, pastor of Trinity United Church of Christ in Chicago, broke ranks with many of his clergy friends by including a sermon entitled, "Good News for Homosexuals." He recounts that preaching this sermon within the mega-African-American church that he pas-

---

Reflections

Progression

How has your church progressed over the years since it was founded? Has your ministry expanded to include people it would have rejected years ago? How have understandings about sex and sexuality progressed since your childhood? What was taught about sex and sexuality at school, at home and in church? What makes sexual orientation such a different issue of diversity from other topics of inclusion on which the church has changed its views, expanded and opened its doors? Can we progress and become inclusive on this issue? If so, how so and what will help? If not, why not and what would help? If a gay or lesbian person invited you to know and understand their suffering a bit better how would you respond? Would knowing their pain and hurt in the church make any difference?

Source

Jeremiah A. Wright, Jr. *Good News! Sermons of Hope for Today's Families* (Valley Forge: Judson Press, 1995).

tors was like being "at a Ku Klux Klan rally talking about the worth and dignity of African Americans." Yet, none of us who know Dr. Wright doubts that he could address such a rally, just as there is no doubt about the good news, psychological data, biological research, and theological/pastoral wisdom he shares with congregations, clergy and the lesbian and gay members who ask for his congregation's respect and support.

In my childhood, news from the pulpit always seemed to be bad for homosexuals. It was a world where the dominant expression of sexual orientation and attraction was straight. Words from the pulpit such as, "God made Adam and Eve, not Adam and Steve," and trite sayings and flippant remarks from people disguising their hate with Christian love, "God loves the sinner, but hates the sin," only served to hurt more than to help gay and lesbian persons who tried to worship there. Philip could have responded in such a way when the Ethiopian eunuch asked him questions about the text from Isaiah (v. 34). Yet rather than interpret the text with bad news to exclude him, he taught in such a way as to "proclaim the good news of Jesus" (v. 35). And when asked, "What is there to prevent me from being baptized," the good news responded, "Nothing at all."

Teaching Tips

A Different World

Have members of the Bible study group imagine a world where heterosexuals are the minority of society and homosexuals are the majority and thus have more power. Imagine that it is abnormal to be attracted to someone of the opposite sex. Have them write a story about what it might feel like to be in this world, what their fears and opportunities would be. When reflecting upon the text, ask members to describe when they first discovered their sexual attraction. Did they feel like they had a choice in deciding it? What have they learned from the example of Philip toward a sexual outcast, like the Ethiopian eunuch?

Living at the Margins Of Diversity: Reviving Youth Culture

Paul and the Resurrection Of Eutychus

During my seven-year ministry as youth minister at Hartford Memorial Baptist Church in Detroit, I noticed a practice that seems to be quite common among youth in many congregations. Just as soon as they arrived with their parents to church, they would leave their parents standing at the main doors, and dart upstairs to the balcony. There, they sat together on the back row, where from the pulpit I would occasionally watch them enjoy their marginal subculture in the sanctuary. Sometimes I was indeed surprised to catch them doing the most unusual things.

On one occasion, when the congregation stood up to sing one of the church's favorite hymns, I looked up from the pulpit to see one of my balcony youth dancing the latest dance of his 1988 Detroit Hip Hop generation: the "Schoolcraft" (popularized by the youth and gangs that lived near Schoolcraft Avenue). In another instance, the youth choir finished singing, took off their choir robes and marched upstairs to the balcony, where they could sit together and look down upon the congregation in protest of the church's rescheduling their youth day without their consent (an action that almost cost their youth minister his job!).

Balcony youth can sometimes do the strangest things, particularly because the focus of most adults in the congregation is on the pulpit and altar, and not on what is happening behind their backs in the balcony. From those years in youth ministry, I learned that there exists a subculture of a different generation, with a language, a form of music, a style of worship, and a list of

Study Bible

See "Paul's Journeys," Map 19 in the back of the *NISB*.

Resources

"To the End of the Earth: Paul's Mission as Light for the Nations," *NIB*, vol. 10, pp. 146-215.

See *NIB* 10: 275-277, top of page, for discussion on Paul's tours.

needs and concerns that often get marginalized to the back row, because congregations fail to create programs and ministries that include and attract this younger generation to the church. When it comes to diversity and inclusion in communities of faith, how often do our theology and practice welcome the voices and needs of the younger generations living at the margins and balconies of our diversity? The narrative of Paul and Eutychus, in Acts 20:7-12, highlights our need to welcome and bring life to many of those voices and needs.

Historical and Theological Context

Much has been said in session two about the progress of salvation history in Luke's writings. The church's mission to expand its welcome to all nations, races, and types of people is carried to the ends of the earth (e.g., Acts 8-9). Paul's missionary trips would extend and expand the church's door of welcome to Diaspora Jews, Greeks, and Romans. During his tours of various cities, Paul not only encountered rejection and persecution, but also found in the homes he visited a warm welcome and a place to break bread with other people who were also seeking to build an inclusive world through the message of Christ.

Acts 20 finds him traveling from Macedonia to Greece and then taking a detour from his proposed trip to Syria, after hearing rumors about the plot to take his life (vv. 1-3.). He returns to Macedonia, then sails from Philippi, and five days later meets his traveling companions in Troas. There he find a place of welcome to celebrate the love feast, the Lord's Supper, and to teach a Bible study with a small community of worshipers who met in the upper room of an apartment building in town. So mesmerized by Paul's teaching, that went longer and longer into the night, neither Paul nor the worshiping community noticed Eutychus sleeping on the windowsill. He could well have been one of my balcony kids, sitting in the back of the congregation, as he appears disconnected from the culture and spirit of his church; he sinks off into a sleep and has a life-threatening fall from the window. Though Eutychus appeared to be dead, Paul declared that his life was still in him. Paul's ministry and witness thus challenges us to welcome, revive, and resurrect the youth who sit at the margins, the windowsills of our communities, whom we sometimes think are worthless, lifeless, and spiritually dead. Two points from the text are most important in this kind of pastoral work:

1. Take ministry to the streets
2. Proclaim life and not death

Take Ministry to the Streets

In her article entitled, "The Generation Down the Red Road," Professor Rachel Buff of Bowling Green State University, describes the importance of youth for cultural and social transformation. Because of their unique position in society, between the tradition of their parents and the culture of the contemporary technological world, youth are cultural innovators. They take the traditions of the past, fuse them with cultural forms (language, art, music) of the present to re-make new worlds for the future. They are key to the creative process of God's Holy Spirit, much like Paul and the apostles in Acts were key transformers of faith and the culture of religion in the biblical witness. Yet communities of faith rarely are able to assist youth in knowing their importance and potential in this regard, because our ministries are more centered on what happens in front of us, in the pulpit and at the altar, than on what may be happening behind us, on the margins, in the streets and subcultures where they gather to find purpose and create meaning.

This was the challenge for the community of worshippers in Troas, where worship became so uncomfortable, and so stuffy in a small room with burning lamps that it caused the young man to drift off, wander away in sleep, and wind up lying almost dead on the streets. His situation was further complicated by Paul's long-winded message. Trying to stay in town as long as he could, Paul shares the longer version of his Bible study that extends to midnight, and then continues until dawn the next day (vv. 9-11). However, the true example of Paul's pastoral concern is that he ends his message, leaves the pulpit, goes downstairs, out to the

Resources

For commentary on the story of Eutychus, see *NIB*, vol. 10, p. 277.

Teaching Tips

Discuss other stories of healed youths:

1 Kings 17:17-24; 2 Kings 4:18-37; Matthew 8:40-42, 49-56; 9:37-43, Mark 5:21-24, 35-43; Luke 7:11-17; 8:40-42, 49-56.

street where the young man is lying, bends down to the young man's level and addresses his need (v. 10). Eutychus's name means "Lucky." He is indeed lucky to have had the church stop its service, and to have Paul end his teaching, at least for while, to head out to the streets, where he is lifted up and embraced in the arms of Pastor Paul. Yet there are so many youth with innovative talent, vision and skill on the streets reshaping their lives and the world, whose names, faces, and experiences make them not so lucky. The challenge of our pastoral ministries is how we might come out of our pulpits and sanctuaries to revive them.

Proclaim Life, Not Death

Some of us have indeed accepted the challenge and invitation to take our ministries to the youth—if not to the streets, then certainly to the balconies and window-sills—to welcome and include youth. Yet what message do we share when we get there and enter into their culturally innovative world? While one sociological reflection sees youth as cultural innovators, social research conducted by Joe Austin and Michael Willard points to the manner in which youth are demonized in society and in social institutions like schools, media, government, courts, family, and church. The decrease in funds for programs to educate them, accompanied by the increase in funds for prisons to hold them when they are arrested, adds to the negative metaphors, stigmas and images we use to describe them. Metaphors that view youth as dangerous, violent, and problematic not only demonize them in society, but also make them feel marginalized, unwelcome, disconnected and spiritually numb in the church. These negative messages will only help to keep them in the balconies and on the windowsills, rather than participating as live, active, and resurrected members of our congregations and churches.

While the rest of the community in Troas may have shaken their heads in disappointment that another young man had messed up and was lying dead on the streets, Paul's message brings life and hope, not death and fear: "Do not be alarmed, his life is still in him" (Acts 20:10). One should take note that most of the

Reflections

Marginalization

Think about the word "marginalization" as it pertains to Eutychus and the church where he worships. If you were a member of that congregation what would you do if you saw him sleeping on the windowsill? If you were preaching that Sunday, would you say anything to him? How many youth can you count in your congregation? Are there more young people around the church than in the church? If so, what might the church do to go to the streets and welcome them in? Do youth make crucial decisions in the church? Do they feel like they are a part of the church, or do they sit in the back? If so, what's needed in your church for them to feel like an active part?

resurrection stories are about children and youth. Exceptions include the raising of Peter's mother-in-law, Mark 1:30-31, and perhaps the resurrection of Lazarus in John 11:38-44. Jesus, who might have been as young as twenty-seven and probably no older than thirty-three, is still young enough to be considered a "cultural innovating" young adult. There is throughout the Bible a major concern in keeping young people and little children excited about life, resurrected and revived, proclaiming to them life and not death. Our hope to create inclusive and diverse communities is limited if we do not encourage the challenging thoughts and innovative, contemporary, technological minds of our youth. The pastoral challenge for inclusion and diversity, thus, is to share with youth the same good news so many teachers of faith proclaimed to us when we were young: "God's goodness is within you. You have life and through you God is going to do great things."

Reflections

Meeting Youth Where They Are

For this lesson it might be helpful to invite the youth of your congregation to Bible study and ask them to describe what they think Eutychus might have been experiencing as he fell asleep on the windowsill. Create space and time during the lesson to pair off youth and adults in groups of two (one adult, one youth) and have them share their stories of being a youth, what is/was most popular, and what they enjoy/enjoyed doing. Ask them to share their thoughts about how to welcome youth to the church. Also, ask the pairs of youth and adults to continue together as prayer partners and pen pals who encourage and revive one another.

Another Plate at the Table: Wait for the Poor

Abuses at the Lord's Supper

They came three times a week to the church where I was pastor, sometimes with headaches from drinking too much the night before—sometimes with body aches from sleeping on the streets of the city, sometimes with heartaches for the friends, jobs, and time they had lost—yet they came to the Fellowship Hall of our congregation where they were sure to get one of the finest home-cooked meals in town. The McGee Avenue Baptist Church food program was the talk of the homeless, the poor, the addicted, the jobless, the battered and abused women and men who live in shelters and traveled upon the streets of our city. About two hundred to three hundred of them came three times a week, not always clean or well kept, sometimes taking the toilet paper out of the bathroom stalls, always leaving a stench throughout the church that sometimes shut down the church office, and leaving no doubt that they had been there. Yet, no matter where they had been, what they had done, or what they planned to do, three times a week they could find a plate and place at the table in the Fellowship Hall to be blessed by the cooking and good service they received from members of the church.

And though we reached out and shared with them a wonderful mission and service of hope, I sometimes wondered if the same sort of welcome they received in the Fellowship Hall on Mondays, Wednesdays and Fridays would be extended to them in the sanctuary on Sunday, were they to walk in, seeking to be members in the body of Christ. Surely we would welcome them, because it is the policy of most congregations not to

Lectionary Loop

**Holy Thursday, Years A, B, and C,
1 Corinthians 11:23-26**

Reflections

Come to the Table

Who is invited to the Lord's Supper? In reality, whom do we welcome, and whom do we unintentionally exclude? What would members of your congregation say to you in private after the service if a group of homeless people joined them for communion one Sunday?

Sources

"The Lord's Supper," *Pastors' Study Bible*, vol. 1, pp. 237-43.
The New Interpreter's Bible Commentary, v.10, pp. 135-138

turn interested people away. Yet, is our welcome slower than it could be? We are quick to bring them into the social hall to break bread with their friends, but we have not once invited them to come to the church on Sunday morning to break bread and share the cup with the worshiping congregation. What are our Communion and Lord's Supper all about? What diversity and inclusion do they symbolize? Whom do we welcome and whom do we exclude? As an initiation ritual and common practice that binds every Christian community together, need we struggle to answer these questions? Perhaps so, when our struggle with welcoming others to the table of Christ is not much different from the questions Paul addressed for the church at Corinth, in 1 Cor 11:17-33.

Historical and Theological Context

The words from 1 Cor 11:17-33 should not be unfamiliar to many of us who hear them recited over and over again, once a month in some churches and every Sunday in others. First Corinthians 11:23-26, in particular, could be recited by memory from the pulpits and hearts of pastors and church members:

> "For I received from the Lord what I also handed on to you, that the Lord Jesus on the night when he was betrayed took a loaf of bread, and when he had given thanks, he broke it and said, 'This is my body that is for you. Do this in remembrance of me.' In the same way he took the cup also, after supper, saying, 'This cup is the new covenant in my blood. Do this, as often as you drink it, in remembrance of me.' For as often as you eat this bread and drink the cup, you proclaim the Lord's death until he comes."

They are the words of institution that carry us back to the moment and time of Christ and his disciples in the upper room, sharing their last meal together before he is soon to depart. Paul was not there as an eyewitness to the event; he "received" the story as a tradition (v. 23) and passed it down to others. Passing down the tradition helps us to cross the barriers of time and space and become one with Christ, one in the upper room with him and his disciples, one with the early church of faithful servants and unwavering martyrs, one with God and one with each other as we eat from the same bread and drink from the same cup. "What a fellowship, what a joy divine" it is indeed to journey back to that time and find oneness with Christ.

But if communion is only about passing on tradition and becoming part of the life of Christ, then we have missed Paul's real message and concern in this text. Paul is not attempting to discuss "the celebration of the Lord's Supper"; his concerns are primarily with "the abuses at the Lord's Supper." What lies behind the ritual of communion is a story about people of faith mistreating one another at the table by discriminating against the poor. When they came together their unity around the table was "not for the better, but for the worse." In his first letter to the Corinthian church, Paul's concern is not merely with the rituals and religious practices, but with the relations between people who live them out and pass them on. And not unlike many churches today, the main attribute that characterized the church at Corinth was its division and conflict. For conflict, the Corinthians were well known, not only in their competition to prove who was more spiritual and more gifted than the other (cf., 1 Cor 3:18-20; 11:19, 12:1-31), but also in the conflict that made them lose sight of the ministry and true call to welcome and provide for the needs of the poor (1 Cor 1:26-29; 11:21-22; 16:1-4; 2 Cor 8-9).

In this text, Paul addresses the class differences that find church folk feasting in the sanctuary, sometimes all by themselves, while forgetting others, relegated to the social hall, who await to eat a few crumbs from the table. We have our potlucks, our fish fries, our men's barbeques, our women's salad bar luncheons, our cake and punch after the 3:00 programs, but are we any closer to each other, or closer to ending the poverty that surrounds us? Are we eating our own supper alone (1 Cor 11: 21), as one "goes hungry" and another "gets drunk?" Our rituals, like communion, are passed down to unite us, but often do not. Our individual strivings cause us not to be patient and wait for others to make their way to the table (vv. 33-34). Indeed, by the time

Reflections

Broken Bread, Broken World

1. How does the broken bread represent the brokenness and division Paul describes in the church, the body of Christ?
2. How is the brokenness of Christ similar to brokenness in the world when it comes to poverty and hunger?
3. How do different classes of people relate to one another in your church?
4. Are working class people and professionals united in what they do?
5. How often do you reach out to the poor, the hungry, the addicted and the homeless? Are they active in your church? If so, what services for them do you provide? If not, what can be done to help them not feel humiliated?
6. What is needed to unite the broken persons and the broken world at the table of Christ?

they get there, the food and spiritual care are just about gone. That should humiliate the church in any age (v. 22).

A New Way to Look at the Bread and Cup

The U.S. Office of Economic Opportunity poverty data reported in 1999 that 35.5 million Americans, "representing 12.7 percent of the population," were categorized as poor. Among these, one out of five children are under the age of eighteen, some of whom come from families and communities that remain poor and become part of a permanent underclass. Chronic hunger, malnutrition, substandard housing, and unemployment lead them to alternative means of finding income on the streets. While many of us argue about theology and are divided by our own self-interest to eat alone and be alone, the poor are standing at the back doors of our churches, looking for food or hope and faith to see another day.

Paul challenges us to look at the bread and cup of Christ in a different way, not only as a tradition to receive and pass down, but also as a call to take on a ministry that does not leave the poor behind (1 Cor 1:21-22, 33). On the one hand, the bread of Christ we share in congregations ought to remind us that there are many who have no bread, no hope, no sustenance, and no strength to believe. On the other hand, the cup ought to remind us that even when the bread box is empty, the anointing Spirit of God still flows from a cup that runs over. Jesus says: "Share this meal in remembrance of me" (v. 25), and when we remember his broken bread we should also remember brokenness in the world that calls for us to share what we have in the cups of our hands.

Sources

Robert Lauer, and Jeanette C. Lauer, *Social Problems and the Quality of Life* (8th Edition), (New York: McGraw Hill, 2002), p. 225.

Teaching Tips

A Formal for the Poor

Cecil Williams, retired pastor of Glide United Methodist Church, San Francisco, is well known for the celebrations and formal gatherings he has sponsored for the poor. From this Bible study, ask the members of your class to think about their own class background, and to share their family's economic journey. Have the class organize a formal celebration, event or ritual like communion for the homeless and poor during a Sunday morning service. How does the example of Paul inspire this ministry? (See Glide United Methodist Church, 330 Ellis Street, San Francisco, CA. 94102, 415-674-6000, info@glide.org, http://www.glide. org/)

There's a New Day Coming: the Power That Makes Us One

The Day Of Pentecost

Upon my graduation from Harvard Divinity School in 1985, I had the opportunity to put into practice the inclusive theology I had learned there. I was invited to Cuba to be part of a summer delegation of young African American church musicians, organized by the Black Theological Research Project to share our cultural heritage and stories of liberation with other economically oppressed peoples in the Caribbean and Central America. One evening following a long, hot day of work in the fields, our group met beneath a tree located on the campsite where we stayed for the first week of our journey. We gathered beneath the tree with others from Cuba, Nicaragua, Guatemala, Chile, and El Salvador for a time of worship, theological reflection and community-based teaching on liberation theology. At the end of worship, our African American delegation was asked to sing. The passion and power of song that we learned from our parents and elders in African American churches not only flowed through us but touched the curiosity and spirit of others whose language we couldn't speak and whose political ideas we were learning better to appreciate and understand.

One woman from Central America approached to ask something in Spanish. I couldn't understand her, so I began speaking in German with a young man from Nicaragua who also knew German. He translated her words to me in German, I responded in German, and he responded back to her in Spanish. Just about that time one of our delegation members from Chicago, who only spoke English and a little Ebonics, joined in

Lectionary Loop

Pentecost, Years A, B, and C, Acts 2:1-21

Teaching Tips

Many Languages, One Voice

As you teach this lesson, have all the members of the class speak all at the same time, testifying to one another in one loud voice about God's goodness. Select a praise song at the opening of the lesson, something with a few easy words (e.g. "God's Been So Good," "Thank You Lord"). As you sing it several times, invite members who might be able to translate the song in another language (e.g., Spanish, Chinese) to translate and sing it to the rest of the group in the language they've selected. Have them reflect upon how this kind of sharing symbolizes that different cultures can be celebrated while the people of God can be one.

the conversation. I translated her words into German for my Nicaraguan friend, who translated them into Spanish for the Central American woman, and just then I realized the power that we had between the four of us to be one inclusive and diverse people. Though our languages were different and perhaps confusing to hear, the Spirit and power of worship and song initiated our interest to find languages in which we could share our hope for a day of liberation where we all would be equal, free and made one. It is that kind of day for which many of us in our faith communities have prayed, a day like the first Pentecost, described in perhaps one of the greatest texts of inclusion and diversity: Acts 2:1-21.

The Day of Pentecost: a Response to the Tower Of Babel

We initiated this discussion on diversity and inclusion by identifying the risk, challenge and sacrifice involved in creating inclusive and diverse communities of faith. In Session 1, the source of this challenge was described as our inability to get along, primarily due to the different cultural norms, languages, ideas, images, and perceptions that make it next to impossible to talk with each other, let alone build inclusive communities in a diverse global world. As in the story of the Tower of Babel (Gen 11:1-9), our languages have been confounded, and we have been confused in our efforts to make everyone the same. Like the people who built the Tower of Babel, we are not recognizing the misuse of power and the perpetuation of hierarchy in the structures we've created in our corporate, social and religious institutions. In sessions 2-7, we not only examined the biblical ideas and theological beliefs that work to exclude cultural, racial, gendered, disabled, sexual, and generational groups, but we also examined— particularly in the "progression" theology in Luke-Acts—how the biblical witness calls us to greater diversity and more inclusive visions.

For those who would put an end to their work on the Tower of Babel ("let us make a name for ourselves" Gen 11:4), the Day of Pentecost comes as an affirmation. The texts from Genesis 11:1-9 and Acts 2:1-21

Sources

See "The Spirit of Prophecy Falls Upon the Community," *NIB* vol. 10, pp. 52-58. The map on p. 56 shows all the places from which the people had come.

are connected by this one thought: though our languages and cultures have been confounded and confused, the power and anointing of God's Spirit will make us one. In Acts 2, the progressive history of the Luke-Acts tradition, which widens and makes more inclusive the Body of Christ, begins anew.

The Day of Pentecost occurred during the Festival of Weeks, at a celebration in the public square outside the Jerusalem temple. Visitors from many places in the world suddenly were filled with power and passion to speak to one another in many different languages (vv. 1-2), not just to be heard, but to hear and understand other stories of faith from other cultures. Galileans, Parthians, Medes, and Elamites, joined residents of Mesopotamia, Judea and Cappadocia, Pontus, Asia, Phrygia, Pamphyilia, Egypt, Libya, Rome, Israel, Crete, and the Middle East to listen to one another speak about the goodness of God. What a great day it was and what a great day it will be for those of us who embrace the power and passion to do the same.

Concluding Thought: It Takes Power and Passion to Become One

One of my mother's old gospel songs says: "Lord, I've never reached perfection, but I'm trying!" And with many years of conversation on diversity and inclusion, I sometimes respond, "I wish we'd hurry up and get there!" However, it takes more than Bible studies, intercultural conventions, and dialogue groups to build diverse communities of faith. In addition to these things, it takes inward strength, passion, and power to help us appreciate every little step we make along the way. One of the most important insights that the Day of Pentecost gives to each of us seeking to do the honest and just work of diversity and inclusion is our need to stay committed and dedicated to this work and vision. The apostles received power when the Holy Spirit came (Acts 1:8). The Holy Spirit provided the power and passion to inspire and propel them toward building an inclusive world, particularly when faced with questions about the religious law (5:17-42), persecution and capital punishment from the government (6:8-7:60), and internal conflict in the church (Rom

Sources

See David Farmer, "The Unselfish Prayer" in *The Pastor's Bible Study* (v.1), especially Session V, pp. 181-183, for discussion of pastoral self care.

Reflections

Power, Passion, and Commitment

1. What's your understanding of the Holy Spirit?
2. How do you understand the many languages and testimonies that were spoken on the Day of Pentecost?
3. Do you think it is possible to have so many different cultural testimonies about God and not be divided?
4. How is commitment to make diversity connected to power? What makes commitment to diversity and inclusion decline?
5. What causes clergy and people working on diversity to burn out?
6. What kind of power from God and passion from the Spirit of Christ will help you stay involved?

14:1-12; 1 Cor 3), circumstances that would make even the strongest want to throw in the towel, give up on the work of diversity and inclusion and cry out, "Take this cup away from me" (Luke 4:42).

No one said it would be easy. Speaking honestly about diversity is always troubling to traditions and powers that resist transformation and change. Yet in my own pastoral ministry, I have been guided by the life of Christ and the life of the apostles to go inward, pray, walk the lake, and refresh my spiritual cup when the crosses that resist diversity and change get a bit too heavy to bear. And my concluding thought to guide your ministry of diversity and inclusion would simply be this: as you attempt to be God's agent of diversity and as you nurture the vision of an inclusive church and world, remember to nurture and refresh yourself in the Holy Spirit. Always remember that God's inclusive community also includes ministry to you.

FAITH AND
THE SPIRITS OF POLITICS

A STUDY BY
THOMAS C. DAVIS

*Thomas C. Davis is pastor of the Hanover Street Presbyterian Church
in his hometown, Wilmington, Delaware.*

FAITH AND THE SPIRITS OF POLITICS
Outline

I. Introduction—Faith and the Spirits of Politics
   A. "Faith"
   B. "Spirits"
   C. "Politics"

II. Session 1—The Politics of Compassion
   A. Interpersonally
      1. Mind Renewal
      2. Loving Others, Even Enemies
   B. Socially
      1. The Necessity of Coercion?
      2. Taking the Leaders' Lead

III. Session 2—The Politics of Isolation
   A. No Biblical Examples
   B. Today's Survivalists
   C. But People Do Withdraw
   D. Jonah: Fear and Flight

IV. Session 3—The Politics of Resentment
   A. Anger with a Lid On
   B. Offended People
   C. The Prodigal's Older, Resentful Brother
   D. Resentful Groups

V. Session 4—The Politics of Domination
   A. Abusers
   B. The Powerful Prey on the Weak
   C. God's Laws Intended to Free
   D. Domination in Religion
   E. Patriarchy
   F. Slavery
   G. "Election" and the Holy Land
   H. A Broken Spirit as Antidote

VI. Session 5—Toward a Politics of Compassion
   A. The Poor in Spirit
   B. Faith
   C. A Power of Spirit
   D. The Transcendent Power

Introduction

The Pastor's Bible Study on Faith and the Spirits of Politics

In the months following the Sept. 11, 2001 terrorist attacks, an upstanding citizen of East Indian descent in the town where I live was rudely accosted in a local restaurant. It seems she was taken for "one of them," an outsider, and perhaps up to no good. Worried that our city was slipping into xenophobia, my church began hosting dinners featuring ethnic food and inviting people whose mere appearance now marked them for suspicion. That's how a dialog about faith started with sheep not of our fold: Hindus from India, Baha'is from Iran, Muslims from Bangladesh and Pakistan, and Buddhists from China. We had much to learn if we in our small way were to turn a tide of ignorance and fear. Around a table we established a safe haven, and after each meal we taught each other about what we believe, and for what we live.

That was a good first step. But now the peacemakers of my neighborhood must venture to explore how our faith informs our politics, for political disputes afflict our globe as much as religious ones, and often the two cannot be untangled. Yet, how should we approach religion and politics, the volatile twins that etiquette advises us to shun in polite company? Can people of good faith but different faiths still remain in good faith when the subject of politics arises? The following lessons address that question. They are entitled, "Faith and the Spirits of Politics." Definitions are now in order.

Faith

"Faith" has two meanings in these lessons:
1) The beliefs of a particular religion or denomination, as in "the Christian faith," or "the Muslim faith," or "the Reformed Faith."

Lectionary Loop
Sixth Week of Lent or Palm/Passion Sunday, Year A, Isaiah 50:4-9

Study Bible
See *NISB*, 1027

Resources
NIB, vol. 6, pp. 435-37.

Sources
James Fowler, *Stages of Faith* (San Francisco: Harper & Row, 1976), pp. 13-14.

2) Trust in a transcendent center of value and power. While many possess both kinds of faith, skeptical persons may lack the first kind, but still possess some of the second. Perhaps Jesus had such persons in mind when he spoke of faith no bigger than a mustard seed.

Spirit

There are many definitions for "spirit," but I will use just two: 1) energy, vivacity, ardor, enthusiasm, and courage. This definition is manifest in the expression, "a spirited person." 2) a temper or disposition of mind and heart, or a group. German writers speak of the spirit, "*geist*," of a people at a particular time in their history. This is the sense of "spirit" in the title of these lessons.

Politics

Finally, although "politics" often refers to the management of nations or states or political parties, I will use the word more broadly here. By politics I mean social relations involving authority and power. So, in addition to civic politics, there can also be a politics of church, tribe, or family—even of couples. The politics of a social system is informed by the spirits of *all* the members of that system, but the spirits of the leaders are most influential, because leaders exercise the most authority and power within the system.

In the following five lessons, we will see how the spirits of political systems are informed by the spirits of the individuals who comprise them, particularly those of their leaders; and also, how faith (trust in a transcendent center of value and power) promotes the movement of both individual spirits and the spirits of politics towards compassion.

For the structure of these lessons, I borrow from the work of pastoral counselors, Donald R. Hands and Wayne L. Fehr. Hands and Fehr introduce three quadrilateral diagrams to help pastors gauge the degree of their intimacy with themselves, others, and God. The intimacy achieved in each of these relationships is determined by a pastor's ego strength (plotted on the vertical axis, with the top indicating high strength, and the bottom, low strength); and secondly, by a pastor's

Read the "Reflections" on faith in the *NIB*, vol. 8, pp. 369 and 635.

Teaching Tips
Have Faith

These lessons will draw upon the faith of all the learners. Read Matthew 17:14-20 and Mark 9:14-24. Discuss how these passages inform your faith.

Teaching Tips
It's All Politics

Discuss ways in which a social group—family, church, city, or nation—develops "politics" out of the spirits of the members and leaders. Share examples. How would the group members define the politics of their own congregation?

Reflections
Teacher and Listener

Read Isaiah 50:4.
1. What do you think the prophet meant when he spoke of listening "with the ears of those who are taught?"
2. How might your answer to this question inform the way you teach these sessions?
3. This verse is part of the third "Servant Song" in Isaiah (Isa 40:4-9).
4. How can a teacher or leader also be a servant?

openness to relationship (plotted on the horizontal axis, with a low relationship to the far left, and a high relationship to the far right). For the purpose of these lessons, I will refer to their diagram that maps self-intimacy and intimacy with others.

Referring to that diagram, we notice four types of persons.

Source

Donald R. Hands and Wayne L. Fehr, *Spiritual Wholeness for Clergy: A New Psychology of Intimacy with God, Self and Others* (New York: Alban Institute, 1993.) Used by permission.

Maximum Power

	Politics of Domination	Politics of Compassion	
	Narcissistic & Self-aggrandizing	Self-intimate & Self-appreciating	
Minimum Relationship			**Maximum Relationship**
	Self-harming Schizoidal	Self-deprecatory & Dependent	
	Politics of Isolation	Politics of Resentment	

Minimum Power

In the top right corner are persons with high ego strength and a high ability to relate to others in a mutually beneficial way. Persons in the bottom left corner have low ego strength and little ability to relate to others. They are withdrawn and unable to form close relationships. Sometimes they are self-harming as well. In the bottom right corner are the self-deprecatory and dependent persons. These have low ego strength and a strong connection to others, and thus tend to be clingy. Finally, in the top left corner are the narcissistic and self-aggrandizing types. These have high ego strength, but little ability to relate to others; (or at least, little concern for doing so).

Types of Leadership

What kind of politics would a society likely obtain if the leaders of a given social system were of Hands and Fehr's top right quadrant? In that case, a *politics of compassion*" would likely ensue. And if the leaders of the system were people of the bottom left quadrant? Let us call that the "*politics of isolation.*" And if the leaders were people of the bottom right quadrant, what

Reflections
Politics Of Compassion

As a leader, you can reflect on the political state of your group or congregation. Has the leadership and spirit of the members produced a politics of compassion, isolation, resentment, or domination? Or does it resemble a mixture of these elements? If you don't like what you see, how can you, as the leader, go about changing it?

Teaching Tips

Take time to explore the four types of leaders. Can the group think of examples of leaders who fit the roles of each? If group members know and trust each other, they might share with the group which quadrant they think most resembles their group or congregation or even themselves personally.

then? A *"politics of resentment"* would result. Finally, what if the leaders were people of the top left quadrant? One would then find a *"politics of domination."*

In the ensuing lessons I will compare and contrast these different politics, which vary according to the different spirits that drive them: the tender-hearted spirit of compassion, the faint-hearted spirit of isolation, the sour-hearted spirit of resentment, and the hard-hearted spirit of domination.

Teaching Tips

Joseph and His Brothers

As a group, read Genesis 50:15-21 aloud. Break into pairs. One partner takes Joseph's role, the other partner, the role of one of Joseph's brothers. Put yourself in the shoes of the character in the scene, as if you are an actor. Express the feelings of your character through a pose or improvised monologue. Finally, come out of character and talk about what you felt. What did the exercise teach you about the difficulty of achieving a politics of compassion when there has been a betrayal? What are the problems in establishing new relationships of authority and power in such a family?

The Politics Of Compassion

We begin our survey with the politics of compassion. Cynics will scoff and say that there is no room for tender hearts in politics. In a dog-eat-dog world; only the meanest, toughest, and shrewdest dogs survive. Politics must therefore become a martial art such as Machiavelli proffered.

Granted, the meanness of the world does weary the human spirit. We are cowed into conformity within systems of domination that have become so common that they seem inevitable. Followers of Jesus, though, are invited to view the world with eyes of faith, and not accept this apparent inevitability. We pray: "Thy kingdom come, thy will be done, on earth as it is in heaven" (Matt 6:10).

"Do not be conformed to this world," wrote the Apostle Paul (Rom 12:2), but be transformed by the renewing of your minds. How our minds should be renewed by the gospel of Jesus Christ is clarified with respect to interpersonal relationships. Many a child knows the golden rule, "In everything do to others as you would have them do to you ... " (Matt 7:12). How this rule looks in practice may be found in Romans 12. Paul spells out there what it means to live in Christ's spirit. He says we must love one another with mutual affection (v. 10). But what if the other doesn't love you? What if mutual affection is impossible? Then, insofar as it depends upon you, Paul says, live peaceably with all (v. 18). Do what you can to promote harmony. People, places, and things may not be under your control, but do what good you can, and leave the outcome to God.

Lectionary Loop

Fifteenth Sunday after Pentecost, Year A, Romans 12:9-21

Sources

Nicolo Machiavelli, *The Prince*. Trans. Christian E. Detmold, (New York: Washington Square Press, 1963).

Teaching Tips

Thy Kingdom Come

Read (or pray) the Lord's Prayer (Matt 6:9-13) and discuss the meaning of the "Kingdom of God." See the excursus on p. 1955 of the *NISB*. Discuss: Do you think we have a part in the coming of God's kingdom? For more discussion, see "The Kingdom of Heaven" in the *NIB*, vol. 8, pp. 288-294.

Politics Of Compassion in the Family and among Nations

The finest example of a politics of compassion within a family is told in the Joseph saga, where older brothers sell their spoiled youngest brother to slavers, fake his accidental death, and forget about him.

Sometimes a politics of compassion arises when one wouldn't expect it, as in Isaiah 56:1-7. This passage dates after 537 B.C.E., when Jewish exiles were returning from Babylon and trying to resettle and rebuild their temple. The going was tough, because the people who had been living there resisted the returnees. They attacked their settlements and frustrated their attempts to rebuild their temple (Ez 4:4-5). The books of Ezra and Nehemiah, reporting about that period, reflect an understandable resentment toward these already resident foreigners (Ez 9-10 and Neh 13). Third Isaiah, however, regards all these people with charity and compassion and insists that the new temple shall be a house of prayer for *all* people.

Romans 12:9-21

Though it is usually very difficult to forgive and love our personal enemies—as Jesus taught (Matt 5:38-48), and as Paul reiterated (Rom 12:9-21)—at least in the interpersonal dimension of Christian ethics we know what we are called to do, and we have a personal model to follow: Jesus. "What would Jesus do?" is a fairly reliable method for deciding how to treat people—in the interpersonal dimension.

But in the social dimension, which concerns group interactions, and personal loyalties and obligations to groups, the going gets murkier. There are two reasons for this: First, the moral teachings of Jesus, found chiefly in parables, are couched in interpersonal terms. Often it is not clear how to apply the principles from that dimension of life to the social one—to the morality of nations, for instance. Particularly in the social dimension, citizens' loyalties and obligations are complex; and this complexity increases the likelihood of moral conflicts.

Reinhold Niebuhr, the founder of the school of "Christian realism," stressed that in the interpersonal

Teaching Tips

What Would Jesus Do?

Compare Paul's advice in Romans 12:9-21 with Jesus' words in Matthew 5:1–7:14. Based on these texts, discuss the answer to the question "What would Jesus do?"

Study Bible

Notes on Isaiah 56:1-7, in *NISB*, 1034-35.

See notes on the Sermon on the Mount on pp. 1754-59 and on Paul's advice in Romans on pp. 2028-29.

Sources

Consult Volume 1 of *The Pastor's Bible Study*, where Thorwald Lorenzen, in his lessons about "Christian Faith and Power" (pp. 185-211), discusses whether Christians must always obey their governors in light of the Scriptures.

See Reinhold Niebuhr's *Moral Man and Immoral Society*. A complete online copy is available at: http://www.religion-online.org.

dimension of ethics, Christians strive to avoid coercion, because of the radically loving, self-surrendering example of Jesus upon the cross. But in politics, some degree of coercion may be required to restore justice and maintain order. However, neither cynicism born of life's hard knocks, nor difficult moral decision-making in the social dimension should dissuade us from pursuing a politics of compassion.

Once in a while, a politics of compassion does appear, even at the level of state. One thinks, for instance, of William Penn's colony, where Native Americans were treated fairly and respectfully. And one thinks of the Republic of South Africa. Considering the history of racial oppression there, one might have expected a politics of resentment or a politics of domination to emerge from the liberated majority; but owing to the moral leadership of the country, that did not happen. Instead, a politics of compassion prevailed. Public confessions and amnesties were conducted to purge the bile of shame and hatred, so that black people and white people could move forward as one nation.

Our diagram suggests that a politics of compassion can arise only when a group's leaders are spiritually mature, strong of spirit, and confident of their own innate worth. Without this inner strength, they will not manage to see God in others, especially in past oppressors or present enemies. Compassion is the ability to feel with others not only empathetically, but sympathetically, so that one recognizes oneself in the other. "Do to others as you would have them do to you." That golden rule doesn't work unless the love of self is first accomplished. Which brings us to session two.

Session 2   Jonah 1:1–4:11; 1 Kings 19:1-18

The Politics Of Isolation

ession one began with an examination of the politics of compassion, which showed that when political leaders rank high in ego strength and the ability to relate cooperatively with others, they are poised to promote arrangements of authority and power that foster justice and reconciliation.

We turn now to political systems of a less mature spirit, and shall begin by considering the politics of isolation. The reader might suppose that a politics of domination is most different from a politics of compassion, but this is not so. A politics of isolation is most different, because people who manifest a faint-hearted and retiring spirit must grow in two directions: in ego strength, and in the ability to relate; whereas people of a domineering spirit already possess ego strength, and must simply learn how to relate to others more cooperatively and compassionately.

In Hands and Fehr's diagram, persons of the bottom left quadrant are labeled self-harming and "schizoidal." These are persons whose egos are so wounded and stunted that they can barely form lasting relationships of any kind, much less become politically committed.

Frightened but Not Isolated

A careful combing of the Scriptures provides instances where frightened individuals run away and hide. Moses resists, at first, God's call to lead the people out of Egypt with the complaint that he is "slow of speech" (Exod 4:10). Jonah runs from God's call (Jon 1:1-17). Elijah runs from Queen Jezebel and hides in a cave (1 Kgs 19:1-18); the disciples all flee and desert

Lectionary Loop

Third Sunday after Epiphany, Year B, Jonah 3:1-5, 10
Third Sunday after Pentecost, Year C, 1 Kings 19:1-15a

Reflections

The Sound Of Silence

During Elijah's time of trembling, God tells him to leave the cave where he is hiding and stand outside. There he is buffeted by a great storm, and threatened by earthquake and fire. The text says that the voice of God was neither in the earthquake nor the fire, but rather, in the sound of "sheer silence." How might this passage support people who are poor in spirit?

Jesus when he is arrested (Matt 26:56); two disciples on their way to Emmaus experience temporary discouragement (Luke 24:13-24).

But one does not find in the Bible a wholesale and permanent retreat from social contact. The people of Israel were indeed isolated during their wilderness wandering—Jesus was alone for forty days in the wilderness, and the disciples of Jesus did retreat for self-protection after his execution (John 20:19), but they did not demonstrate a politics of isolation. They stayed in community with each other. On first inspection it might seem that the Jewish sectarians called Essenes had a politics of isolation, for they retreated to the desert to escape corruption. One might also suppose that the many different groups of Christians who formed monastic communities during the dark ages also exemplified an ecclesiastical politics of isolation. But these communities were still quite vigorous in spirit, so one cannot legitimately place them in the bottom left quadrant of our diagram.

People with very low ego strength tend to withdraw from lasting association. They are averse to participating in politics. They resist entering into arrangements of authority and power, because their own personal power is so meager.

Examples of a politics of isolation are "survivalists"—those who are convinced that the end of the world is coming, who have stockpiled food and water and ammunition, and who are prepared to defend their domiciles against the rest of humanity. Survivalists manifest the spirit of isolation. They do not form political systems, because they are finished with politics. They believe the world is beyond fixing. It's everyone for himself or herself now; and to survive one must be ready, if necessary, to shoot one's best friend.

Weak-spirited withdrawers rarely attract notice, unless they become violent. Haiti's wretched rural poor build their huts far from roads to escape molestation by the powers that be. The world scarcely ever pays attention to the withdrawers. Society is made aware of these withdrawers when their slide into poverty of spirit carries them to the ragged edge of

Reflections

From Isolation to Compassion

1. Where have you seen a "politics of isolation?"
2. How can groups and individuals be helped toward a politics of compassion?

Sources

In order to understand the link between depression and male violence, see Terrance Real's *I Don't Want to Talk About It: Overcoming the Secret Legacy of Male Depression* (New York: Fireside Press, 1998).

See also the website of the National Institute of Mental Health, http://www.nimh.nih.gov.

humanness, and they explode in a fit of indignant fury, like Timothy McVeigh in Oklahoma City, or the boys who shot up Colombine High School near Denver.

As a society, we need to discern spirits much better than we do, and pay better attention to those who are poor in spirit, not only because withdrawers may go ballistic, but because they belong to us, these raggedy souls so close to the edge.

Jonah the Withdrawer

The story of Jonah concerns a withdrawer, and God's way—both firmly and tenderly—of dealing with him. The book was written sometime after the Jews returned from exile in Babylon, in the fifth century B.C.E.. As mentioned before, this was a difficult time for the returnees, who resented the harsh welcome they received from foreigners residing in the land which they had been forced to vacate. Not all Jews were resentful, however. The postexilic voices of Third Isaiah (see Isa 56:1-7) and Jonah's author both criticize their compatriots' xenophobia and resentment.

The character Jonah is both comical and pitiful. God assigns to him the terrifying mission of preaching repentance to Nineveh, the capital of Assyria. The Assyrians had conquered Israel, and so for Jews, Ninevah stood as a symbol of domination. Poor in spirit but not too weak in the knees to run, Jonah flees in the opposite direction. His attempt to escape the reach of a relentlessly loving God fails utterly, and he is consigned to a three-day continuing education retreat in the belly of an aquatic beast.

After emerging from the deep, Jonah reluctantly goes to Nineveh, and fulfills his preaching assignment, which, to his consternation, succeeds. The Ninevites repent, and Jonah sulks. No sooner does his fear abate and his spirit strengthen, than he must deal with the next spiritual hurdle: resentment. This brings us to session three.

Study Bible

See notes on Jonah, *NISB*, 1297-1301.

Teaching Tips

Running with Jonah

Jonah's is an evocative story, tailored for drama. Play with it. Invite your students to slip into Jonah's running shoes. Ask them to recall a time when they heard God's call and headed in the opposite direction. Get them to read aloud Jonah's lament, 2:1-6, and then ask them to recall a time when they fell into an abyss, and didn't know whether they would ever see the light of day again. Finally, ask them if they, like Jonah, have ever begrudged something good happening to bad people.

Session 3 Matthew 20:1-16; Luke 15:11-32

The Politics Of Resentment

Resentment is the anger instinctually felt whenever one is wronged. My dictionary adds that "pride and selfishness are apt to aggravate this feeling until it changes into a criminal animosity." Cain was filled with resentment when God preferred Abel's gift to his own for no apparent reason, so he rose up and killed his brother (Gen 4:1-8). Though resentment does sometimes explode into rage, we see it also in cooler, calculated revenge, as in the case of Joseph's brothers, who seethed with envy and malice (Gen 37). Usually though, resentment does not erupt, at least not for a long, long time. It festers just below the surface, like pus in a boil. Resentment is anger with the lid on.

Parable Of the Laborers

In Jesus' parable (Matt 20:1-16), the laborers who began working much earlier in the day were paid the same as those who started later. With good reason, those who worked all day became resentful. In this case, they did not suppress their anger. They complained right away to the man who paid them, the person best able to correct a perceived injustice. Their behavior demonstrates strength of spirit. It takes courage and self-esteem for laborers to protest to a land owner!

Often, though, offended people behave neither courageously nor sensibly. They don't even try to use their anger well. Either they rage and do stupid, destructive things, or else they ventilate their resentment sideways. For instance, in parish politics, resentment often gets aired in the church parking lot.

Lectionary Loop

Eighteenth Sunday after Pentecost, Year A, Matthew 20:1-16
Fourth Sunday of Lent, Year C, Luke 15:1-3, 11b-32

Teaching Tips

Handling an Injustice

Suggest to the group that several of the laborers from the Matthew 20:1-16 parable decide to file a class action suit against the landowner for unfair labor practices. The landowner convenes lawyers to defend himself against the charge. Break into four groups: plaintiff team, defense team, judges, and court observers. Conduct a mock trial. Then poll the judges for their opinions. Finally, ask the observers what they think of the case, legally, morally, and spiritually.

Questions for discussion:
1. In what circumstances do you think it is appropriate for Christians to express anger?
2. Why do many Christians nurse their resentment, and ventilate it sideways?

(Continued on Page 286)

Parable Of the Prodigal Son and His Brother

To better understand the dynamics of resentment, let's look at the Prodigal Son Parable (Luke 15:11-32). Many readers halt at verse 25. Why ruin a nice story about forgiveness and reconciliation? But if you omit the older brother part of the story, you miss an essential insight: That the father loves both sons, the one whom he forgave, and the one who can't forgive; and he loves them both equally. If you stop the story at verse 25, you have a happy ending. The lost son is back and everybody's partying. But if you read on to verse 32, the ending is tragic. Think of what has happened from the father's point of view: First he lost one son to dissolute living; then, as soon as that one came home, he lost the other to resentment. He wants both sons at his table, but it seems he can't have both. That's tragic.

The ending doesn't have to be tragic, of course. The older brother could change. He could try to like his brother more, let bygones be bygones. But look at Hands and Fehr's diagram. You will notice that the way to exit the resentment quadrant is not by connecting better to others, although intuition says so. A person in the bottom right quadrant is already a strong relater. No, the one who is full of resentment must come to love *himself* more. His self respect must grow. That's the way out. The older brother must increase his love for himself to feel better about his brother. Consider the text. The older brother complains to his father: "You never killed a fatted calf for me!" That isn't just anger talking, it's hurt. He feels his father doesn't love him as much. After all, his father just handed that rebel everything that he wanted, then forgave him in a wink when he blew it all. What an injustice (see Deut 21:18-21)! You have to wonder whether the older brother ever asked his father for anything. Probably not. He probably kept slogging along like Martha (Luke 10:38-42), fuming all the while.

Some people are like that. They expect the duty they render to elicit affection. They can't just ask for love. They can only complain when they don't get it. The people who get bogged down in resentment, who just can't forgive, are often the ones who have felt rotten

(Continued from Page 285)

3. Do you think Christians tend to do this more than other people, and if so, why?
4. Finally, what can you remember from the Scriptures how Jesus handled his anger?

Resources

See John T. Carroll and James R. Carroll, "When Grace is Not Fair," in *Preaching the Hard Sayings of Jesus* (Peabody: Hendrickson, 1996) 18-24.

Study Bible

See notes on the Parable of the Laborers (Matt 20:1-16), *NISB*, 1782.

Resources

See Kenneth Bailey's discussion of the son's resentment in *Poet and Peasant* and *Through Peasant Eyes* (combined edition, Grand Rapids: Eerdmans, 1983), 142-206.

See also Bernard Brandon Scott, *Hear Then the Parable* (Minneapolis: Fortress, 1989), 99-125.

about themselves all along. So the problem isn't really with the other. It's with oneself. The father in the parable says to the older son: "See, all that I have is yours," meaning, "I love you too, just as much!" But the older brother won't have it, because he doesn't feel loved or lovable.

Groups get resentful, too, like people. I have seen some groups struggling for freedom and dignity who have not quite shaken loose their oppressors' stigma. They've swallowed it, and it's holding fast in them, deep down. So they can't get a clear picture of themselves, nor of other groups struggling as they are. They can't see that they're all the same, like the two brothers whom the father loves equally. They can only claw and snipe, playing at the oppressor's game, wrestling to stay one up in the pecking order of the stigmatized, trying to earn respect by claiming they've suffered more. That's the politics of resentment.

It's futile. Nobody gets free that way. Hasn't Jesus taught us that it doesn't matter how much we've suffered? Early workers—late workers—what's all that to God? God loves us all the same.

Teaching Tips

How Would You Feel about It?

Focus for a moment on the feelings of the elder son.

1. If you were in his place, would you feel resentment toward your younger sibling?
2. Compare the elder brother to Martha in the Mary-Martha story (Luke 10:38-42).
3. Compare Jesus' reply to Martha with the father's reply to his elder son. What similarities and differences do you see?

Reflections

Indignant Displeasure

Where have you seen politics of resentment? What must be done to free a group from the politics of resentment?

M. Scott Peck said that in many situations a person must decide if he or she wants to be right or healthy. What do you think he meant? When is it time to let go of self-justification? See M. Scott Peck, *Road Less Traveled*, *A New Psychology of Love, Traditional Values, and Spiritual Growth* (New York: Simon & Schuster, 1980).

Session 4   Deuteronomy 24:16-22; Leviticus 25:8-22

The Politics Of Domination

W e turn finally to the top left quadrant of Hands and Fehr's diagram, where the narcissists and abusers are located—those persons whose ego strength is high, but whose ability or inclination to relate to others is low. They tend to abuse others not because they are sadistic, but because they focus so much on their own needs, interests, and desires. When their spirit prevails in a social system, a politics of domination results.

The politics of domination has been and continues to be the most common arrangement of authority and power in the world. Walter Wink notes that in the Christian Scriptures the word for "world," "*cosmos*" in Greek, sometimes means fallen society and nature, where the powerful and rapacious prey upon the weaker. The world, in the eyes of the first Christians, was a domination system.

Trading in a Politics Of Dominance

Between the time that the Hebrews inhabited the land of Canaan and the beginning of the first kingship, their politics was tribal and their leadership charismatic. This was the period of the judges. In one sense, the judges were like warlords. Their followers believed that they were divinely appointed to protect them, for they possessed vision, courage, and military shrewdness. In peaceful times, judges may also have had judicial and governmental duties.

When the wise, well respected, and aging Samuel passed his judging duties to his three sons, they turned out to be not as wise and beneficent as he was. Disappointed with those three, the people demanded that

Sources

Walter Wink, *Engaging the Powers: Discernment and Resistance in a World of Domination* (Minneapolis: Fortress Press, 1992), see especially pp. 51-63.

Dennis T. Olson, Introduction to the book of Judges, *NIB*, vol. 2, 723–28.

Sources

Bruce Birch, comments on 1 Samuel 8:1-18, *NIB*, vol. 2, 1022-31. See especially his "Reflections" on pp. 1030-31. See also the lesson on First and Second Samuel in this volume (2) of *The Pastor's Bible Study*.

Thomas Hobbes's treatise on government, *The Leviathan*, chapters 13 and following. Text is available at website: http://oregonstate.edu/-instruct/phl302/texts/hobbes/leviathan-contents.html.

Study Bible

See Genesis 14:1-10, *NISB*, 30-31.

Samuel anoint for them a king, such as the nations around them had. Samuel warned them that they didn't know what they would be getting into (1 Sam 8:1-18). A king would exploit them for his gain. He would confiscate their best fields and livestock. He would conscript their sons for his wars and their daughters for his kitchens. He would tax them a tenth—as much as God demands!—and pass the purse to his retinue. Samuel warned them earnestly, but they turned a deaf ear, and gave in to the politics of domination.

Genesis 14:1-10 gives a thumbnail sketch of the politics of domination among nations: warring, shifting alliances, and more fighting. Clearly, the rule of kings often is no better than that of warlords. The English philosopher, Thomas Hobbes, wrote that citizens hand over their freedom to a sovereign because without strong authority human existence is anarchic; life is "solitary, poor, nasty, brutish, and short." But of course, unless one's sovereign is benign, life is likely to turn out that way anyway, which was precisely Samuel's point.

Biblical Call for Relationship and Justice

The precious laws of Yahweh were supposed to protect against a politics of domination, not only by requiring justice, but also by urging compassion. For instance, when a landowner cut his grain crop, or picked his olive grove, or harvested his vineyard, according to Deuteronomy 24:19-22, he was forbidden to take all that there was. He was supposed to leave a little for the sojourner, the poor widow, the orphan. And when debts piled up over many years, so that the poor were losing their land and their homes, Leviticus 25 mandated a Jubilee year every fiftieth, when debts were to be canceled, and land returned to the original owners. Such rules were supposed to make God's love real in the land of Israel. But as long as there were people with callous, domineering, and abusive spirits, most especially in positions of leadership, rules would not suffice. Somehow, mused the prophet Jeremiah, who lived during a time of corrupt and turbulent leadership, God's rules would have to be written on people's hearts, so that from the richest and most power-

Study Bible

See notes on Deut 24:16-22, *NISB*, 282.

See notes on Leviticus 25:8-22, *NISB*, 183.

Study Bible

See introduction to Paul's Letter to Philemon and notes, *NISB*, 2147-50. The author of Colossians, likely a disciple of Paul's, tells slaves to obey their masters! (Col 3:22).

See "Special Note" on slavery, *NISB*, 2112-13.

See also Cain Hope Felder's comments on slavery in Philemon in *NIB*, vol. 11, pp. 885-87.

ful person to the poorest and meekest, everyone would know God intimately, and be moved to reflect the spirit of God in their conduct. (Jer 31:33-34).

Patriarchy: Politics Of the Domination Of Men

A recurring moral challenge for godly people is to recognize and articulate the ways in which a spirit of domination insinuates itself into their religion, so that politics of domination seem not only proper, but divinely ordained. Patriarchy serves as an excellent example. Patriarchy is a politics in which men enjoy more authority and power than women simply because they are men. Patriarchy was so much an accepted part of the ancient cultures in which Judaism and Christianity developed that it shaped the ancients' ideas about the nature of God, and God's intentions for the conduct of family and community life.

Slavery: Politics of Domination of the Master

Slavery is another prominent example of a politics of domination. The Apostle Paul, the first Christian theologian and arguably the founder of Christianity, argued that Onesimus was not Philemon's slave but a brother "both in the flesh and in the Lord" (Phlm 10-16). Nevertheless, Paul did not question the legitimacy of slavery as an institution.

Land: Politics Of Dominance in Ownership

A third politics of domination relates to the doctrines of election and holy land. Some Jews and Christians maintain that God's gift of land to God's chosen people justified and continues to justify Israel's ruthless suppression of her enemies. The following texts have been used to support this claim, Deuteronomy 7:1-8, and the war song of King David, 2 Samuel 22:33-51. The moral difficulty with such passages is that they portray God as a bully and tyrant. Michael Prior writes: "A major problem with some of the traditions of the Old Testament, especially those concerned with the promise of land, is their portrayal of God as . . . a racist, militaristic xenophobe, whose views would not be tolerated in any modern democracy." But there are other voices in the Scriptures that are not bel-

Source

Walter Wink calls this challenge of discernment "unmasking the domination system," *Engaging the Powers: Discernment and Resistance in a World of Domination* (Minneapolis: Fortress, 1992), 87-104.

Teaching Tips
The Bible Says . . .

Have two women in the class read, in a firm and vigorous voice, the following: 1 Timothy 2:1-4, 9-15; and 1 Corinthians 14:34-35. Then, discuss those passages. Ask whether the behaviors urged in them are still practiced by your congregation; if not, why not? See also *NISB*, 2056, 2132.

The Abolitionists read the same Holy Scriptures as the slave owners in The United States of America, but reached very different moral conclusions. Discuss how this was possible.

Discuss: Is it all right to disagree with the moral opinions of the founders of your religious tradition, especially when they are expressed in Holy Scripture?; if so, on what grounds?

Sources

Michael Prior's *The Bible and Colonialism* (Sheffield, England: 1997), 263. See also see this author's sermons entitled "God's Abode" and "Everywhere Lies Holy Ground" at http://www.hanoverchurch.org/your-ti22225.html]

licose and self-righteous, but rather imbued with compassion, especially for strangers. As I have already indicated, Isaiah 56:1-7 is one of these. Isaiah 9:1-7 is another.

Outgrowing the Need to Dominate

Our diagram reminds us that the human spirit matures in two directions: towards vitality of ego and intimacy with others. People in the top left quadrant already have strong egos. They don't need more elevation in that direction! But neither do they need to "be knocked down a peg," which is the proverbial wisdom for dealing with people "too full of themselves." Their vitality of ego is fundamentally good for them and society. What they need is to be drawn toward intimacy with others and to have more concern for them. Trying to force them in that direction won't work. Coercion is the *modus operandi* of the system of domination. Resorting to it only reinforces a spirit of domination. God's message must be written upon people's hearts, said Jeremiah (31:33). But how can God write on the hard heart of a dominating spirit? The heart must be broken to render it tender enough to receive what shall be written there. The psalmist sings to Yahweh: "My sacrifice is this broken spirit; you will not scorn this crushed and broken heart" (Ps 51:17). We will ponder this insight in session five.

Reflections

From Domination to Compassion

1. Where have you seen the "politics of domination?"
2. How can groups and individuals be helped toward the politics of compassion?

Both Martin Luther King, Jr. and Nelson Mandela were individuals that worked at change from domination to compassion.

Toward a Politics Of Compassion

The Sermon on the Mount (Matt 5-7) begins with blessings for people on the bottom of the heap in systems of domination. Blessed are the meek, Jesus taught. Blessed are the persecuted; and blessed are the poor in spirit. That last teaching seems contrary to what we have learned in these lessons: that strength of spirit (plotted on the vertical axis of our diagram) is key to the maturation of individuals, and also the political systems in which they participate. So why would Jesus say that being poor in spirit (lower on the scale) is a blessing? Because people poor in spirit are more likely to recognize their need for God than the strong ones. Satisfied folk don't crave nourishment; the hungry do (Matt 5:6). By faith, the poor in spirit open their hearts, reach out for help, and receive it, which is why they're blessed.

Does Our Faith Lead to Compassion or Division?

Often we think of faith as a set of firm beliefs by which we make a stand in the world. By this definition (number one in the text box), faith is a strength. But faith can also be understood (by definition two) as trust in a transcendent center of power and value, which implies a certain poverty of spirit, a dependence, a need. In the introduction of these lessons I posed this question: Can people of good faith, (that is, honest and well-meaning people), but of different faiths (according to definition one), remain in good faith when the subject of politics arises?

Recently a clergy support group in my neighborhood began, comprised of a Muslim *imam*, a Jewish cantor, a Roman Catholic priest, and several Protestant

Lectionary Loop

Fourth Sunday after Epiphany, Pentecost, All Saints Day, Year A, Matthew 5:1-12

Lent, Ash Wednesday, Year A, B, C, Matthew 6:1-6, 16-21

Thanksgiving, Pentecost. Year B, Matthew 6:25-33

Second Sunday after Pentectost, Year A, Matthew 7:21-29

Study Bible

Read the study notes about the Sermon on the Mount, *NISB*, 1754-59.

Reflections

Keep the Faith

At the beginning of this study, we defined faith in two ways:

1. The beliefs of a particular religion or denomination, as in, "the Christian faith," or "the Muslim faith," or "the Reformed Faith."

2. "Trust in a transcendent center of value and power."

The similarities and differences between these two approaches to "faith" are the topic of the next part of the lesson.

pastors. Would my colleagues and I in this group be able to remain in good faith if the subject of a Palestinian homeland were to arise in our conversation? Could we remain in good faith if some recent Catholic bishops' threats to excommunicate liberal Catholic politicians were to be mentioned? Our good faith might break if faith by the first definition were the only kind we possessed. But it isn't. We have another kind of faith: We all acknowledge our need for God. Therefore, we might be able to see each other as poor souls with a common spiritual need, instead of just adversaries on opposite sides of political fences.

The desire to be more connected to others moves people toward greater intimacy (from left to right on the horizontal axis). But that drive alone is insufficient to bring about a politics of compassion. The distrust and animosity between vying groups in society impedes that possibility, unless the individuals within them can identify a common need, and thereby recognize their own vulnerability, their own humanness, in their adversaries. Faith, as a common dependence upon a transcendent center of power and value, can make that possible. For instance, Mahatma Gandhi sincerely cared for India's British oppressors. He used methods of liberation intended to free them as well as his own people. Martin Luther King, Jr. sincerely cared for racists and worked to liberate them as well as his own people. Both leaders worked toward a politics of compassion because they trusted in a transcendent center of power and value, and recognized that within the center, their enemies were as valued as highly as they.

Helping the Isolated and Resentful toward Compassion

The diagram indicates that people in the bottom quadrants need to know themselves better and have their spirits lifted, so that they can relate to others in a mutually beneficial way. By strengthening individuals' spirits, we increase the pool of persons sufficiently strong to become politically active. Thus, the care of souls through Christian education and pastoral care can contribute indirectly to a politics of compassion.

Teaching Tips
Campaigning for Compassion
In these five lessons we have explored the psychological and theological groundwork for a politics of compassion. Based on what we have discussed, how might we work toward a politics of compassion?

Reflections
How Big Is Your God?
Read Acts 17:22-28 and discuss the God in whom "we live and move and have our being." Is your understanding of God big enough to embrace both people of religious belief (definition one) and those who trust in value or power that is greater than themselves (definition two)?

Study Bible
Read the excursus "No One Comes to the Father Except Through Me" (John 14:6), *NISB*, 1937.

Teaching Tips
Do You Know the Way?
Read John 14:6 and discuss how the two definitions of faith (as a particular religious view or as trust in a transcendent center of value and power) might inform your understanding of this verse. Even if Jesus has ultimate meaning for us as the way to God, does that necessarily preclude others of different faiths from finding and enjoying God in their own ways? Read Philippians 4:8. Should *(Continued on Page 295)*

Helping the Dominators toward Compassion

We need to persuade people in the top left quadrant to see themselves more clearly, to be more keenly aware of the needs and interests of others, and to hold those in higher regard. We need to find more clever ways to soften hard hearts. Scolding almost never works. Jesus employed entertaining stories to lure the unsuspecting into compassion.

We need to explore further the relationship between faith by definition one (the beliefs of a particular religion or denomination) and faith by definition two ("Trust in a transcendent center of value and power.") Faith by the second definition tends to promote a politics of compassion, but faith by the first may impede it. All people who trust in a value or power that transcends themselves share a common spiritual kinship despite their different belief systems.

(Continued From Page 294)
not these virtues and values be praised when they are also observed and practiced in other religions? See "Declaration on the Relationship of the Church to Non-Christian Religions" in *The Documents of Vatican II* (Baltimore: The America Press, 1966), 660-68.

Teaching Tips

From Anger to Compassion

Discuss means by which the spirits of those who are isolated and resentful could be nourished toward a politics of compassion. How might Jesus' words in Matthew 10:16 be a helpful principle for nonviolent engagement in this regard? See also Wink, *Engaging the Powers, 209-30.*

Teaching Tips

Welcome Back

At the conclusion of *The Chosen* by Chaim Potok (New York: Simon & Schuster, 1967) there is a moving scene in which the very conservative Jewish rabbi welcomes home his liberal-thinking son, Danny. Read Luke 15:11-32 again. Have each person in the group write or tell an ending to the parable that brings the elder son back into the family. Share your endings.

SOURCES

SOURCES

The Gospel of Mark

Barks, Coleman and John Moyne, trans. *The Essential Rumi*, San Francisco: HarperSanFrancisco, 1995.

Blount, Brian. *Go Preach! Mark's Kingdom Message and the Black Church Today.* Maryknoll: Orbis Books, 1998.

Carnes, Robin Deen and Sally Craig. *Sacred Circles: A Guide to Creating Your Own Women's Spirituality Group.* San Francisco: HarperSanFrancisco, 1998.

Elliot, John H. "Temple Versus Household in Luke-Acts: A Contrast in Social Institutions." In *The Social World of Luke-Acts: Models for Interpretation*, edited by Jerome H. Neyrey. Peabody, Mass.: Hendrickson Publishers, 1991.

Juel, Donald H. *Master of Surprise: Mark Interpreted.* Minneapolis: Fortress Press, 1994.

Horsley, Richard A. *Jesus and Empire: The Kingdom of God and the New World Disorder.* Minneapolis: Fortress Press, 2003.

Malina, Bruce J. *The New Testament World: Insights from Cultural Anthropology.* Louisville: Westminster John Knox Press, 1981.

Malina, Bruce J. and Richard Rohrbaugh. *Social Science Commentary on the Synoptic Gospels.* 2nd ed. Philadelphia: Fortress, 2003.

McFague, Sallie. *Speaking in Parables.* Philadelphia: Fortress Press, 1975.

Minor, Mitzi. *The Power of Mark's Story.* St. Louis: Chalice Press, 2001.

_____ *The Spirituality of Mark.* Louisville: Westminster John Knox Press, 1996.

_____ "Exegesis: Mark 7:31-37, 8:27-37, 9:30-37, 9:38-50." In *Lectionary Homiletics* XIV (2003), 41-42, 47-48, 55-56, 61-62.

Myers, Ched. *Binding the Strong Man: A Political Reading of Mark's Gospel.* Maryknoll: Orbis Books, 1988.

Oliver, Mary. "Maybe." In *House of Light.* Boston: Beacon Press, 1990.

_____ "Logos." In *Why I Wake Early.* Boston: Beacon Press, 2004.

Peck, M. Scott, *People of the Lie: Toward a Psychology of Evil.* New York: Simon & Schuster, 1998.

Pilch, John J. and Bruce J. Malina, eds. *Biblical Social Values and Their Meaning.* Peabody, Mass.: Hendrickson, 1993.

Rohrbaugh, Richard, ed., *The Social Sciences and New Testament Interpretation*. Peabody, Mass.: Hendrickson, 1996.

Shea, John. *An Experience Named Spirit*. Allen, Texas: Thomas More, 1983.

Wieder, Laurance and Robert Atwan, eds. *Chapters Into Verse: Volume Two*. New York: Oxford University Press, 1993.

Wiesel, Elie, *From the Kingdom of Memory*. New York: Schocken Books, 1990.

Witherington, Ben. *The Gospel of Mark: A Socio-Rhetorical Commentary*. Grand Rapids: Eerdmans, 2001.

Wright, N. T., *The New Testament and the People of God*. Minneapolis: Fortress Press, 1992.

The Ten Commandments

Banner, Stuart. *The Death Penalty: An American History*. Cambridge, Mass: Harvard University Press, 2002.

Childs, Brevard S. *The Book of Exodus: A Critical Theological Commentary*. Old Testament Library. Philadelphia: Westminster, 1974.

Cline, Donald. "The Los Lunas Stone," in *Epigraphic Society Occasional Publications* 10, 1982.

Craige, Peter C. and David L. Jeffrey. "Ten Commandments." In *A Dictionary of Biblical Tradition in English Literature*, David L. Jeffrey, editor. Grand Rapids: Eerdmans, 1992.

Dahood, Mitchell. *Psalms 1:1-50*. Anchor Bible 16. Garden City, N.Y.: Doubleday, 1966.

DeMille, Cecil B. "Why We Need the Ten Commandments." *The Eagle Magazine*, September, 5-6, 2001.

Fell, Berry. *America B.C: Ancient Settlers in the New World*. New York: Pocket Books, 1976.

Freedman, David N. *The Nine Commandments: Uncovering a Hidden Pattern of Crime and Punishment in the Hebrew Bible*. New York: Doubleday, 2000.

Freedman, David. N., M. P. O'Connor, and H. Ringgren. "YHWH," in *The Theological Dictionary of the Old Testament*. Grand Rapids: Eerdmans, 1986, 5: 500-521.

Gordon, C. H. *Ugaritic Textbook*. Analecta Orientalia 38. Rome: Pontifical Biblical Institute, 1965.

Harrelson, Walter J., General editor. *The New Interpreter's Study Bible: New Revised Standard Version with Apocrypha*. Nashville: Abingdon Press, 2003.

____ *The Ten Commandments and Human Rights*. Overtures in Biblical Theology. Philadelphia: Fortress Press, 1980.

Hester, Joseph P. *The Ten Commandments: A Handbook of Religious, Legal, and Social Issues*. Jefferson, N.C.: McFarland Publishers, 2003.

Horne, Charles F. *The Sacred Books and Early Literature of the East*. (New York: Parke, Austin, & Lipscomb, 1917.

Khan, M. Z. *The Quran: Arabic Text with a New Translation*. London: Curzon, 1971.

Kroncke, Francis X. *The Religious Dimension of the Rise of the Penitentiary Movement 1787–1822*, 1978.

Kramer, Heinrich and James Sprenger. *Malleus Maleficarum*, 1486. Available online at http://www.malleusmaleficarum.org/.

Lambert, W. G. *Babylonian Wisdom Literature*. Oxford: Clarendon Press, 1960.

Lambert, W. G. and A. R. Millard. *Atra-hasis: Babylonian Story of the Flood*. Oxford: Clarendon Press, 1969.

Lane, Edward W. *Arabic-English Lexicon*. 8 volumes. Edinburgh: Williams and Norgate. Reprinted 1956. New York: Unger.

Lehmann, Paul L. *The Decalogue and a Human Future: The Meaning of the Commandments for Making and Keeping Human Life Human*. Grand Rapids, Mich.: Eerdmans, 1955.

Lovelace, Wicasta. *Malleus Maleficarum: Introduction to the 1948 edition with Translation and Notes by Montague Summers*, 2003. http://www.malleusmaleficarum.org

McDaniel, Thomas. *The Los Lunas, New Mexico, Decalogue*, 2003. http://www.ebts.edu/tmcdaniel/LosLunas.html.

Neusner, Jacob. *Genesis Rabbah: The Judaic Commentary to the Book of Genesis: A New American Translation*. Brown Judaic studies; no. 104-106. Atlanta, Ga.: Scholars Press, 1985.

Phillips, Anthony. *Ancient Israel's Criminal Law*. Oxford: Basil Blackwell, 1970.

Phillips, Anthony. *Essays on Biblical Law*, JSOTSup 344. Sheffield: Sheffield Academic Press, 2002.

Plaut, W. Gunther. *The Torah: A Modern Commentary: Genesis*. New York: Union of American Hebrew Congregations, 1974.

Poteat, Edwin McNeill. *Mandate to Humanity*. Nashville: Abingdon Press, 1953.

Pritchard, James Bennett. *Ancient Near Eastern Texts Relating to the Old Testament* Princeton, N.J.: Prentice Hall, 1969.

The Protection Project, Johns Hopkins University School of Advanced International Studies in Washington, D.C. http://www.protectionproject.org/main1.htm

Stonebreaker, Jay. "A Decipherment of the Los Lunas Decalogue Inscription," *Epigraphic Society Occasional Publications* 18, 1989.

Underwood, L. Lyle. "The Los Lunas Inscription," *Epigraphic Society Occasional Publications* 10, 1982.

Weinfeld, Moshe. *Deuteronomy 1–11: A New Translation with Introduction and Commentary*. Anchor Bible 5. New York: Doubleday, 1991.

Cultural Diversity and Inclusion

Andersen, Margaret and Patricia. HillCollins, *Race, Class, Gender Anthology,* 4th ed. Belmont, Calif.: Wadsworth, 2001.

Brown, R. E., J. A. Fitzmyer, R. E. Murphy, eds. *Jerome Biblical Commentary*. Englewood Cliffs, N.J.: Prentice Hall, 1968.

"Can we all get along?" Rodney King, May 1, 1992; *Time*: Rodney King Riots Cover, May 11, 1992. (http://www.time.com/time/newsfiles/rodneyking/#)

Edles, Laura. "Introduction: What is Culture and How Does it Work?" In *Cultural Sociology in Practice*. Boston: Blackwell, 2002.

Eiesland, Nancy L. *The Disabled God: Toward a Liberatory Theology of Disability*. Nashville: Abingdon, 1994.

Farmer, David. "The Unselfish Prayer," in *The Pastor's Bible Study,* vol. 1, 181-183.

Feldman, Corey. "Can't We All Just Get Along," in *Business to Business,* May 15, 2000.

Gagnon, Robert. *The Bible and Homosexual Practice*. Nashville: Abingdon, 2001.

Grenx, Stanley J. *Welcoming But Not Affirming: An Evangelical Response to Homosexuality*. Louisville: Westminster John Knox, 1998.

Horner, Tom. *Jonathan Loved David*. Westminster Press: Philadelphia, 1978.

Lauer, Robert, and Jeanette C. Lauer. *Social Problems and the Quality of Life. 8th Edition*, New York: McGraw Hill, 2002.

Lorenzen, Thorwald. "Liberating Discipleship." In *The Pastor's Study Bible,* vol. 1, 215-250.

Morrison, Toni. *The Bluest Eye*. Plume Books: NY, 1994.

Smith, Archie. "Not Everyone Feels Welcome," in *Navigating the Deep River*. Cleveland: United Church Press, 1997.

Snowden, Frank. *Blacks in Antiquity: Ethiopians in the Greco-Roman Experience*. Cambridge, Mass.: Harvard University Press, 1970.

Soards, Marion L. *Scripture and Homosexuality: Biblical Authority and the Church Today*. Louisville: Westminster John Knox, 1995.

Takaki, Ron. "In A Different Mirror," in *Race, Class, and Gender: An Anthology,* Edited by Margaret L. Andersen and Patricia Hill Collins. 4th ed. Belmont, Calif.: Wadsworth, 2001.

Weber, Max. "Open and Closed Economic Relationships," in *Economy and Society*, Roth, Guenther and Claus Wittich, eds. Berkeley: UC Berkeley Press, 341-343.

West, Cornel. *Prophesy Deliverance*. Philadelphia: Westminster, 1982.

Wright, Jeremiah A., Jr. *Good News! Sermons of Hope for Today's Families*. Valley Forge: Judson Press, 1995.

Faith and the Spirits of Politics

Bailey, Kenneth. *Poet and Peasant and Through Peasant Eyes,* combined edition. Grand Rapids: Eerdmans, 1983.

Brueggemann, Walter. *The Prophetic Imagination,* revised edition. Minneapolis: Fortress, 2002.

Hands, Donald R. and Wayne L. Fehr. *Spiritual Wholeness for Clergy: A New Psychology of Intimacy with God, Self and Others*. New York: Alban Institute, 1993.

"Declaration on the Relationship of the Church to Non-Christian Religions" in *The Documents of Vatican II*. Baltimore: The America Press, 1966.

Hands, Donald R. and Wayne L. Fehr. *Spiritual Wholeness for Clergy: A New Psychology of Intimacy with God, Self and Others*. New York: Alban Institute, 1993.

Hobbes, Thomas. *The Leviathan.* http://oregonstate.edu/instruct/phl302/texts/hobbes/leviathan-contents.html

Machiavelli, Nicolo. *The Prince*. Translated by Christian E. Detmold. New York: Washington Square Press, 1963.

Niebuhr, Reinhold. *Moral Man and Immoral Society.* New York: Simon & Schuster, 1930.

Peck, M. Scott. *The Road Less Traveled: A New Psychology of Love, Traditional Values, and Spiritual Growth*. New York: Simon & Schuster, 1978.

Potok, Chaim. *The Chosen*. New York: Simon & Schuster, 1967.

Prior, Michael. *The Bible and Colonialism*. London: Sheffield, 1997.

Real, Terrance. *I Don't Want to Talk About It: Overcoming the Secret Legacy of Male Depression*. New York: Fireside Press, 1998.

Scott, Bernard Brandon. *Hear Then the Parable*. Minneapolis: Fortress, 1989.

Thomas Hobbes's treatise on government, *The Leviathan*, chapters 13 and following. http://oregonstate.edu/instruct/phl302/texts/hobbes/leviathan-contents.html

Walter Wink. *Engaging the Powers: Discernment and Resistance in a World of Domination*. Minneapolis: Fortress Press, 1992.

LECTIONARY

LECTIONARY

Year A

Year B

Year C

SCRIPTURE INDEX

Scripture Index

Notes

Notes

How to Use the Compact Disk

The compact disk located in the back of *The Pastor's Bible Study: Volume Two* may be used to supplement and enhance the study experience. The disk includes:

◆ A QuickTime® video introduction to *The Pastor's Bible Study: Volume Two* by general editor David Albert Farmer

◆ The full text of *The Pastor's Bible Study: Volume Two* in Adobe Reader® (.pdf) format, plus several versions of Adobe Reader® software

◆ PowerPoint® presentations containing outlines for each study within the volume, in both PowerPoint® Presentation (.ppt) and PowerPoint® Show (.pps) format

◆ Study outlines and reflection questions in rich text file (.rtf) format that may be edited, printed, and given to group participants.

To access any of this material, insert the compact disk into the CD-ROM drive of your computer and browse to the item(s) you wish to select using your PC Windows Explorer, or your Macintosh Browser.

Viewing the QuickTime® Introductory Video

To view the QuickTime® introductory video of *The Pastor's Bible Study: Volume Two*, you must have QuickTime® software installed on your computer. If you wish to install this free software, download it from the web at www.apple.com/quicktime/download/.

Note: The QuickTime® program is not included on The Pastor's Bible Study: Volume Two *disk. Technical support for QuickTime® is available at www.apple.com.*

Once QuickTime® is installed on your computer, browse to the file named **Video** on the disk and double click on it to play it.

Using the Adobe Reader® Book

To use the Adobe Reader® book containing the full text of *The Pastor's Bible Study: Volume Two*, you must have Adobe Reader® software installed on your computer. If you wish to install Adobe Reader®, browse to the **Adobe_Installation** folder on the disk and select the correct version.

Make your selection by referring to the chart below. Once you have determined the correct version to install, double click on the file and follow the onscreen instructions for installation.

Note: Technical support for installation of the Adobe Reader is available at www.adobe.com.

Once Adobe Reader® is installed on your computer, browse to the file named **PBS_Vol_2.pdf** on the disk and double click on it to open it. After opening the **PBS_Vol_2.pdf**, you may search any keyword or phrase in *The Pastor's Bible Study: Volume Two*.

Another useful feature of the Adobe Reader® file is the addition of links to other resources on the supplemental disk. These links are at the beginning of each of the six studies at the bottom the study's outline page. Clicking on a link will open the selected resource on your computer in its default program. Just be sure that *The Pastor's Bible Study: Volume Two* compact disk is in your CD-ROM drive.

Platform	OS	Acrobat Reader® Version	Acrobat Reader® File
Windows	XP	6.0.1	AdbeRdr60_enu.exe
	2000	6.0.1	AdbeRdr60_enu.exe
	ME	6.0.1	AdbeRdr60_enu.exe
	NT	6.0.1	AdbeRdr60_enu.exe
	98SE	6.0.1	AdbeRdr60_enu.exe
	98	5.05	rp505enu.exe
	95	5.05	rp505enu.exe
Palm	1.1		accrreadpalmosv11.exe
	2.0	English Windows	arpos_winv20enu.exe
	2.0	English Mac Palm Desktop 2.6.3	arpos_macv20pd263enu.sit
	2.0	English Mac Palm Desktop 4.0	arpos_macv20pd40enu.sit
	3.0	English Windows	AdobeReader305-PalmOS.exe
	3.0	English Mac Palm Desktop 4.0	AdobeReader305-PalmOS.dmg
Pocket PC	2002		acrobatreader-ppc2002.exe
	English ARM		acrobatreader-ppcarm.exe
	English MIPS		acrobatreader-ppcmips.exe
	English SH3		acrobatreader-ppcsh3.exe
Mac	10.2.2-10.3	6.0.1	AdbeRdr60_enu.dmg
	9.1-10.2.1	5.1	AcroReader51_ENU.bin
	8.6-9.0	5.05	ar505enu.bin
	8.1-8.5	4.05	rs405eng.bin
	7.5.3	4.05	rs405eng.bin

Viewing PowerPoint® Presentations

There are twelve PowerPoint® files on the disk, two for each of the six studies. These two PowerPoint® files contain presentations of study outlines. All PowerPoint® files are in a folder named **PowerPoint**. To view the PowerPoint® files that accompany *The Pastor's Bible Study: Volume Two*, you must have Microsoft PowerPoint® software or PowerPoint® Viewer installed on your computer.

.PPT files: The .ppt files are files associated with the full version of Microsoft PowerPoint®. If you have the full version of PowerPoint® software installed on your computer, you may double click on the .ppt files to open them in PowerPoint® and customize your study presentations.

> *Note: The Microsoft PowerPoint® program is not included on* The Pastor's Bible Study: Volume Two *disk. Technical support for PowerPoint® is available at www.microsoft.com.*

.PPS files: The .pps files are "stand alone" files that may be viewed using the PowerPoint® Viewer, which is installed on most computers. If you wish to install this free software, download it from Microsoft at http://www.microsoft.com/downloads/details.aspx?FamilyID=428d5727-43ab-4f24-90b7-a94784af71a4&DisplayLang=en.

In most cases, using the .pps files will be the best choice for presenting the outlines to study participants. To begin the presentation:

◆ Place the disk in your computer's CD-ROM drive.

◆ Click on the link found on the appropriate study outline in Adobe Reader® to start the presentation. (Or, you may open the .pps file by browsing to it on the disk and double-clicking it.)

◆ Click anywhere on the slide, or use the Page Down button, to move through the presentation.

Note: If you click past a point in the outline and wish to go back, use the backspace or Page Up button on your computer's keyboard.

Using Study Outlines

Study outlines for all six sections are in a folder named **Study_Outlines**. Double-click on an outline to open the rich text format (.rtf) file in your computer's default word processing program. You may then customize your study experience by making changes to the outline. You may also access these files by clicking on the links provided in the study outline in Adobe Reader®.

Note: At the end of each session outline, participant assignments for the upcoming sessions are noted, including Scripture reading assignments and New Interpreter's Study Bible references. Providing the outlines to participants will enhance their study experience.

Using Reflection Questions

Reflection questions for all six studies are in a folder named **Reflection_Questions**. Double click on an outline to open the rich text format (.rtf) file in your computer's default word processing program. You may then customize your study experience by making changes to the reflection questions. You may also access these files by clicking on the links provided in the study outline in Adobe Reader®.

Contacting Technical Support

To contact one of our Technical Support Representatives, call: **1-615-749-6777, Monday through Friday, 8:00 A.M. to 5:00 P.M.**, Central time.

Notes

Notes

Notes

Notes

Notes

Notes